Gender and Politics in Contemporary Canada

Edited by

François-Pierre Gingras

Toronto
Oxford University Press
1995

Oxford University Press
70 Wynford Drive, Don Mills, Ontario M3C 1J9

Oxford   New York
Athens   Auckland   Bangkok   Bombay
Calcutta   Cape Town   Dar es Salaam   Delhi
Florence   Hong Kong   Istanbul   Karachi
Kuala Lumpur   Madras   Madrid   Melbourne
Mexico City   Nairobi   Paris   Singapore
Taipei   Tokyo   Toronto

and associated companies in
Berlin   Ibadan

Oxford is a trademark of Oxford University Press

Canadian Cataloguing in Publication Data

Main entry under title:

Gender and politics in contemporary Canada

Includes bibliographical references and index.

ISBN 0–19–541011–4

1. Women in politics – Canada. 2. Sexism – Canada.
3. Women – Government policy – Canada.
I. Gingras, François-Pierre.

HQ1236.5.C2G4 1995   305.42'0971   C95–932200–0

Design: Brett Miller

CONTENTS

ACKNOWLEDGEMENTS

Ever since I joined the Political Science Department at the University of Ottawa, back in 1976, I have enjoyed the good fortune of working in an environment where sound scholarship and dedicated teaching are valued equally highly. My first thanks naturally go to my colleagues for providing me with such a stimulating atmosphere throughout the years.

Among my colleagues, a very special mention goes to Caroline Andrew, whose social commitment I have always admired. I am particularly pleased that she agreed to write a short but superb concluding chapter to this book. Andrew, it must be mentioned, supported this project from the very beginning, when I suggested she be a co-editor of a selection of gender-related papers presented at the annual meetings of the Canadian Political Science Association. I believed that, as former president of the association and a respected feminist scholar, she was the natural choice for that task. After reading the first version of the texts assembled here, she persuaded me to go ahead on my own. I thank her for this expression of confidence.

I must also thank the editors of Oxford University Press: first, Brian Henderson for his initial support, then Phyllis Wilson and Olive Koyama for their unbelievable patience, and Freya Godard for her numerous editorial revisions and suggestions for making the manuscript more easily understandable by the intended audience.

Finally, I owe to my wife, Susan McDougall-Gagnon-Gingras,[1] special gratitude for tolerating my exponentially increasing frustration with the computer in the last stretch of this enterprise, for this machine designed to make our lives easier eventually gave me ulcers.

Some essays originally intended for this collection could not be used for various reasons. They include an examination by Dina Iordanova of Canadian immigration policy and its effect on refugee women, a report by Claudia Wright on the disposition of sexual harassment complaints, and a study by Évelyne Tardy of gender differences in municipal politics. Deadlines and limitations of space prevented the inclusion of many other contributions proposed by authors who showed an interest in this project. I wish they could all have been part of this collection.

---

[1]Using a three-barrelled name in her career is how this soft-spoken feminist decided to defy the Quebec legislation that forces women to use solely their maiden name, even when they do not wish to.

INTRODUCTION

Antigone's Legacy to Canadians

François-Pierre Gingras

Ismene: *O think, Antigone; we are women; it is not for us to fight against men; our rulers are stronger than we. . . . I cannot act against the State, I am not strong enough.*

Antigone, daughter of Oedipus: *Let that be your excuse, then. . . . But I know what my true duty is.*

Creon, king of Thebes: *Proud thoughts do not sit well upon subordinates. Keep them inside: this is the proper place for women.*

Chorus: *Antigone, you have gone your way, to the outermost limit of daring. You will be the victim of your own self-will.* (Sophocles [440 BC] 1947)

And Creon had his niece Antigone entombed alive because she defied him.

Sophocles' Antigone is often presented as the archetype of the feminist (Irigaray 1989; Dumais 1992). Proud and determined, she is confident that she has justice on her side. But in the context of antiquity, Antigone was essentially a tragic character, dedicated to a hopeless task. While women in western post-industrial societies have made substantial gains, some women in Canada still live tragic and hopeless lives every day. They are harassed, battered, and murdered *because they are women* and are therefore considered less worthy than men. Needless to say, the situation is still much worse in some other countries. But Antigone must remain present in our minds so that we do not forget all of this when we narrow our focus to gender and politics in Canada.

At the time of Antigone, in ancient India, Greece, and Rome, a woman was always a dependent of some man: first of her father, then of her husband, later (when her husband had died) of her sons or other male relatives. She could not be obeyed in her own right, she was not a citizen (Fustel de Coulanges 1963). Things were not much different in the early decades of this country, and Canadian women were constitutionally recognized as 'persons' only in 1929.

However defined, citizenship has always involved rights and duties, benefits and responsibilities. In a democracy, it also involves not only being subjected to political decisions but also having the opportunity to participate in making those decisions.

All Canadians, women as much as men—and sometimes women more than men—are affected by the political process in which needs are expressed, authorities elected, priorities established, policies developed, and resources allocated. This collection of essays explores some aspects of the relevance of gender to the Canadian political process.

Canadians of both sexes are affected by the subjects covered in this book, which was written with a broad audience in mind. All 14 authors are scholars and well-respected researchers; in total they are affiliated with 11 Canadian universities. Some contributors are also activists, and, although this is not a militant book filled with radical feminist claims, many readers will find ample support here for their militancy. In addition, this eclectic collection will expose both undergraduate and graduate students to original material highly relevant to courses in communication, political sociology, public policy, and women's studies.

Indeed, this book is intended primarily to show a few of the very diverse ways in which gender is related to politics. All the chapters report findings of research projects conducted by the authors themselves. In many cases, preliminary findings were presented at conferences held under the auspices of the Social Sciences Federation of Canada, the Canadian Federation of Humanities, or the Association canadienne-française pour l'avancement des sciences.

This collection provides a good balance of quantitative and qualitative evidence, of detailed analysis, and broad generalizations. Many findings reported here could be replicated either systematically by students in the course of research for essays or informally by any attentive observer of Canadian politics. All chapters have methodological implications. Readers are urged to challenge their own views with the interpretations offered by the authors, since most essays confront theories with empirical evidence and many propose alternative, innovative explanations.

Although the 12 chapters may be read in any order, the sequence adopted here is not arbitrary. The design is similar to a series of concentric waves: although the book is divided into three parts for the purpose of concentrating on specific questions, the last chapter of each part leads naturally to the first chapter of the next.

For many Canadians, elections and political parties are at the heart of domestic politics; that is why the book begins with gender and the party system, moving from case studies to a broad theoretical discussion. The next 'concentric circle' of politics is often associated with governments and their policies; therefore, Part II deals with public policy in relations to gender and moves from proposals for achieving equality to the influence of women on the constitutional debates. Finally, because our impressions of what and who is politically important are influenced by the media, Part III addresses the portrayal of gender in the media and ends with a methodological note on some pitfalls in gender-relevant social research.

GENDER AND THE PARTY SYSTEM

The first three chapters discuss women's interests in the context of parties and elections. In the search for attitudinal differences between male and female party activists and candidates, two chapters rely heavily on a quantitative analysis of survey data. In the first chapter, 'The Gender Gap among Party Activists', Alan Whitehorn and Keith Archer present a case study of activists in the New Democratic Party. Using historical documents and survey data gathered at NDP federal conventions, Whitehorn and Archer explore gender differences over a range of social and political attitudes among male and female delegates. They conclude with an evaluation of the relative importance of gender compared to other demographic variables such as region, type of membership, age, and religion.

In 'Gender and Support for Feminism: A Case Study of the 1989 Quebec General Election', Manon Tremblay uses data collected among candidates to investigate empirically the hypothesis that women vying for positions of political power are more likely than men to support feminist demands. The underlying assumption is that a greater number of female members in legislatures could bring a transformation in gender relations in society at large. Tremblay's use of frequency tables and factor analysis will present a considerable challenge to some readers; the resulting insight will be well worth the effort. This chapter raises the question of whether more women in electoral politics make a difference. It begins a discussion that is continued in the next chapter.

Is the significance of sex parity symbolic or real? If there were more women in Parliament, would issues of concern to women be considered more important? While all women matter, do all women have similar interests? How can we ensure that the full range of their interests will be represented? In 'A Job Well Begun. . .: Representation, Electoral Reform, and Women', Jane Arscott discusses the present condition of theorizing about women and their electoral under-representation in the light of the final report of the Royal Commission on Electoral Reform and Party Financing. The low level of 'women-sensitivity' of political parties found by Arscott, is actually also characteristic of government policies, as demonstrated in Part II.

GENDER AND PUBLIC POLICY

Part II of the book comprises five chapters, beginning with three that examine different routes to gender equality—and stumbling blocks on the way. In the first part of 'Gender and Public Policy: Making Some Difference in Ottawa', Sandra Burt examines the recent agenda of the Canada-wide feminist lobby groups as reflected in their proposals and assesses their current commitments. Of great interest here is the evolution of the feminist claims over a 10-year period, during which Burt observes an increased emphasis on equal rights. She then examines the evolution, during the same period, of federal government policies of special interest to women in the fields of justice, social services, health and safety, and employment.

This last issue is taken up in 'Equity and Opportunity,' in which Lesley Jacobs discusses legislative measures for addressing gender inequality in the workplace: he argues that there has been much confusion between the expected effects of such legislation (the reduction of the wage gap) and its rationale and justification (equality of opportunity). Jacobs raises an important question for any evaluative research: when policies are about principles, should their success be evaluated by the way in which new processes have been adopted or by the results of those processes, which may be observable only in the long term?

The experiences of many Canadians are ignored by empirical researchers, dismissed by politicians, and forgotten by theorists. These are the experiences of those who tend to participate less in surveys and in institutionalized politics: those who are assumed to have no potential because they are illiterate,[1] poor, or homeless. In fact the homeless are of so little interest to our 'system' that no way has been found even to enumerate them properly.[2] Needless to say, homeless women tend to be doubly disregarded. In 'Homeless Women and the New Right', Meredith Ralston asks whether neo-conservatism can explain, and provide solutions for, the situations of women who are homeless or addicted to alcohol or drugs. Ralston's case study has the invaluable merit of illustrating the importance of listening to the experiences of women, in particular the most silenced.

The women's movement and public policy is the subject of the two other chapters in Part II. Both investigate the ambivalent relationship between women and political authorities when the structural gender inequalities in a political system are challenged by women while the authorities wish to mobilize women in support of nationalism. In the first part of this discussion, 'Pronatalism, Feminism, and Nationalism', Roberta Hamilton concentrates on the often hostile but sometimes friendly relationship between nationalism and feminism in Quebec. She discusses contradictory historical interpretations of the roles of women in *la survivance* of French Canadians and, with considerable insight for an 'outsider', shows convincingly how these attitudes keep percolating through the present constitutional debates.

In 'Women of Quebec and the Contemporary Constitutional Issue', a welcome addition to the English literature on the women's movement in Quebec, Micheline Dumont presents her own feminist, but clearly nationalist, analysis of the confrontation between the present-day independence movement and Quebec's own brand of new institutionalized feminism. Dumont explores the many divisions, based on party and language, within the feminist movement and their manipulation by political leaders. These divisions, she finds, make it easier for the male political establishment to ignore women's voices. The next section shows that these voices are also less likely than men's to be reported in the mass media.

PORTRAYING GENDER

Historians tell us very little about women of any political (or even artistic) importance in the times of Antigone.[3] Today's journalists are not always much more articulate, despite the fact that the media play a major role in the portrayal of politicians. Two of the four essays of this section are concerned with the media. In 'The Portrayal of Women Politicians by the Media: The Political Implications', Gertrude Robinson and Armande Saint-Jean look at the implications of the different ways in which female and male politicians are described by the media.

In 'Daily Male Delivery: Women and Politics in the Daily Newspapers', François-Pierre Gingras presents a quantitative contents analysis revealing that, despite considerable variations from one newspaper to the other, the media magnify the under-representation observable in politics and portray women politicians as relatively unimportant. The findings of Gingras as well as those of Robinson and Saint-Jean confirm the persistence of sex-role stereotyping in the Canadian media, despite a recent editorialist's claim that the arrival of women in politics has civilized the exercise of power (Maltais 1995).

While the data presented by Tremblay as well as by Robinson and Saint-Jean would support the view that the present generation of women politicians is committed to a feminist agenda, the brief tenure, in 1992 and 1993 respectively, of Mary Collins and Kim Campbell as defence ministers definitely did not have much influence on the attitudes of the military. In 'Gender and the Canadian Military: Attitudes Toward Peace and Ethical Issues', Gingras uses survey data to probe gender differences in the attitudes of the Canadian military to ethical questions related to peace and peacekeeping. This chapter and the next one by David Northrup are of particular interest in that, unlike most reports of surveys, they show some limitations of survey research.

In 'Gender-of-Interviewer Effects and Level of Public Support for Affirmative Action', Northrup examines several methodological questions relevant to social science research. He uses three surveys conducted by the Institute for Social Research at York University to measure the extent to which the sex of the interviewer affects the respondents' answers. The implications are many, for Northrup suggests that standard practices of survey firms may result in the incorrect reporting of attitudes about issues related to gender.

The book concludes with a reflection by Caroline Andrew, 'The Fine Line: Strategies for Change'. I shall not say much about this piece, to avoid spoiling the pleasure of the reader, who will find there a discussion of how the various chapters may contribute to transforming scholarship on gender relations.

Any assortment of essays on the topic of gender and politics is necessarily incomplete, because the field is so wide and scholarship is expanding so rapidly. Instead of seeing this as a shortcoming, I consider it a marvellous opportunity. May this dissemination of knowledge stimulate more research and an improved understanding of the imperfect world we live in. There are many tasks left for the Canadian spiritual descendants of Antigone.

NOTES

1 Statistics Canada's 1989 *Survey of Literacy Skills Used in Daily Activities* shows that one-third of all native-born Canadians aged 16 to 69 are functionally illiterate; the proportion is higher among older and foreign-born persons. There are many definitions of illiteracy; in Canada someone who can't use the *Yellow Pages* or who can't fill in a simple medical information form is considered to be functionally illiterate.

2 Statistics Canada has no reliable data on the homeless; its Cardex indicates only that 8,000 Canadians spent one Saturday night of January 1987 in one of the shelters across the country. Using data from a study it sponsored in 1987, the Canadian Council of Social Development estimates that there were at that time 260,000 homeless Canadians, and that their numbers have certainly increased since.

3 In fact, 'the earliest depiction of a woman artist at work' is that of a vase painter appearing on a Greek pottery of *circa* 450 BC, about the time Sophocles wrote *Antigone*. It has been remarked that 'even the subordinate role played by [this] female vase painter must have been a significant step on the road to equality' (Janson 1986: vol. 1: 109). This must have been a long road, as 'women began to emerge as distinct artistic personalities around [AD] 1550' (Janson 1986: vol. 2: 501)—fully two thousand years later.

BIBLIOGRAPHY

Dumais, Monique (1992), *Les droits des femmes* (Montreal: Paulines).

Fustel de Coulanges, Denys Numa (1963), *La cité antique* (Paris: Hachette).

Irigaray, Luce (1989), *Le temps de la différence* (Paris: Livre de Poche).

Janson, Horst Woldemar (1986), *History of Art*, 3rd edn (New York: Henry Abrams and Englewood Cliffs, NJ: Prentice-Hall).

Maltais, Murray (1995), 'Vers l'égalité,' *Le Droit*, 8 Mar., p. 20.

Sophocles ([440 BC] 1947), *Antigone:* in *Three Theban Plays*, trans. E.F. Watling (Harmondsworth: Penguin).

PART I

Gender and the Party System

CHAPTER 1

The Gender Gap Amongst Party Activists:

A Case Study of Women and the New Democratic Party

Alan Whitehorn and Keith Archer

Throughout history, most societies and political organizations have been characterized by inequality. One enduring form of stratification has been that based on sex (Armstrong and Armstrong 1978; Connelly 1978; Lovenduski and Hills 1981; Brodie 1985b; Prentice *et al.* 1988; Anderson 1991; McLaughlin 1992). Canadian politics provides yet another setting for this phenomenon. For example women first obtained the right to vote in federal elections in 1918. There have also been delays in the election or appointment of women to important political posts, such as Member of Parliament (1921), Senator (1930), leader of a provincial party (1951),[1] federal cabinet minister (1957), Supreme Court (1982), Governor General (1984), leader of a major federal party (1989), premier (1991), and Prime Minister (1993).

Since the modern democratic polity channels the bulk of conventional participation through political parties, it is useful to ask the following questions: 'To what degree do political parties continue today the past pattern of gender inequality?' and 'How prevalent are differences of opinion along gender lines within political parties?'[2]

This chapter examines those questions in relation to the federal New Democratic Party. Like so much of women's studies, this has been a neglected area of research until recently.[3] The case study begins with a brief history of the issue of gender in the NDP. We will then examine the degree of participation by women at the various levels of the party hierarchy, ranging from the mass membership at the bottom to the leadership posts at the top. The chapter will then shift from the historical methodology to the social science mode of analysis and focus upon selected data from two national surveys conducted at NDP federal conventions in 1983 and 1987. These surveys should provide insight into the behavioural and attitudinal differences between female and male party activists.

HISTORICAL AND ORGANIZATIONAL BACKGROUND

Over most of the twentieth century there have been two principal organizations for social democrats in Canada. The first was the Co-operative Commonwealth Federation, which emerged in 1932 in the midst of the Great Depression. The second was the New Democratic Party, which appeared three decades later in 1961 in a more urban and relatively prosperous Canada. During the CCF era, only a small percentage (11.1 per cent) of the electorate voted for the party (Whitehorn 1992: 3) and a disproportionate number who did were men.[4] Though at first this gender imbalance continued for the NDP,[5] recent surveys have shown that more women than men now vote for the NDP (Brodie 1991: 22; Wearing and Wearing 1991; Pammett 1989: 127).[6] It seems plausible that a party with a changing base of support will also exhibit a similar alteration in its membership profile and leadership positions. Similarly one would expect also to observe some modifications in the party's policies to reflect better the opinions of its newer clientele (Carbert 1994).[7]

PARTICIPATION OF WOMEN IN THE
NEW DEMOCRATIC PARTY

Extra-parliamentary Wing

The New Democratic Party is an example of a 'mass party' with extra-parliamentary origins and activities (Duverger 1963) that has endeavoured to build a large membership. In the late 1980s, it had the most members of any Canadian political party (Stanbury 1989: 363). Bashevkin (1985b; 1989; 1993) and others (Brodie and Vickers 1981; Brodie 1985b) have shown in the past how the participation of women in Canadian political parties declined as one moved up the levels of the party pyramid (see Figure 1). It may be useful to explore to what degree this is so in the New Democratic Party.

Until recently, no formal membership data were available on the numbers or percentage of female party members for any Canadian party. Previous interviews with several NDP officials and earlier research (Kornberg et al. 1979: 186-7; Vickers and Brodie 1981: 62; Sangster 1989: 205; Bashevkin and Holder 1985: 276) found that there were more male than female members,[8] although the imbalance has been lessening in recent years. A number of women's organizations, such as study clubs, auxiliaries, committees, and conferences operated at various times within the CCF (Manley 1980; Beeby 1982; Bashevkin 1985b: 85, 106-13; Sangster 1989: 104-21, 209-22; Melnyk 1989: 78-9, 95-103). For over two decades there has been a Participation of Women (POW) committee (Bashevkin 1985b: 111). It is currently one of the main standing committees of the NDP. Its purpose is to

FIGURE 1 WOMEN'S PARTICIPATION IN MAJOR CANADIAN PARTIES, 1980S

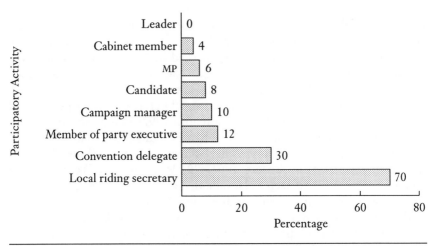

SOURCE: BASHEVKIN 1985b: 452; 1989: 452.

'encourage women's participation in all forms of political activity.' There are POW committees in all of the provincial and territorial sections of the party. Certainly, the creation of the POW Committee and the hiring of a women's organizer helped recruit more women into the party, encouraged those already in the party, and fostered their promotion into more senior levels (Bashevkin 1985b: 110-12; Brodie and Vickers 1981: 334; Sangster 1989: 224; Brodie 1991: 28).[9] Though the figures for the gender of members of the federal NDP are still unavailable, for the first time data on one of the party's major provincial sections has been made available to the authors. As of September 1992, slightly fewer than half of the Ontario NDP's members were women (see Figure 2).[10] This new finding suggests that the Ontario NDP has taken one step closer to having equal numbers of men and women.

There are more reliable and long-term data on women's involvement in the NDP for higher and more visible levels of the party. Starting at the first step in the party's management pyramid—the riding association executive— Bashevkin and others (Bashevkin 1985a; 1985b: 58; Bashevkin and Holder 1985; Brodie 1985b; Bashevkin 1989; 1991: 62-5) have noted the continuing presence of a pink-collar ghetto. That is, more women occupy the support position of riding secretary than that of president or treasurer.[11]

Nevertheless, the same researchers have found a trend toward more women in executive positions. Indeed, a comparison of delegates at recent federal NDP conventions shows that the percentage of female delegates who were also members of federal riding association executives had gone up from 36.9 per cent in 1983 to 42.5 per cent in 1987. A similar increase was evidenced for provincial riding association executives (from 45.1 per cent to

FIGURE 2 PARTICIPATION OF WOMEN IN THE
NEW DEMOCRATIC PARTY 1989, 1990

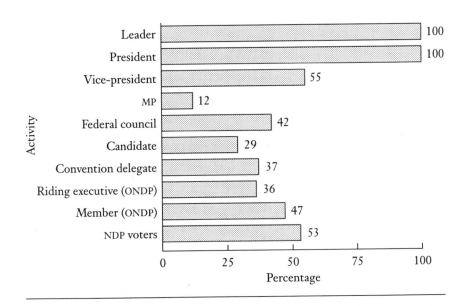

54.2 per cent). Indeed the rate for both types of riding associations was higher than that for men.[12]

In the aftermath of the 1988 federal election, outgoing leader Ed Broadbent encouraged the creation of the 'councils' of federal ridings, a body that was inserted mid-way between the riding association executive and the national federal council in an attempt to give more vitality to the federal operations of the party between elections. It is a structure that has not worked well because it suffers from inadequate funding and too infrequent meetings. Nevertheless, it is worthy of study. According to the federal NDP constitution, there are no requirements for gender parity for election to the councils, but in practice the party is trying informally for parity. A strong example, however, is set in the constitutional requirement for parity in the selection of representatives from the councils of federal ridings to attend the national federal council.

Since its birth in 1932, the CCF-NDP has held conventions to determine policy and leadership. Canadian society in the 1930s was very much stratified along gender lines, and this was no less so for the the CCF. The early CCF conventions were overwhelmingly male affairs, although a few women were prominent.[13]

While the most recent surveys show that a growing proportion of delegates are women (see Table 2), men still predominate by about two to one (see Whitehorn 1988; Bashevkin 1985b: 64, 163; 1989; Archer 1991;

TABLE 1 WOMEN ELECTED TO ONTARIO NDP PROVINCIAL RIDING EXECUTIVES

	1973	1981	1985	1990
President	8.5	28.8	30.4	34.6
Treasurer or chief financial officer		41.6	36.8	29.2
Secretary		67.2	69.3	48.5

SOURCES: BASHEVKIN 1985a: 277; 1985: 58; 1991

Whitehorn 1992).[14] One reason is that NDP conventions are attended primarily by two types of delegates—those from party riding associations and those from affiliated trade unions. While ridings have increasingly made strides toward choosing equal numbers of male and female delegates, unions, given the preponderance of men in their membership,[15] have not progressed as dramatically (Hayward and Whitehorn 1991). For example Bashevkin (1985b: 64) reports that whereas 41 per cent of federal riding delegates in the early 1980s were women, only 11 per cent of affiliated union delegates were women. By 1987, the percentage of female union delegates had increased only slightly, to 16.5 per cent (Archer and Whitehorn 1993: 10).

Between conventions, the paramount decision-making body of the NDP is its federal council. The current constitution of the federal party calls for important elements of gender parity on the party's national federal council. For example, 10 of 20 council members elected by the federal convention must be women.[16] In addition, two of the ten women must be aboriginal and another two from visible minorities. The newly created councils of federal ridings also send representatives to the federal council, and again gender parity is required for those delegates. Similarly, at least one of the two representatives on federal council elected by the provincial conventions must be a woman. As an official party committee, POW is entitled to send one woman from each provincial or territorial section to the federal council.

All these changes have certainly increased the number of women on the federal council. For example, the percentage of women members at the

TABLE 2 PERCENTAGES OF MEN AND WOMEN AT NDP
FEDERAL CONVENTIONS: 1971-1989

	1971	1979	1983	1987	1989
Men	73.9	74.4	69.1	67.0	63.2
Women	26.1	25.6	30.9	33.0	36.8
N	747	519	395	738	995

SOURCES: WHITEHORN 1988; 1992; ARCHER AND WHITEHORN 1990, 1991;
ARCHER 1991.

March 1977 federal council meeting and before the gender parity features were implemented was 20.8 per cent. Just over a decade later, in 1989-90, 41.5 per cent of the federal council were women.[17] However, without provisions for gender parity in affiliated unions, which also send delegates to council, the federal council is not likely to achieve full gender parity. Even if full numerical equality in male and female representation were to emerge at some future date, this would not necessarily guarantee that both groups would be equal in influence, as Pitkin (1967) and others (Kornberg et al. 1979: 186; Jennings and Farah 1981: 469; Gelb 1989; Jennings 1990: 246) point out. Clearly, attitudinal factors such as status, bias, and forcefulness can affect the distribution of power. Still, a vast distance has been travelled since the first councils in the 1930s, when very few women were members.

Before a woman was first elected as federal party leader, important political gains were made in a number of executive posts. For example, since the early 1980s the federal party has 'balanced' the vice-presidents along gender parity lines (for example, four to four in 1983; currently six to five in favour of women). In addition, according to the party's constitution, either the party president or the associate president must be a woman.

Formal charts of a party hierarchy often fail to list important positions. Election planning has always been a central task for political parties. In the television age of mass advertising and public opinion polling, the pivotal positions include principal secretary to the leader, chair of the election planning committee (SEPC), party pollster, caucus research director, and federal secretary. Even as recently as 1984, all of these positions were filled by men. However, by January 1993 in the run-up to the election, three of these five positions were held by women (Sandra Mitchell as principal secretary, Julie Davis as chair of SEPC, and Tessa Hebb as research director). This is a dramatic contrast to the NDP's earlier history and that of other parties even today (Bashevkin, 1993: 76). The changes in gender make-up of principal federal NDP posts were no doubt influenced by the party's first female leader.

In the days of the CCF, all of the national presidents[18] and chairmen were men. However, there was one female vice-chair in the CCF era. Thérèse Casgrain was first elected to that post in 1948 (Engelmann 1954). It was not until 1975, well into the NDP era, that a woman, Joyce Nash (Scotton) was elected president of the party. Her election ended four decades of male dominance of this post. In keeping to some degree with the shift in the party's base of support and a desire to project a progressive image, the last four federal NDP presidents have been women (Marion Dewar, Joanna den Hertog, Sandra Mitchell, and Nancy Riche).

From the time of the party's founding in 1932 until 1989, almost six decades later, the CCF-NDP was led by men. One step towards the historic election of a female leader was taken in 1975, when Rosemary Brown (1989; Roy 1992) challenged Ed Broadbent and three other men for the party leadership. The fact that she came a close second to Broadbent and won 41 per cent of the vote on the final ballot was a sign of both the growing power of the women's movement in the party and increased acceptance in the party and society of women as political leaders. With the election of Audrey McLaughlin in Winnipeg in 1989 (see Archer 1991; Whitehorn and Archer 1994), the highest bastion of male ascendancy was finally breached.[19] The announcement of a new feminist leader was made amidst the stirring strains of Tracy Chapman's 'Talking about Revolution' (McLaughlin 1992: 67, 73). Not surprisingly, the party's first female federal leader has strongly advocated accelerating the pace of the party's commitment to gender parity and affirmative action.[20] The adoption by the 1991 NDP convention of a resolution to promote greater numbers of female candidates for Parliament is one example of the party's efforts to foster still further organizational changes on the gender question. Another possible example in the eyes of some is the recent decision by the party's federal council to open up the leadership selection process to include a direct ballot of all party members just before the next leadership convention. Whether that will democratize the political process still further or create new financial barriers to female leadership candidates remains to be seen.

Parliamentary Wing

Despite its extra-parliamentary origins and activities the NDP involved itself in the traditional electoral process. From the founding of the CCF, women ran as candidates (Melnyk 1989: 78; Webster n.d.; Roome 1989: 106; Sangster 1989: 208). The number, however, was very small,[21] and success was more likely at the municipal level, where the prestige was lower and it was easier to combine family work and political activism (Vickers and Brodie 1981: 58; Brodie 1985b: 20; Bashevkin 1989: 450; Howard 1992; Surrey-Newton NDP 1994). Historical data are available on the participation of women both as candidates for Parliament and their success (Bashevkin 1985b: 72, 73; Brodie and Vickers 1981: 324; Gotell and Brodie 1991; Brodie 1991; Sharpe 1994: 226).[22] One thing is clear. The CCF-NDP has never had as many female as male candidates. Nevertheless, the party has made slow but recently accelerating progress in the number and percentage of female candidates (see Table 3). From fewer than 6 CCF candidates on average in the 1940s, the NDP ran just over 60 in the 1980s, a tenfold increase. In 1988, the party nominated more female candidates than any other party (28.5 per cent).[23] To encourage this trend the party created the Agnes Macphail Fund to provide modest financial assistance to female candidates. The current NDP constitution and a policy approved at the 1991 convention call for greater efforts towards 'affirmative action' and permit the party's federal council to oversee greater female involvement in local nominations. One method employed has been the 'clustering' of ridings in each region to ensure that enough female candidates emerge. Nominations can be frozen for an entire cluster until a more inclusionary nomination process has been achieved (McLaughlin 1992: 220). As a result, the 1993 federal election campaign saw the NDP nominate more female (113) (Canada 1993; Whitehorn 1994) and visible minority candidates than ever before and more than any other party.

The first woman elected to the House of Commons was Agnes Macphail in 1921 (Stewart and French 1959; Pennington 1989; Crowley 1990). Although she was elected as a member of the United Farmers of Ontario (UFO) and more than a decade before the formation of the CCF, she did become one of the pioneering figures in the birth of the CCF. Only a handful of women from any party were elected to Parliament in the 1930s and 1940s. Unfortunately, Macphail was defeated in her efforts at re-election in 1940. She did not run successfully for the CCF until 1943, when she and fellow CCFer Rae Luckock became the first women to be elected to the Ontario legislature.

The CCF record for the election of women to Parliament, like that of other parties in the first half of the twentieth century, was abysmal (Lazarus 1983; Kome 1985; Gotell and Brodie 1991; Brodie 1991). Only one female CCF candidate (Gladys Strum from Saskatchewan) was elected to Parliament in the entire CCF era (see Table 4). At the beginning of the NDP era there was a slight improvement, but not until the 1970s did the party have more than one woman in the House of Commons at the same time. One reason there were so few female social democratic MPs was that the CCF was a third party that never got more than 28 seats. As the NDP era progressed, so did the

TABLE 3 WOMEN CCF-NDP FEDERAL CANDIDATES BY DECADE

Decade	Total No. of Women	No. of Elections	Average per Election
CCF era			
1930s	7	1	7.0
1940s	16	3	5.3
1950s	31	3	10.3
NDP era			
1960s	56	4	14.0
1970s	119	3	39.7
1980s	182	3	60.1
1990s	113	1	113.0
Total	524	18	

SOURCE: CORRESPONDENCE WITH ABBY POLLENETSKY, FORMER DIRECTOR OF WOMEN'S ORGANIZATION, NEW DEMOCRATIC PARTY; UNPUBLISHED REPORT BY DIANE LEDUC.

party's vote, number of seats, and number of women elected. In the thirty-fourth Parliament a record number of five women were elected for the party. The percentage of women in the caucus (11.6 per cent) was still low but was above the average of 4.3 per cent for the history of the CCF-NDP.[24] However, in the next election, in 1993, the NDP suffered an electoral setback; Audrey McLaughlin was the lone female New Democrat elected.

Optimists might suggest that the overall record represents progress. Others would note that the gains came very late and that the number of women is still woefully low. In more than six decades, the number of women in the social democratic caucus averaged fewer than one per election—17 in 18 elections (see Table 4). Of course, the bias in the electoral system against third parties made it even more difficult for female CCF-NDP candidates.

Despite a less encouraging note on the parliamentary side, the participation of women in the NDP in the late 1980s improved (see Figure 2). Certainly, the decline in women's participation rate as one moves up the party hierarchy is far less severe today. Still, there is room for improvement, and the party's 1993 election nomination plans sought to remove some of the remaining obstacles to gender equality. Unfortunately, the results were disappointing for feminists. The fact that the party plummeted in seats and votes to its worst showing ever in the NDP era raises the question of why women still seem to be less successful candidates than men. In general, does having more women candidates help or hinder a party's electoral chances? For a third- or fourth-place party, such as the NDP, are the risks even greater?

TABLE 4 WOMEN ELECTED AS CCF-NDP FEDERAL MPS BY DECADE

Decade	Total No. of Seats	No. of Elections	% of Party's Total
CCF era			
1930s	0	1	0
1940s	1	3	2.0 (1/49)
1950s	0	3	0
NDP era			
1960s	2	4	2.5 (2/79)
1970s	3	3	4.1 (3/73)
1980s	10	3	9.5 (10/105)
1990s	1	1	11.1 (1/9)
Total	17	18	X = 4.5 (17/378)

SOURCE: CALCULATIONS BY WHITEHORN.

Is there any way of alleviating this problem of under-representation? Perhaps more women would have been elected had they been candidates in stronger CCF-NDP ridings. Would more funding for women have helped?[25] Would matters have improved if we had an electoral system based on proportional representation (Megyery 1991)? In any case, while the number of female NDP MPs went down, the combined total of women elected by other parties went up, suggesting the election of women to Parliament may actually be easier in other parties.

PROFILE OF NDP CONVENTION DELEGATES[26]

It has already been noted that there have been far more male than female delegates at federal NDP conventions (see Table 2). One can also ask whether there were important demographic differences between the profiles of female and male delegates.[27]

While the overwhelming majority of delegates were chosen from constituency associations, a higher percentage of women (89.1 per cent in 1983 and 75.8 per cent in 1987)[28] came to the convention by this means than was the case for men (73.4 per cent in 1983 and 63.2 per cent in 1987). The second-largest category of male delegates for both conventions was from trade union locals (9.6 per cent and 16.7 per cent). By contrast only 1.7 per cent and 5.8 per cent of women came by this route. Of course there are more men than women in trade unions. Nevertheless, given the above differences, it may be that the oft-described friction between delegates from labour union locals and constituency associations (Brodie 1985a) is related partially to the gender issue and may be worthy of further exploration in future research.[29]

While the overwhelming majority of NDP delegates said they had some university or college education, at both conventions more women (81.1 per cent and 85.5 per cent) than men (63.7 per cent and 74.6 per cent) had a university or college education.[30] One suspects that one reason is that more male delegates were from working-class trade unions. This will become clearer when we analyse occupation and class variables.

As might be expected from the above data, there was a difference in the leading occupations listed by the male and female delegates. Of the occupations given by 10 per cent or more of the respondents in 1983, women were most likely to describe themselves as skilled white-collar (20.7 per cent), followed by home-maker (18.2 per cent), educator (11.6 per cent), and retired (11.6 per cent). In 1987 the ranking by women was similar: skilled white-collar was first (28.3 per cent), followed by home-maker (11.2 per cent) and educator (11.2 per cent). Reflecting in part the increase in the percentage of women in the paid work-force, the percentages selecting skilled white-collar increased while home-maker declined. By contrast the job listed most frequently by the male delegates in 1983 was skilled blue-collar (14.0 per cent), retired (11.8 per cent), skilled white-collar (11.2 per cent), professional (11.1

per cent), union administrator (10.0 per cent), and student (10.0 per cent). By 1987, more men listed skilled white-collar (20.0 per cent), followed by skilled blue-collar (12.9 per cent) and union representative (12.1 per cent).

About two-thirds of the survey respondents said they could identify the social class to which they belonged. Again, as might be expected from some of the data on education and occupation, women were slightly more likely to describe themselves as middle-class (53.8 per cent and 46.0 per cent) compared to (40.4 per cent and 40.3 per cent) among men. Similarly, a slightly higher percentage of men than women picked working class (30.2 per cent and 26.5 per cent compared to 23.5 per cent and 23.8 per cent respectively).

Not surprisingly, most convention delegates said they did not intend to be an NDP candidate in an upcoming election. The rate was higher, however, for women than for men (77.6 per cent and 68.6 per cent compared to 68.7 per cent and 57.0 per cent). Interestingly, the gender gap was greatest at the federal level.[31] Despite the fact that more women had a higher level of formal education, a larger percentage of women gave as the most common reason for not running as a candidate 'lack of experience' (33.3 per cent compared to 20.5 per cent for men). Though formal education is not an equivalent to experience, it is likely that part of the explanation can be found in a socialization process that often diminishes the importance and status of women's experiences. This theme even emerges in the autobiography of party leader Audrey McLaughlin (1992: 199, 200, 214).

NDP DELEGATES' ATTITUDES TOWARD SELECTED ISSUES: 1983 AND 1987

All political questions, whether they relate to war and peace, the environment, or the constitution, are of interest to women as well as men. There are, however, a number of questions (for example, abortion and gender parity) that have been noted by women as being of more immediate relevance to them (see Tables 5 and 6). To begin our analysis we will observe the summary replies of all the delegates (both men and women) to some of these questions.

Though there has been an increase over the years in the number of women attending NDP conventions, as noted earlier women have still in general been outnumbered by men by a ratio of about two to one. Despite this discrepancy, most respondents (77.9 per cent in 1983 and 71.6 per cent in 1987)[32] did not believe that 'Women are discriminated against within the NDP'.[33]

In both surveys an overwhelming majority (86.5 per cent and 88.2 per cent) of convention delegates thought that 'more women should be candidates for the NDP'. And when asked if they thought 'women are as effective as men as candidates', almost all (92.3 per cent and 92.8 per cent) said that they are.[34]

A large majority (72.1 per cent and 83.9 per cent) of delegates believed that 'the NDP should ensure that a significant percentage of its candidates and Party officers are women.' In 1983 many delegates were less likely to support the entrenchment of parity of the sexes on the federal council (47.8 per cent were in favour, and 36.7 per cent were opposed).[35] Nevertheless, beginning at that convention, half of the council members and vice-presidents elected by convention were required to be women. Such measures certainly helped to raise the proportion of women in the executive levels of the party. On a positive note, only four years later a declining number (23.4 per cent) disagreed and a sizeable majority (62.3 per cent) agreed with the parity provisions.

TABLE 5 RESPONSES TO SELECTED STATEMENTS BY GENDER, 1983

Statement	Percentage in Agreement		
	Men	Women	Difference
Pornography should be banned.	42.6 41.1D	63.2	20.6
Fifty per cent of the Federal Council should be composed of women.	38.9 42.7D	66.9	28.0
There should be no censorship of any kind.	66.3D	78.8D	12.5
The NDP should ensure that a significant percentage of its candidates and Party officers are women.	67.2	82.5	15.3
Women are discriminated against within the NDP.	82.4D 10.3	65.5D 30.2	16.9 19.9
Abortion is a private matter which should be decided between the woman bearing the child and her doctor.	79.7 19.2D	95.8	16.1
On the whole, women are as effective as men as candidates for elected office.	92.2	93.4	1.2
More women should be candidates for the NDP.	83.2	92.5	9.3 X = 15.0

Notes: 1. D indicates percentage in disagreement.
2. Average sample size = 385.

SOURCE: WHITEHORN (1992)

TABLE 6 RESPONSES TO SELECTED STATEMENTS BY SEX, 1987

Statement	Percentage in Agreement		
	Men	Women	Difference
Pornography should be banned.	38.2	61.1	22.9
	38.9D		
Fifty per cent of the Federal Council should be composed of women.[1]	58.3	73.5	15.2
	57.4	75.2	17.8
There should be no censorship of any kind.	52.0D	64.6D	12.6
	29.8	13.9	15.9
The NDP should ensure that a significant percentage of its candidates and Party officers are women.[1]	81.0	86.2	5.2
	83.4	88.7	5.7
Women are discriminated against within the NDP.[1]	81.6D	63.6D	18.0
	9.3	23.8	14.5
	75.8D	65.5D	10.3
	12.4	24.0	11.6
Abortion is a private matter which should be decided between the pregnant woman and her doctor.[2]	81.8	94.1	12.3
On the whole, women are as effective as men as candidates for elected office.	92.4	96.2	3.8
More women should be candidates for the NDP.	87.3	93.3	6.0
Government sponsored child care service should be greatly expanded.[3]	92.4	93.8	1.4
Overall, sexism is on the decline.[3]	48.3	35.2	13.1
		45.3D	
			X = 11.1

[1]Three statements appeared twice in the questionnaire, both early and later in the survey. The twinned sets of responses thus provide an indication of the consistency in responses over the 300-item survey.
[2]Different wording than in 1983.
[3]Statement not included in 1983.

Note: D signifies percentage in disagreement.
     Average size of sample = 722.

Several social issues are of great interest to women in particular. Abortion, like the language issue, is a topic that arouses strong feelings on both sides. The NDP has long supported the right of women to seek medical abortions.[36] Not surprisingly then, an overwhelming number of NDP delegates (84.6 per cent) agreed with the statement 'Abortion is a private matter which should be decided between the woman bearing the child and her doctor.' In 1987 a slightly different question (see Table 6) received virtually the same degree of support (85.1 per cent). The rate of support is somewhat higher among NDP delegates than among either Liberal or Conservative delegates (Brodie 1988; Blake 1988; Archer and Whitehorn 1990; 1991). [37] As might be expected, the overwhelming majority of NDP delegates, male and female alike (92.4 per cent and 93.8 per cent), believed that 'Government sponsored child care services should be greatly expanded.' Again the rate seems to be higher than for the Liberal and Conservative convention delegates (Brodie 1988: 181).[38]

Many people believe pornography fosters sexist and violent attitudes and behaviour towards women and perpetuates gender inequalities. While there are no survey data on NDP attitudes to censorship and pornography before the 1980s, our impression is that many NDP members have shifted their position in recent years away from previous, more libertarian viewpoints to one more compatible with a radical feminist perspective.

In the 1983 and 1987 surveys respectively, 69.8 per cent and 55.8 per cent of the delegates disagreed with the statement 'There should be no censorship of any kind.' Though most were willing to accept the principle of censorship, the number supporting a 'ban on pornography' was lower (49.0 per cent in 1983 and 44.8 per cent in 1987), although it was still the dominant viewpoint.[39]

GENDER GAP IN NDP DELEGATES' ATTITUDES

Differences between parties are a crucial part of democratic choice in a modern pluralistic polity. In any large mass party, however, differences within the party can also be quite important. No major political party, composed as it is of tens of thousands of members, can possibly represent perfectly for each member, let alone for every group, all the possible points of view on every issue. Consequently, though any large political party may find considerable agreement on some issues, on others there may be significant disagreement among members.[40] Such differences can add strain on an organization, contribute to its lack of cohesion, and convey a confused image of the party to the public at large.

In a federal country of continental size such as Canada, there are often regional variations and differences in a party. The importance of regionalism can also be observed in the fact that the reports of regular Gallup polls offer regional breakdowns of public opinion. However, with the increasing participation of women in the paid work-force and greater involvement of women in politics it is essential to study more systematically the gender differences within political parties. In earlier decades, political parties in Canada, as elsewhere, were largely male organizations, and therefore gender differences within parties were less obvious and, in some ways, more difficult to study. As the number of women in political parties has increased, it may be more significant to ask the question 'How salient are the gender differences in Canada's parties?'

In an earlier report on the 1983 survey (Whitehorn 1988: 289-91; 1992: 131-2),[41] it was shown that some policy areas (such as priority women's issues) enjoyed greater consensus in the party.[42] For example, of the 52 survey questions for which the replies were broken down by gender, a difference of 10 per cent or more was found on only 17. Nevertheless, one would also expect that a disproportionate number of these 17 items would involve issues considered by women as central to their concerns. This indeed proved to be the case in that 6 of the 8 priority items had a gender difference greater than 10 per cent (see Table 5). By far the most divisive item on gender lines in 1983 was gender parity on federal council. Women strongly supported the measure, whereas men were more inclined to disagree. But after a decade of the successful functioning of this policy, it is largely taken for granted in the 1990s (see for example the 1987 data in Table 6). The second-most divisive issue along gender lines in 1983 was the banning of pornography. Whereas women strongly favoured a ban, men were split on the issue (see Table 5).

A similar analysis was conducted on a sample of 30 items from the 1987 survey. Again on the items targeted by women (see Table 6) there was more likely to be disagreement within the NDP on gender lines ($X = 11.1$) than there was on the other sampled items ($X = 4.8$). Not surprisingly, the most divisive issue of this cluster in 1987 was whether to ban pornography. Women still favoured a ban, and men were still divided. The gender difference on this item had not diminished.

Interestingly, when the average gender difference for the eight targeted items in 1983 was compared to the average gender difference for comparable items in 1987, it was found that the gender gap had narrowed. How significant a change is this? Certainly, there were more survey items in 1987, and this might be a minor contributing factor to the amount of change.[43] Another more likely explanation is that with the greater participation and representation of women at NDP conventions, councils, and even now in the leadership, issues of particular interest to women are probably being dealt with more fully. It also appears that greater numbers of men are more willing to accept the policies and measures favoured by the majority of NDP women (such as gender parity). Evidence of this can be found in Table 7 which records the change in men's and women's attitudes between 1983 and 1987 on the selected issues. The table also indicates whether the direction of the attitude shifts is towards the views held by women or by men. As monitored by these items, men's attitudes on average shifted further. In addition, on six of eight policy statements, men moved closer to the women's views.

Finally, it should be noted that the gap between men and women may not be the greatest existing at NDP conventions. When different demographic factors were explored to see which were associated with the greatest frequency of differences, gender was ranked third in 1983 behind education and size of community (see Whitehorn 1992: 134; Archer 1992).[44]

Another way to study this question is to build upon work presented previously by Brodie (1988), Blake (1988), and Archer and Whitehorn (1990; 1991) on comparisons of parties. These latter accounts noted differences between members of the NDP at one end of the political spectrum and Liberals and Conservatives on the other (see Archer and Whitehorn 1990: Table 1; 1991: Table 1). Given the existence of differences both between and within parties, one can pose the question as to which is the greater. Is the gap, for example, between male NDP delegates and female NDP delegates greater than the gap between all NDP delegates and all Liberals or between all NDP delegates and all Conservatives? If a party is to survive, the internal party differences should be less. Figure 3 suggests a hypothesized distribution on the political spectrum.

The thesis we postulate is that internal party differences between male and female delegates (that is, the gap from 1 to 3) is in general likely to be less than differences between the NDP and other parties (that is, between 2 and 4 or between 2 and 5) (see also Kirkpatrick 1976). This thesis can be tested empirically by re-analysing data from an earlier study of the NDP by Archer and Whitehorn (1990: 104; 1991: 146-7) and by drawing upon the work of Perlin (1988), Brodie (1988), Blake (1988), and others on the Liberals and Conservatives. Thirty items were taken from the 1987 NDP survey to determine whether gender differences in the party were less than differences between parties (for details of the latter see Archer and Whitehorn 1990: Table 1; 1991: Table 1). As expected, differences within the party were smaller in 28 cases, a finding similar to that of Brodie's (1988: 179, 182).[45] One can postulate that since differences between parties were greater, the gender gap within the NDP was not wide enough to cause excessive internal division.

CONCLUSION

The rise of the women's movement has left no political party, left or right, free of charges of gender bias and inequality. Despite their commitment to cultural change, socialist parties world-wide have in the past not shown themselves immune to elements of male chauvinism (Whitehorn 1992: 64, 250-1, 254-5). One way of reducing gender inequality has been to require

TABLE 7 SHIFTS IN NDP ATTITUDES, 1983 AND 1987

| | Percentage in Agreement | | | | | |
| | Men | | | Women | | |
Statement	1983	1987	Differences	1983	1987	Differences
Ban on pornography	42.6	38.2	4.4	63.2	61.1	2.1
50% council	38.9	57.9[a]	19.0	66.9	74.4[a]	7.5
No censorship	66.3D	52.0D	14.3	78.8D	64.6D	14.2
Significant percentage of women	67.2	82.2[a]	15.0	82.5	87.5[a]	5.0
Discrimination in NDP	82.4D	78.7D[a]	3.7	65.5D	64.6D[a]	0.9
Abortion	79.7	81.8	2.1	95.8	94.1	1.7
Women as effective candidates as men	92.2	92.4	0.2	93.4	96.2	2.8
More women candidates	82.2	87.3	4.1	92.5	93.3	0.8
			X = 7.9			X = 4.4

[a]In 1987 some survey items were duplicated; the percentage here is the average score for the duplicated items.

Notes:
See Tables 5 and 6 for full text of the survey statements.
D signifies disagreement.

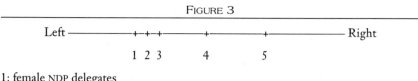

FIGURE 3

1: female NDP delegates

2: all NDP delegates (both male and female)

3: male NDP delegates

4: Liberal convention delegates

5: Conservative convention delegates

parity in important party posts. Recent NDP constitutional amendments have ensured that this one obstacle to women's political equality has been significantly lessened. Still, the progress in women's participation at other levels (for example, at conventions, as candidates, and as MPs) is less striking. Nevertheless, there has been progress in participation rates overall (see Figure 2).

As to gender differences in attitudes among New Democrat activists, it can be observed that a gap exists but (1) the gender difference seems to be less divisive than some others; (2) the male-female divide seems to be greatest on so-called targeted women's issues; (3) the gender gap in attitudes seems to be lessening; and (4) differences along gender lines within the NDP are less than those between members of the NDP and other parties. Overall, a case can be made that the divisions and inequality along gender lines, are lessening at least in the NDP.

However, lest we conclude on an excessively optimistic note, it may be useful to recall the replies of NDP delegates to the 1987 survey item which asserted that 'overall, sexism is on the decline'. Men were more likely to agree, whereas women were more likely to disagree (see Table 6).[46] It seems that important aspects of the gender gap still exist.

NOTES

This is an expanded and revised version of a paper presented by Alan Whitehorn to the annual meeting of the Canadian Political Science Association, Charlottetown, May 1992.

We wish to thank Fraser Green, federal secretary, Leslie Kerr, Director of Organization, and Abby Pollenetsky, the former Director of Women's Organization of the federal NDP, and Ed Dale, the Director of Administration for the Ontario NDP, for providing data for portions of this paper. Comments on an early draft were gratefully received from Sylvia Bashevkin, Dawn Black, Sandra Burt, Wendy Hughes, and Dale Poel.

1 Thérèse Casgrain was elected leader of the provincial CCF in Quebec in 1951 (see Casgrain 1972; Trofimenkoff 1989). Alexa McDonough became the first female leader of the Nova Scotia NDP in 1980.

2 It should be noted that this study is confined to conventional participation in a political party. The increasing importance of interest groups and unconventional forms of participation, particularly for so-called out groups such as women, is not discussed here.

3 For example, two recent major election studies (Johnson et al. 1992; Clarke et al. 1991) somewhat surprisingly do not list the categories of female, gender, sex, or women in their indexes.

4 For confirmation of this see the various CIPO/Gallup reports available from the 1940s onwards. See for example, no. 214, October 1951; no. 230, July 24, 1953; no. 267, March 1958; no. 282, May 1961. The authors are indebted to the Carleton University data archives for help in obtaining and processing these data. See also Brodie and Vickers (1981: 334); Bashevkin (1985b: 38, 40, 46, 48, 50, 51). Quebec may have been an exception, but the sample for the Quebec NDP is very small (132-3).

5 See for example CIPO (July 1974); Meisel (1975); Clarke et al. (1980: 88); Vickers and Brodie (1981: 62).

6 A number of commentators, including Gelb (1989: 67-8); Brodie (1988: 174, 179; 1991: 20-3); and Brackman et al. (1988: 223); Everitt (1994), have suggested that a reason for this new gender gap in party support may be in part that modern women appear to be more progressive than men on a number of social issues. One would expect this pattern of greater female support for the NDP to continue, if not increase, given the NDP's selection of a female federal leader in 1989. The long-term reasons for the shift in party support are important but in general beyond the scope of this chapter. But worthy of note are the decline of male-dominated religion, the rise in the education level of women, the opening of more vocations to women, and the corresponding increase in the number of women in the paid workforce, and a decline in the fertility rate for women.

7 Evidence for this can be seen in the greater number of references to women in the more recent party's manifestos (see Sangster 1989a: 121; Whitehorn 1992: chap. 3). Regrettably, the latter author did not cite the number of references to women in his statistical summary of the content analysis of CCF-NDP manifestos. It could be argued that the party's commitment to sexual equality and feminism in some ways predated the gender swing in membership and support. So for example 'it was the NDP, the party with the lowest proportion of women supporters in 1974, that developed the most aggressive and coherent campaign to attract women voters in 1979' (Brodie and Vickers 1981: 334).

8 Partial confirmation of this fact can be found in the percentage of federal convention delegates who are men (see Table 2). This preponderance of men is even more pronounced among the affiliated members from the unions linked with the NDP. Data partially confirming this can be found in surveys reported by Archer and Whitehorn (1993).

9 One analyst has provocatively suggested that 'the women's caucus is now the most powerful lobby group within the NDP and was a major force in the election of Audrey McLaughlin as Broadbent's successor' (Whitehorn 1992: 204). For a discussion of the central role of the women's network in her election as leader see McLaughlin (1992: 52, 54); Archer (1991); Whitehorn and Archer (1994).

10 Correspondence from Ed Dale, Director of Administration of the Ontario NDP 30 Sept. 1992. These data do not, however, include the affiliated trade union members.

11 Sangster (1989a: 99, 101, 103, 205) observes that this phenomenon also occurred during the CCF era. Bashevkin and Holder (1985: 279) note that when a woman was president, it was often in a weak riding association. Nevertheless, Bashevkin (1991: 64, 68) has found the ghettoization of women less evident in the NDP than in either the Liberal or Conservative party.

12 The corresponding federal riding executive rate for men was 39.6 per cent in 1983 and 38.7 per cent in 1987 and for provincial riding executives 52.7 per cent in 1983 and 49.9 per cent in 1987. Some caution should be used in analysing the data since the sample consists primarily of convention delegates and only secondarily of executive members of riding associations. Thus the many members of riding association executives who do not attend conventions would not appear in the survey sample.

13 For example, Sangster (1989a: 247) states that 16 per cent of delegates at the 1933 federal CCF convention (21 of 131) were women. (See also Roome 1989: 106.) Among those attending was Grace MacInnis, the daughter of the new CCF leader, J.S. Woodsworth (Lewis 1993; Farrell 1994). It has also been noted that two women, Louise Lucas (Wright 1965) and Agnes Macphail (Stewart and French 1959; Pennington 1990; Crowley 1990), introduced two of the fourteen sections of the Regina Manifesto.

14 For a comparison with the Liberals and Conservatives, see Brodie 1988. According to Bashevkin and Holder (1985: 280) as early as 1982 the Ontario NDP approved affirmative action for the party's conventions and executive. A recent Ontario NDP provincial executive report (September 1992) on the provincial convention of that year noted that 52 per cent (391 of 758) riding delegates were women. These figures, however, do not include union delegates. As of 1992 gender parity of NDP federal riding delegates was not required, but it was strongly encouraged. Certainly, the features of mandatory parity at senior levels of the party set an important tone for lower levels in the organizational hierarchy. One of the consequences of greater numbers of women attending conventions is the emergence of day care for delegates.

15 Given the decline in the economic sector of heavy industry and the rise in the service sector, one would expect the difference in the rate of unionization of women and men should diminish. For an early account of women and unionization, see E. Sufrin (1983), who was a long time CCF-NDP activist.

16 The 1983 survey of NDP delegates posed a question on gender parity at the convention at which the issue was debated and voted on (see Table 5).

17 When the names of the delegates at the 1977 and 1989 federal councils were being coded, it was not possible to discern the sex of two persons in 1977 and of 12 in 1989. Hence, the data are based on a slightly smaller sample. While no detailed statistics are offered here on the gender breakdown of specialized committees of the federal council, the party has come close to achieving gender parity on these bodies as well (McLaughlin 1992: 48; correspondence and data from Dawn Black to Whitehorn, 16 Nov. 1992). For data on the Ontario NDP provincial council, see also Bashevkin (1985b: 66; 1989: 457; 1991: 68) for partial data on other provincial sections see Kornberg et al. (1979).

18 Some caution in the comparisons should be used given that the nature of the position as well as the title changed over the years.

19 Although the final vote for Audrey McLaughlin was the lowest ever for a federal NDP leader, it should be noted that there has been a steady decline in support for the winner in NDP leadership races. This is partly explained by the increase in the number of candidates, although one suspects another reason may well be the lower esteem in which political leaders are held today. As of late 1994, the NDP had three elected female leaders: McLaughlin at the federal level, Alexa McDonough in Nova Scotia, and Elizabeth Weir in New Brunswick. However, like Thérèse Casgrain in Quebec several decades ago, none of these leaders had much chance of forming the government.

20 Indeed, both ideas are enshrined in the NDP's current constitution.

21 One pleasant partial exception was the British Columbia provincial election of 1941, in which three CCF women were elected.

22 For data on the Ontario NDP see Bashevkin and Holder (1985: 283-4); Bashevkin (1985b: 73); Brodie (1991: 38); Bashevkin (1991: 69). For data on Saskatchewan, see Carbert 1994.

23 Of course many of the female NDP candidates ran for the party in regions where it had little electoral strength, such as Quebec (Brodie and Vickers 1981: 329; Sangster, 1989a: 208). In short, the women were often sacrificial lambs.

24 Although CCF-NDP women have won a total of 17 seats in general elections over seven decades, those seats were held by only 10 women: Gladys Strum, Grace MacInnis, Pauline Jewett, Margaret Mitchell, Lynn McDonald, Marion Dewar, Audrey McLaughlin, Dawn Black, Lynn Hunter, and Joy Langan (1988). NDP provincial election victories in Ontario in 1990 and in Saskatchewan and British Columbia in 1991 saw a record number of women elected and appointed to cabinets.

25 In 1991 the Royal Commission on Electoral Reform and Party Financing recommended that parties receive financial compensation for recruiting female candidates and having them elected. As yet the federal government has not acted on that recommendation.

26 The 1983 data and much of the commentary in this section are derived from Whitehorn (1988, 1992). The 1987 data are derived from Whitehorn and Archer. See Archer and Whitehorn (1990, 1991). For an earlier profile of women in parties see Kornberg et al. (1979).

27 Since income was listed as family income only, no analysis is offered here on gender differences in income.

28 Unless otherwise indicated, the first percentage given in each case is for 1983 and the second for 1987. The sample size in the 1983 survey was 395 persons and that for the 1987 survey was 738 persons (see Table 2).

29 Regrettably the index of a recent book-length study of unions and the NDP does not list the categories of female, gender, sex, or women (Archer 1990). By contrast, Bashevkin (1985b: 48) provides a gender breakdown among unionists supporting the NDP.

30 This finding is at variance with observations made earlier by others (Brodie 1988: 177).

31 Some caution should be exercised in the interpretation of the data, given the small number of people who replied in the affirmative on this particular question, especially in the 1983 survey. See also Kornberg et al. (1979: 207).

32 Because of changes in the research instruments, some caution should be used in comparing the delegates' responses over time. The 1983 NDP survey, permitted respondents to reply to the policy statements with 'agree' 'disagree' or 'no opinion'. That format permitted more inter-party comparison but was less satisfactory for measuring the distribution of opinions on any single item. Accordingly, in the 1987 survey, a five-point Likert scale was employed with the following responses: 'strongly agree', 'agree', 'uncertain', 'disagree', and 'strongly disagree'. Clearly, the 'uncertain' and 'no opinion' categories are not fully equivalent, nor was their placement on the page the same.

33 The statements selected by political scientists for use in surveys are at times as interesting as the responses of the delegates. What is striking about earlier social science research drawn from an era when there were fewer female university professors is how little attention was given to the gender question. Yet another example of this is the virtual absence of items related to women's issues in the earliest surveys (1971 and 1979) of NDP delegates.

34 Interestingly, women's election success rate has not been as high as that of men's (Brodie and Vickers 1981: 325; Brodie 1985b: 124; 1991: 7; Young 1991: 83; Sharpe 1994: 226). The reasons offered by commentators include low winnability of ridings selected, lack of income and other resources, family duties, cultural bias (McLaughlin 1992), and background of the candidates.

35 Bashevkin (1985b: 87-9) reports on the responses of members of the Ontario NDP to a similar question.

36 Even in the CCF era, women were active on the issue of birth control (Sangster 1989a; Melnyk 1989: 80; Lewis 1993; Farrell 1994). As early as 1967 a resolution was passed by an NDP convention favouring the legalization of abortion (Scotton 1977).

37 Some caution should be used in making comparisons because the coding of the questionnaires for the Liberal and Conservative surveys was different from that for the NDP study.

38 Some caution should be exercised since the question was worded differently in the NDP survey.

39 Significantly, 21.3 per cent in 1987 said they were undecided.

40 This situation is accentuated by the existence of a number of caucuses. For example, there is not only a caucus for women (POW), but also one for youth, for each of the provincial sections, and for unionists. See also Archer (1992).

41 For comparison, a similar analysis of areas of issue disagreement within the Conservative Party can be found in Perlin (1980: 154-5).

42 Some caution should be exercised with this assertion since degree of controversy is also a function of the statements that are posed. Summarizing the gender differences on the 52 items, Whitehorn reported, 'Male delegates were more likely to wish to have the NDP present a moderate image, oppose cooperation with communists and expel ultra-leftists from the ranks of the party. Female delegates, not surprisingly, were more favourable to support greater participation by women in politics, a ban on pornography, and the right to abortion. They also showed a stronger desire for the party to shift to the left, to embrace unilateral disarmament, to be concerned about pollution, and to support the rights of homosexuals.' He speculated that 'it may be possible that the trade unionist influence may be contributing to the male pattern of responses. The data on women's attitudes and the 1989 leadership victory of Audrey McLaughlin give some justification to the argument posed by some party members that there may be a potential coalition of compatible interests within the party amongst feminists, radicals, gays, and ecologists. Needless to say, these are neither mutually inclusive nor exclusive categories!' (Whitehorn 1992: 135).

43 A decline occurred even when only the same items were compared over time.

44 One important observation in the surveys was that of the 52 statements posed in 1983, in an overwhelming number of cases (35) the difference in responses between men and women was less than 10. In the 1987 survey, of the 30 general statements studied, the average difference was only 4.8.

45 The average for Liberal/NDP differences was 26.3, for PC/NDP differences 42.7, and for differences between male and female members of the NDP only 4.8.

46 Among men 48.3 per cent agreed, 24.9 per cent were uncertain and, 26.8 per cent disagreed. In contrast, among women 45.3 per cent disagreed, 19.5 per cent were uncertain, and 35.2 per cent agreed.

BIBLIOGRAPHY

Adamson et al. (1988), *Feminist Organizing for Change: The Contemporary Women's Movement in Canada* (Toronto: Oxford University Press).

Anderson, D. (1987), *To Change the World: A Biography of Pauline Jewett* (Richmond Hill, Ont.: Irwin).

——— (1991), *The Unfinished Revolution: The Status of Women in Twelve Countries* (Toronto: Doubleday).

Archer, K. (1990), *Political Choices and Electoral Consequences: A Study of Organized Labour and the New Democratic Party* (Montreal and Kingston, McGill-Queen's University Press).

—— (1991), 'Leadership Selection in the New Democratic Party', in H. Bakvis, ed., *Canadian Political Parties: Leaders, Candidates and Organization* (Toronto: Dundurn).

—— (1992), 'New Politics and New Democrats: Materialist and Postmaterialist Issues and the NDP', paper presented to the Canadian Political Science Association, Charlottetown, June.

Archer, K., and A. Whitehorn (1990), 'Opinion Structure among New Democratic Party Activists: A Comparison with Liberals and Conservatives', *Canadian Journal of Political Science* 23, no. 1 (March).

—— (1991), 'Opinion Structure of New Democrat, Liberal and Conservative Activists', in Thorburn (1991).

—— (1993), *Canadian Trade Unions and the New Democratic Party* (Kingston: Queen's University Industrial Relations Centre).

Armstrong, P., and H. Armstrong (1978), *The Double Ghetto: Canadian Women and Their Segregated Work* (Toronto: McClelland and Stewart).

Bashevkin, S. (1985a), 'Women's Participation in the Ontario Political Parties', in S. Bashevkin, ed., *Canadian Political Behaviour: Introductory Readings* (Toronto: Methuen).

—— (1985b), *Toeing the Lines: Women and Party Politics in English Canada* (Toronto: University of Toronto Press).

—— (1989), 'Political Parties and the Representation of Women', in A. Gagnon and A.B. Tanguay, eds, *Canadian Parties in Transition: Discourse, Organization and Representation* (Scarborough, Ont.: Nelson).

—— (1991), 'Women's Participation in Political Parties', in Megyery (1991).

—— (1993), *Toeing the Lines: Women and Party Politics in English Canada*, 2nd edn (Toronto: Oxford University Press).

Bashevkin, S., and M. Holder (1985), 'The Politics of Female Participation', in D. MacDonald, ed., *The Government and Politics of Ontario* (Toronto: Nelson).

Beeby, D. (1982), 'Women in the Ontario CCF, 1940-1950', *Ontario History* 74, no. 4.

Blake, D. (1988), 'Division and Cohesion: The Major Parties', in Perlin (1988).

Brackman, et al., (1988), 'Wedded to the Welfare State', in J. Jenson et al. (1988).

British Columbia (1994), Ministry of Women's Equality, *Women Count* (Victoria: British Columbia Government).

Brodie, J. (1985a), 'From Waffles to Grits: A Decade in the Life of the New Democratic Party', in Thorburn (1985).

—— (1985b), *Women and Politics in Canada* (Toronto: McGraw-Hill).

—— (1988), 'The Gender Factor and National Leadership Conventions in Canada', in Perlin (1988).

—— (1991),'Women and the Electoral Process in Canada', in Megyery (1991).

Brodie, J., and J. Jenson (1980), *Crisis, Challenge and Change: Party and Class in Canada* (Toronto: Methuen).

—— (1988), *Crisis, Challenge and Change: Party and Class in Canada Revisited* (Toronto: Methuen).

Brodie, J., and J. Vickers (1981), 'The More Things Change . . . Women in the 1979 Federal Campaign', in Penniman (1981).

Brown, R. (1989), *Being Brown: A Very Public Life* (Toronto: Random House).

Brym, R., and B. Fox (1989), *From Culture to Power: The Sociology of English Canada* (Toronto: Oxford University Press).

Burt, S., et al. (1988), *Changing Patterns: Women In Canada* (Toronto: McClelland and Stewart).

Bush, P., et al. (1991), *Women and Politics, 1980-1990: A Selected Bibliography* (North York, Ont.: Dept. of Political Science, York University).

Canada (1993), Chief Electoral Officer, *Official Voting Results* (Ottawa: Elections, Canada).

Carbert, L. (1994), 'Governing on "the Correct, Compassionate, the Saskatchewan Side of the Border"' (unpublished manuscript).

Casgrain, T. (1972), *A Woman in a Man's World* (Toronto: McClelland and Stewart).

Clarke, H., et al. (1980), *Political Choice in Canada* (Toronto: McGraw-Hill Ryerson).

—— (1991), *Absent Mandate* (Toronto: Gage).

Connelly, P. (1978), *Last Hired, First Fired: Women and the Canadian Work Force* (Toronto: Women's Press).

Crowley, T. (1990), *Agnes Macphail and the Politics of Equality* (Toronto: Lorimer).

Duverger, M. (1963), *Political Parties* (New York: Wiley).

Engelmann, F. (1954), 'The Cooperative Commonwealth Federation of Canada: A Study of Membership Participation in Party Policy-Making', Ph.D. diss., Yale University.

Everitt, J. (1994), 'The Gender Gap on Social Welfare Issues: 1966-1990', paper presented to the Canadian Political Science Association, Calgary.

Farrell, A. (1994), *Grace MacInnis* (Toronto: Fitzhenry and Whiteside).

Frizzell A., et al. (1984), *The Canadian General Election of 1984: Politicians, Parties, Press and Polls* (Ottawa: Carleton University Press).

—— et al. (1989), *The Canadian General Election of 1988* (Ottawa: Carleton University Press).

Fry, J., ed. (1979), *Economy, Class and Social Reality: Issues in Contemporary Canadian Society* (Toronto: Butterworths).

Gelb, J. (1989), *Feminism and Politics: A Comparative Perspective* (Berkeley: University of California Press).

Gotell, L., and J. Brodie (1991), 'Women and Parties: More than Issue of Numbers', in Thorburn (1991).

Hayward, S., and A. Whitehorn (1991), 'Leadership Selection: Which Method?' paper presented to the Douglas-Coldwell Foundation, Ottawa, Apr.

Howard, I. (1992), *The Struggle for Social Justice in British Columbia: Helena Gutteridge, the Unknown Reformer* (Vancouver: University of British Columbia Press).

Jennings, K. (1990), 'Women in Party Politics,' in L. Tilly and P. Gurin, eds, *Women, Politics and Change* (New York: Russell Sage)

Jennings, K., and B. Farah (1981), 'Social Roles and Political Resources: An Over-Time Study of Men and Women in Party Elites', *American Journal of Political Science 25*, 3.

Jennings, K., and N. Thomas (1968), 'Men and Women in Party Elites: Social Roles and Political Resources', *MidWest Journal of Political Science 12*; no. 4.

Jenson J., et al., eds (1988), *Feminization of the Labor Force* (New York: Oxford University Press).

Johnson, R., et al. (1992), *Letting the People Decide: Dynamics of a Canadian Election* (Montreal and Kingston: McGill-Queen's University Press).

Kealey L., and J. Sangster, eds (1989), *Beyond the Vote: Canadian Women and Politics* (Toronto: University of Toronto Press).

Kirkpatrick, J. (1976), *The New Presidential Elite: Men and Women in National Politics* (New York: Russell Sage).

Kome, P., ed. (1985), *Women of Influence: Canadian Women and Politics* (Toronto: Doubleday).

Kornberg, A., et al. (1979), *Citizen Politicians—Canada: Party Officials in a Democratic Society* (Durham, N.C.: Caroline Academic Press).

Lazarus, M. (1983), *Six Women Who Dared* (Toronto: Carswell).

Leduc, D. (1991a), 'Women in Politics: Women Elected for the Co-operative Commonwealth Federation or the New Democratic Party' (Ottawa, unpublished report).

———(1991b), 'Statistics on Women Candidates for the Co-operative Commonwealth Federation or the New Democratic Party, 1932-1991 (Ottawa, unpublished report).

———(1991c), 'Women Candidates for the New Democratic Party, 1961-1991' (Ottawa, unpublished report).

Lewis, S. (1993), *Grace: The Life of Grace MacInnis* (Madeira Park, BC: Harbour).

Lovenduski, J., and J. Hills, eds (1981), *The Politics of the Second Electorate: Women and Public Participation* (London: Routledge).

Manley, J. (1980), 'Women and the Left in the 1930s: The Case of the Toronto CCF Women's Joint Committee', *Atlantis* 5, no. 2.

McKie, C., and K. Thompson, eds (1990), *Canadian Social Trends* (Toronto: Thompson).

McLaughlin, A. (1992), *A Woman's Place: My Life and Politics* (Toronto: Macfarlane, Walter and Ross).

Macpherson, K. (1994), *When in Doubt, Do Both* (Toronto: University of Toronto Press).

Megyery, K., ed. (1991), *Women in Canadian Politics: Toward Equity in Representation*, vol. 6 of the research studies of the Royal Commission on Electoral Reform and Party Financing (Ottawa and Toronto: RCERPF/Dundurn).

Meisel, J. (1975), *Working Papers on Canadian Politics* (Montreal: McGill-Queen's University Press).

Melnyk, O. (1989), *No Bankers in Heaven: Remembering the CCF*, Toronto (McGraw-Hill Ryerson).

Michels, R. (1962), *Political Parties: A Sociological Study of the Oligarchic Tendencies of Modern Democracy* (New York: Free Press).

Mueller, C., ed. (1988), *The Politics of the Gender Gap: The Social Construction of Political Influence* (Newbury Park, CA.: Sage).

Pammett, J. (1989), 'The 1988 Vote', in Frizzell et al. (1989).

Penniman, H. (1975), *Canada at the Polls: The General Election of 1974* (Washington, D.C.: American Enterprise Institute).

—— (1981), *Canada at the Polls: 1979 and 1980: A Study of the General Elections* (Washington, D.C.: American Enterprise Institute).

—— (1988), *Canada at the Polls, 1984: A Study of the Federal General Elections* (Durham, N.C.: Duke University Press).

Pennington, D. (1990), *Agnes Macphail: Reformer, Canada's First Female MP* (Toronto: Simon and Pierre).

Perlin, G. (1980), *The Tory Syndrome* (Montreal and Kingston: McGill-Queen's).

Perlin, G., ed. (1988), *Party Democracy in Canada* (Scarborough, Ont.: Prentice-Hall).

Pitkin, H. (1967), *The Concept of Representation* (Berkeley: University of California Press).

Poole, K., and L. Zeigler (1985), *Women, Public Opinion and Politics: The Changing Political Attitudes of American Women* (New York: Longman).

Porter, J. (1967), *Canadian Social Structure: A Statistical Profile* (Toronto: McClelland and Stewart).

Prentice, A., et al. (1988), *Canadian Women: A History* (Toronto: Harcourt, Brace Jovanovich).

Rinehart, S. (1992), *Gender Consciousness and Politics* (New York: Routledge).

Roome, P. (1989), 'Amelia Turner and Calgary Labour Women, 1919-1935', in Kealey and Sangster (1989).

Roy, L. (1992), *Brown Girl in the Ring: Rosemary Brown: A Biography for Young People* (Toronto: Black Women and Women of Colour Press).

Sangster, J. (1989a), *Dreams of Equality: Women on the Canadian Left, 1920-1950* (Toronto: McClelland and Stewart).

——— (1989b), 'The Role of Women in the Early CCF, 1933-1940', in Kealey and Sangster (1989).

Sauve, R. (1990), *Canadian People Patterns* (Saskatoon: Western Producer Prairie Books).

Scotton, A., ed. (1977), *New Democratic Policies 1961-1976* (Ottawa: Mutual).

Sharpe, S. (1994), *The Gilded Ghetto* (Toronto: Harper Collins).

Stanbury, W.T. (1989), 'Financing Federal Political Parties in Canada, 1974-1986', in A. Gagnon and A.B. Tanguay, eds, *Canadian Parties in Transition: Discourse, Organization and Representation* (Scarborough, Ont.: Nelson).

Stewart, M., and D. French (1959), *Ask No Quarter: A Biography of Agnes Macphail* (Toronto: Longmans).

Sufrin, E. (1983), *The Eaton Drive* (Toronto: Fitzhenry and Whiteside).

Surrey-Newton NDP (1994), *Then and Now: A Celebration of CCF/NDP Women* (Surrey, BC: n.p.).

Thorburn, H., ed. (1979), *Party Politics in Canada*, 4th edn (Scarborough, Ont.: Prentice-Hall).

——— (1985), *Party Politics in Canada*, 5th edn (Scarborough: Prentice-Hall).

——— (1991), *Party Politics in Canada*, 6th edn (Scarborough, Ont.: Prentice-Hall).

Toennies, F. (1963), *Community and Society* (New York: Harper and Row).

Trofimenkoff, S. (1989), 'Thérèse Casgrain and the CCF in Quebec', in Kealey and Sangster (1989).

United Nations (1991), *The World's Women; 1970-1990: Trends and Statistics* (New York: United Nations).

Vallance, E. (1979), *Women in the House: A Study of Women Members of Parliament* (London: Athlone).

Vickers, J. (1989), 'Feminist Approaches to Women in Politics', in Kealey and Sangster (1989).

Vickers, J., and J. Brodie (1981), 'Canada', in Lovenduski and Hills (1981).

Wearing, J. (1988), *Strained Relations* (Toronto: McClelland and Stewart).

Wearing, P., and J. Wearing (1991), 'Does Gender Make a Difference in Voting Behaviour?' in J. Wearing, ed., *The Ballot and Its Message: Voting in Canada* (Toronto: Copp Clark Pitman).

Webster, D. (nd), *Growth of the NDP in BC, 1900-1970* (Vancouver: BC NDP).

White, J. (1980), *Women and Unions* (Ottawa: Government of Canada).

———— (1993), *Sisters and Solidarity: Women and Unions in Canada* (Toronto: Thompson Educational Publishing).

Whitehorn, A. (1988), 'The New Democratic Party in Convention', in G. Perlin (1988).

———— (1992), *Canadian Socialism: Essays on the CCF-NDP* (Toronto: Oxford).

———— (1994), 'The NDP's Quest for Survival', in A. Frizzell et al., *The Canadian General Election of 1993* (Ottawa: Carleton University Press).

———— (1995), 'Women and Politics: A Social Democratic Perspective' (unpublished manuscript).

Whitehorn, A., and K. Archer (1994), 'Party Activists and Political Leadership: A Case Study of the NDP', in M. Mancuso et al., eds, *Leaders and Leadership in Canada* (Toronto: Oxford University Press).

Wilson, S. (1982), *Women, the Family and the Economy* (Toronto: McGraw-Hill).

Wright, J.F.C. (1965), *The Louise Lucas Story: This Time Tomorrow* (Montreal: Harvest House).

Young, L. (1991), 'Legislative Turnover and the Election of Women to the Canadian House of Commons', in K. Megyery (1991).

CHAPTER 2

Gender and Support for Feminism

A Case Study of the 1989 Quebec General Election

Manon Tremblay

During the last 20 years, Canadian politics has been altered by the increase in the number of women in Parliament and the legislatures. But we still do not completely understand the implications for Canadian society in general—and its female population in particular—of the arrival of these new actors on the parliamentary scene. As long as women were barely visible in political institutions, we could blame that for the lukewarm reception of governments to the demands of feminist movement. However, as the number of women in politics increased, the hope developed that these elected women would defend, in the political arena, proposals that were likely to improve women's living conditions.

Some research has suggested a relationship between the presence of women in the political system and the promotion of feminist demands: if more women entered Parliament, the political system would become more receptive to the demands of the feminist movement. This assumption is inspired by the work of Rosabeth M. Kanter (1977), who says that when a minority in an organization such as women in parliament reaches a proportion of about 35 per cent its commitment to a cause becomes more intense because it may question the dominant—in this case, male—culture (for empirical evidence see Mezey 1978; Saint-Germain 1989; Thomas 1991). In addition, the inclusion of feminist demands on the political agenda could inspire women to become politically active (Black and McGlen 1979; Smith and Wachtel 1992: 24).

This hope is certainly encouraged by the presence of female politicians who support the demands of the feminist movement. The best-known examples are Flora MacDonald, Lucie Pépin, and Audrey McLaughlin in the House of Commons (McLaughlin 1992; Sharpe 1994), and Louise Harel and Lise Payette in the Quebec National Assembly (Payette 1982). In 1991 the female members of the House of Commons demonstrated as a group that women make a difference in politics when they lobbied against Bill C-43, which would have recriminalized abortion (Sharpe 1994: 208-11).

But the debate has also been sustained by the interest of the feminist movement in the question of power. This interest is based on the idea that political and parliamentary power may be used to reach socio-political and economic equality between women and men by enforcing the law, adopting new legislation or rules favourable to women, and lobbying interest groups. That idea was supported by the creation of FRAPPE (Femmes regroupées pour l'accès aux pouvoirs économiques et politiques, Women for Access to Political and Economic Power) in 1985 and the holding of symposia on the role of women in politics.[1] In May 1992, the Quebec coalition of women's groups, 'Québec féminin pluriel', proposed that a solidarity fund be set up to support feminists interested in becoming active in political parties (*Le Devoir*, 1 June 1992).

Canadian and Quebec political parties had already shown some receptiveness to feminist demands; that is not insignificant considering their importance in providing access to the House of Commons, as well as the Quebec National Assembly. Consider, first, the debate between the leaders of the three major parties during the 1984 Canadian general election campaign concerning questions of particular interest to women; second, the Parti Québécois (PQ) leadership race in 1985 in which for the first time two women competed; and, third, the 1989 election of Audrey McLaughlin as leader of the New Democratic Party. Moreover, as much in Ottawa as in Quebec, the parties have committed themselves to reaching a fairer representation of women and men, notably by recruiting more female candidates for winnable constituencies or by establishing special funds to support them financially.

Those circumstances—that is, female parliamentarians favourable to feminist demands, the interest of feminist movement in political power, and the receptivity of political parties to feminist demands—together with the election of a greater number of women since the 1970s, have facilitated the integration into the formal political arena of issues which were previously considered private (such as violence against women, child care, marital rape, and the status of women working with their husbands in a family business). One of the most obvious consequences was a questioning of the split in political thought and socio-political life between the public (male) and private (female) spheres. As well, women's status as second-class citizens by virtue of their sex became clear.

Thus, it is essential to know more about the reactions of female politicians to feminist demands, since an improvement in the social status of women depends at least in part on the intervention of the state (be it only in such matters as abortion, sexual harassment in the workplace, or pay equity). Furthermore, when the satisfaction of feminist demands remains dependent on the government's perception of its own role, the political parties that favour a neo-conservative philosophy could be tempted to recruit women to give the impression of agreeing to feminist demands—or at least to certain minimal requirements regarding representatives of the female population. In reality, these female politicians were more loyal to their party than to feminism (Gotell and Brodie, 1991).

Research by political scientists (mostly women) is another way to explore the connection between a greater number of women in places of power and a positive response to feminist demands. It is this Canadian and Quebec literature which will now hold our attention.

FEMALE POLITICIANS AND FEMINIST DEMANDS IN CANADA AND QUEBEC

Eichler (1979) questioned 300 members of parliament and in the provincial legislatures, both female and male, on matters concerning employment (such as access to jobs and vocational training, pay discrimination and probability of being fired before men), access to leadership positions, housework and child care. She reports that men gave less importance than their female counterparts to equality between the sexes, and they are less conscious of the inequalities in their relationships. She concludes: 'To get more women into decision-making positions must, therefore, be an integral part of the effort to realize sex equality in Canada' (p. 72). In a more recent article, Burt (1988) supports the same hope for an end to the traditional gender roles due to the effect of an increased presence of women in Parliament. Bashevkin expresses the same point of view in two articles, one published in 1985, the other in 1989. In the first, she wishes to know to what extent the delegates, both female and male, to the 1982 conventions of the New Democratic, Progressive Conservative, and Liberal parties of Ontario supported affirmative action for women in political party. In all the parties, not only did a majority of the female respondents support affirmative action, but they did so more strongly than the men. In addition, as in Eichler's (1979) research, more women than men thought there was discrimination against women in their party. In reference to affirmative action and discrimination, Bashevkin (1985) notes a difference among women according to their party affiliation, as observed in related research conducted in the United States (Berkman and O'Connor 1993; Leader 1977; Norris 1986; Sapiro and Farah 1980; Thomas 1991). In her 1989 article Bashevkin says that the goal adopted by the Ontario New Democratic Party in 1982, and by the federal party in 1983, of achieving equal representation of women and men in the party is 'an important example of party women pursuing structural reforms in order to increase numerical and, hence, substantive representation' (p. 458; see also Bashevkin and Holder 1985). Bashevkin (1989) thus establishes a causal relationship between 'quantitative representation' (that is, the number of women elected) and 'qualitative representation' (female politicians speaking and acting for women in the population).

Following the example of Bashevkin (1985), Brodie (1987) also became interested in political delegates of both sexes but this time at the federal level, specifically at the Progressive Conservative convention of 1983 and the Liberal Party convention of 1984. On those two occasions, women were significantly (from a statistical point of view) more favourable to feminist demands than their male counterparts; that applied especially to free choice for women in regard to abortion and the commitments made to sexual equality. Regarding government spending for child care, the female-male gap was statistically significant only in the Liberal Party. Free choice regarding abortion was supported by almost identical proportions of the female Conservative and Liberal delegates, but the question about publically financed day care reveals important differences between the female delegates in the two parties. Brodie (1987) believes that the female-male gap explains why feminist demands are always situated at the bottom of the political priority scale; in the present state of things men, who predominate in the important positions in the political parties, are less strongly committed to women's issues than their female counterparts. Among the female and male members of the Canadian New Democratic Party during the 1980s, Whitehorn and Archer (in this volume) identify the spreads between the opinions of women and those of men on the women's issues (particularly of abortion and pornography).

We know little about the attitude of Quebec female politicians toward feminist demands. Gingras, Maillé, and Tardy (1989) interviewed 148 Quebec female and male activists during the second half of the 1980s, with the goal of understanding gender differences in political parties and unions. According to them, in those organizations only women defend women's interests (p. 175). Their results are in line with those from English Canada (Bashevkin 1985; Eichler 1979): fewer women than men rejected affirmative action measures, probably because women are more conscious than men of their minority status within their organization.

In a study of female and male candidates of the New Democratic Party, the Liberal Party, and the Parti Québécois during the 1989 Quebec general election, I concentrated on the reaction of women in politics to the demands made by the feminist movement. Even though a strong majority of women and men endorsed the transformation in the social status of Quebec women during the last few years and the actions of the feminist movement in that direction, female candidates were more inclined than male candidates to consider that women politicians have a particular responsibility to represent the interests of the female population. The female and male candidates of the Liberal Party were the most resistant to such a conception of the political role of women, and to the feminist movement (Tremblay 1992). In a general way, female candidates expressed opinions more in keeping with feminist goals than men did; this difference was especially marked in relation to the family and reproduction, employment, and culture, but not politics. Nevertheless, sometimes sex proved to be a weaker determinant than political party and political philosophy (Tremblay 1993).

This chapter is part of the same research project, in that it examines the opinions of women and men in politics about the demands of the feminist movement. More precisely, I want to understand better if a larger number of women in positions of power may cause the political system to become more receptive to feminist demands and, accordingly, favour a transformation in gender relations. To that end I will investigate two hypotheses, both of which follow the line of thought of the research mentioned previously: the first proposes that women in politics support unconditionally all demands made by the feminist movement, and more strongly than the men; the second states that women in politics react uniformly to feminist demands. Three questions will be asked: (1) What feminist demands do women in politics support? (2) Do female politicians give a uniform answer to these demands? (3) Which demands divide the sexes?

METHODOLOGY

After the 1989 Quebec general election, I mailed a self-administered questionnaire (see Appendix) to all the candidates of the three major political parties: the New Democratic Party of Quebec (NDPQ), the Liberal Party of Quebec (PLQ), and the Parti Québécois (PQ). There were 305 candidates, and 157 of them completed and returned this form, for a response rate of 51.5 per cent. The questionnaire consisted of 22 statements using the Likert's scale of responses (that is, 'agree strongly', 'agree', 'neither', 'disagree', 'disagree strongly', 'don't know'). The questions concerned gender relations and were inspired by the demands made by the principal Quebec feminist groups during the last 15 years (which corresponds with the second wave of feminism). In asking so many questions, my aim was to learn the opinions of the candidates on a large inventory of feminist demands, and not only on a few claims considered in an isolated fashion, as most other studies have done.

The statements refer to two models of gender relations central to feminist thought, the hierarchical (or segregated) model and the egalitarian model. The feminist movement wants to change the socio-political relations between women and men by substituting an egalitarian relationship for the hierarchical relationship. Thus, I tried to identify the opinions that support the equality option and that reject the unequal perspective, a point of view in agreement with the feminist goal of changing gender relations. The statements in the questionnaire correspond to four principal subjects addressed by the demands of Quebec feminist groups: (1) the family and reproduction, a category that includes such issues as equality of partners, the sharing of parental responsibilities, and freedom of choice for women in regard to abortion; (2) employment, which includes child care, equal pay for work of equal value, and affirmative action; (3) politics, which includes numerical parity for the sexes in positions of power, systemic discrimination, and the specialization of female politicians in portfolios viewed as feminine like health, family, or social security; and (4) culture, which mainly concerns education. This organization of statements by themes permitted a more complete and diversified evaluation of female and male candidates' opinions.

Frequency tables with percentages are used for the presentation of results. In order to analyse the relationship between gender and feminist demands, I have carried out chi-square tests. Factor analysis has also been done, in order to isolate the influences of variables such as age, education, occupation, political party, and political philosophy[2] on political women's opinions of feminist demands.

THE FINDINGS

Female Candidates and Feminist Demands

Do Quebec political women support the demands of the feminist movement? Do certain demands divide women? If so, which are they and which variables permit us to understand these divisions? These questions are answered in part by Tables 1, 2, 3, and 4. The tables show that a majority of the female candidates in the 1989 Quebec election express support for feminist goals; for 19 of the 22 statements the female respondents either endorse the feminist position or reject the conception of unequal gender roles. Fifteen of these 19 statements received the support of at least three female respondents out of four; those 15 statements included all the feminist demands pertaining to employment, and a majority of those related to the family and reproduction and to education, but only two related to politics.

The tables also show that female candidates do not all share the same opinion about feminist demands. In fact, some questions divide women. This is the case notably with freedom of choice for women on abortion (only 66.7 per cent of the female respondents support this demand); the primacy of the maternal role (only a little more than half of the female respondents believe that women with young children should work outside the home); systemic discrimination in the political system (close to two female respondents out of five do not see that the rules of the political game prevent women from being fully integrated into parliamentary life); and affirmative action in politics (almost one woman in three rejects this means of increasing the number of women in positions of political power).

TABLE 1 DISTRIBUTION OF RESPONSES TO FEMINIST DEMANDS
CONCERNING FAMILY AND REPRODUCTION, BY SEX

	Agree		Disagree		Other Responses	
	Women	Men	Women	Men	Women	Men
1[a] Mothers in the home	4	23	23	60	13	34
	10%	19.7%	57.5%	51.3%	32.5%	29.1%
3 Abortion, anti-choice	1	18	32	84	5	14
	2.6%	15.5%	84.2%	72.4%	13.2%	12.1%
5 Working mothers	34	78	4	21	2	13
	85%	69.6%	10%	18.8%	5%	11.6%
9 Abortion, pro-choice*	26	49	7	46	6	22
	66.7%	41.9%	18%	39.3%	15.4%	18.8%
15 Sharing of family tasks	38	108	0	4	2	5
	95%	92.3%	0%	3.4%	5%	4.3%
16 Paternity leave	39	96	1	9	0	9
	97.5%	84.2%	2.5%	7.9%	0%	7.9%

[a]Numbers correspond to statements in the questionnaire (see Appendix).
*p < .05.
Note: Each figure in italics is the N corresponding to the percentage on the line below.

TABLE 2 DISTRIBUTION OF RESPONSES TO FEMINIST DEMANDS
CONCERNING EMPLOYMENT, BY SEX

	Agree		Disagree		Other Responses	
	Women	Men	Women	Men	Women	Men
6[a] Child care facilities	36	99	2	9	2	8
	90%	85.3%	5%	7.8%	5%	6.9%
8 Affirmative action in employment*	4	23	32	67	4	25
	10%	20%	80%	58.3%	10%	21.7%
10 Financial needs	0	8	39	103	1	3
	0%	7%	97.5%	90.4%	2.5%	2.6%
13 Equal pay for work of equal value	39	116	1	0	0	0
	97.5%	100%	2.5%	0%	0%	0%
19 Non-traditional jobs for women	1	5	37	99	2	12
	2.5%	4.3%	92.5%	85.3%	5%	10.3%

[a]Numbers correspond to statements in the questionnaire (see Appendix).
*p < .05.
Note: Each figure in italics is the N corresponding to the percentage on the line below.

TABLE 3 DISTRIBUTION OF RESPONSES TO FEMINIST DEMANDS
CONCERNING CULTURE, BY SEX

	Agree		Disagree		Other Responses	
	Women	Men	Women	Men	Women	Men
7[a] Home economics	1	8	38	94	1	14
	2.5%	6.9%	95%	81%	2.5%	12.1%
11 Sporting activities*	31	63	4	25	4	27
	79.5%	54.8%	10.3%	21.7%	10.3%	23.5%
17 Domestic and maternal skills*	3	7	34	92	3	16
	7.5%	6.1%	85%	80%	7.5%	13.9%
20 Homosexuality*	11	29	15	69	11	15
	29.7%	25.7%	40.5%	61.1%	29.7%	13.3%
22 School textbooks and education	39	99	1	8	0	10
	97.5%	84.6%	2.5%	6.8%	0%	8.6%

[a]Numbers correspond to statements in the questionnaire (see Appendix).
*p < .05.
Note: Each figure in italics is the N corresponding to the percentage on the line below.

TABLE 4 DISTRIBUTION OF RESPONSES TO FEMINIST DEMANDS
CONCERNING POLITICS, BY SEX

	Agree		Disagree		Other Responses	
	Women	Men	Women	Men	Women	Men
2[a] Affirmative action in politics	22	43	12	55	6	18
	55%	37.1%	30%	47.4%	15%	15.5%
4 Responsibility, family and education	13	17	16	74	10	26
	33.3%	14.5%	41%	63.3%	25.6%	22.2%
12 Rules of the game in politics*	21	35	15	63	2	14
	55.3%	31.3%	39.5%	56.3%	5.3%	12.5%
14 Improvement of political life*	32	34	1	41	6	37
	82.1%	30.4%	2.6%	36.6%	15.4%	33%
18 Representation in decision-making positions*	39	59	0	24	1	33
	97.5%	50.9%	0%	20.7%	2.5%	28.5%
21 Access to decision-making positions*	30	69	6	30	1	18
	81.1%	59%	16.2%	25.6%	2.7%	15.4%

[a]Numbers correspond to statements in the questionnaire (see Appendix).
*p < .05.
Note: Each figure in italics is the N corresponding to the percentage on the line below.

Moreover, more than two female respondents out of five do not consider that homosexuality should be presented as a normal form of sexual behaviour by the schools, thus rejecting the most radical demand of the feminist movement. More than four female respondents out of five believe that the presence of more women in politics would improve political life, reminding us of the concept of patriarchy propounded by Elshtain (1974) in a classical article entitled 'Moral Woman and Immoral Man'. Furthermore, one female candidate out of three considers that women in politics have a particular responsibility for the 'feminine' portfolios of the family and child rearing—thus defining women as primarily private human beings. In reference to that phenomenon, Sapiro (1983: 73) says, 'Even where women are involved in public life, as in the workforce and politics, their activities and concerns are expected to be imbued with the private significance of being a woman.'

If women do not share a uniform view of the feminist demands, what other variables allow us to understand and predict their opinions? To answer this question, we have proceeded to factor analyses.[3] The variables used here are of two types: the socio-professional variables (like age, level of education, occupation and party affiliation) and the variables inherent to the objectives of this study (political philosophy and attitude toward feminist demands). Figures 1, 2, 3, and 4[4] can thus be thought of as a map of the feminist demands related to a theme on which is superimposed socio-professional characteristics and a normative sketch that represents a liberal or conservative view of political society. The percentages at the end of the internal axes of the figures represent the inertia explained by each axis. For example in Figure 1 the first factorial axis D_1 (19.2 per cent) explains almost 20 per cent of the sum of all the other axes theoretically possible and the second factorial axis D_2 contributes 13.8 per cent. In this way, the first and second factorial axes together represent 33 per cent of all the relations between variables; that prompts us to use caution in the interpretation of Figure 1, since it yields only a part of the total information. Nevertheless, even though this percentage appears weak, these two axes account for almost a third of the cloud of points belonging to the 20 axes that compose the model of the relations on the theme of family and reproduction; this demonstrates the importance of the first and second axes in this abstract model. The purpose of the numbers along the horizontal and vertical axes of the figures is simply to facilitate the positioning of each point (or vector) in the quadrant along the first and second axes (D_1 and D_2). Finally, each point in the figures represents the mean of a candidate's responses to the questions on a specific theme.

Two preliminary observations should be made about the figures. The factor analysis refers to women only, not to women and men. The reason for that decision is not only my goal of understanding and predicting better the responses of women to feminist demands, but also my desire to contribute to the debate on feminist strategy in regard to power. This debate is expressed in these terms: must we try to increase the number of women in the democratic institutions simply to make them more numerous—notwithstanding their feelings towards feminist demands—or should we support only those women that would be the most likely to endorse feminist goals? If so, how can those women be identified? A second remark concerns the limitations of factor analysis which, even though it gives a global picture of a phenomenon, does not allow us to assume a causal relation between two variables closely situated on the graph. For example, for a female candidate, membership in the NDPQ does not necessarily imply that she will have feminist opinions. Rather these figures must be understood as an ideal type of female candidate supportive of feminist demands, depending on the particular variable.

Figures 1, 2, 3, and 4 illustrate the socio-professional and philosophical variables used for the analysis of feminist and anti-feminist opinions. The second ordinal axis (D_2) is the most significant to the analysis. It contrasts the female NDP and PQ candidates with the Liberal candidates; the female candidates aged between 18 and 49 with those 50 and over; the women that have a university education with those that do not; the female candidates that are employed in high-level jobs with those who work in a subordinate position; and finally, the women with a liberal political philosophy with those with a conservative political philosophy. In other words, the young female candidates of the New Democratic Party of Quebec and of the PQ, university-educated, working as professionals or at a management level, and of liberal philosophy present a similar feminist profile, while the liberal female candidates in their fifties, who have not attended university, working in a subordinate position, and who have a conservative political philosophy are united in their opposition to feminist demands.

Since factor analysis simply offers a general survey of the relations between variables without any quantification, I have also done chi-square tests. I was thus able to confirm that there are significant differences (statistically speaking, 19 times out of 20) among women in their support for feminist demands:

- On issues related to the family and reproduction (see Figure 1), there is a difference between women aged 18 to 49 and those who are 50 and over (F: 7.85; df: 1; 36; P: 0.0081);[5] between the female candidates who have attended university and those who have not (F: 5.28; df: 1; 37; P: 0.0273); and between the female candidates with a liberal and conservative political philosophy (F: 13.59; df: 1; 37; P: 0.0007).
- On the subject of employment (see Figure 2), there are differences between the university and the non-university female candidates (F: 4.74; df: 1; 37; P: 0.0358) and between the women of liberal and conservative philosophy (F: 14.49; df: 1; 37; P: 0.0005).
- On the subject of politics (see Figure 3), a single difference was found to be significant, the one between women who have graduated from university and those who have not (F: 6.36; df: 1; 37; P: 0.0161).

FIGURE 1 FACTOR ANALYSIS — SUBJECT: FAMILY AND REPRODUCTION

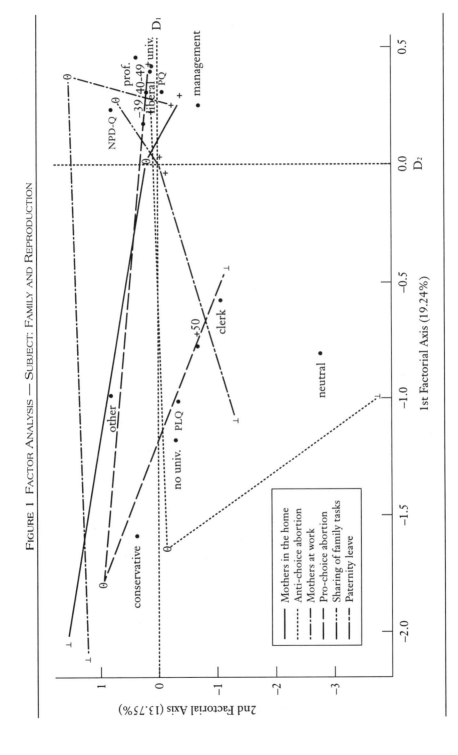

FIGURE 2 FACTOR ANALYSIS — SUBJECT: EMPLOYMENT

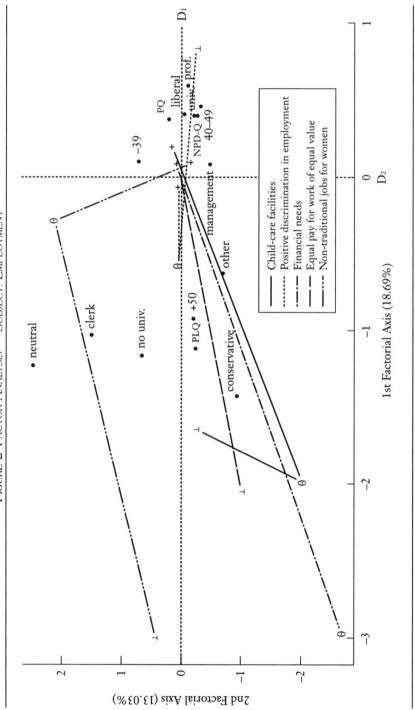

FIGURE 3 FACTOR ANALYSIS — SUBJECT: POLITICS

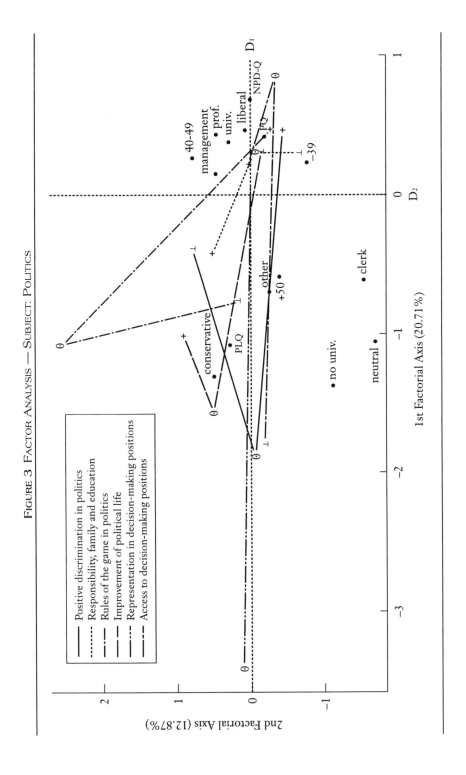

FIGURE 4 FACTOR ANALYSIS — SUBJECT: CULTURE

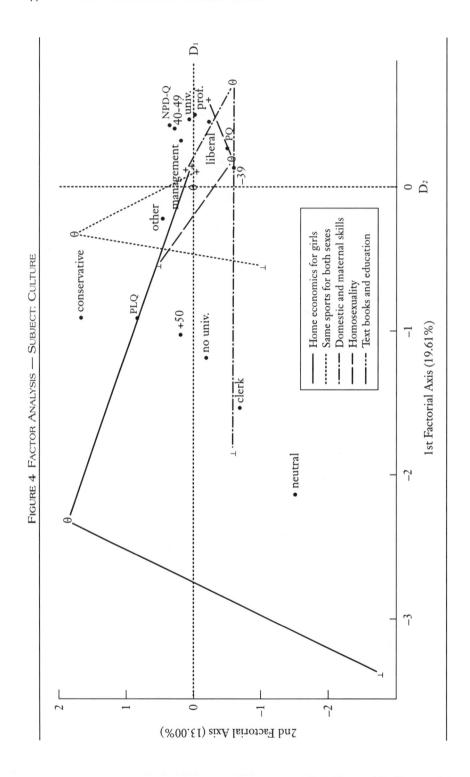

- Finally, on the subject of culture (see Figure 4), women are divided by age (F: 6.00; df: 1; 36; P: 0.0193) and political philosophy (F: 6.08; df: 1; 37; P: 0.0185).

The variables for type of employment and political party also account for a distinction among women's responses to feminist demands, even though the differences are not statistically significant.

It seems that a woman who belongs to a political party with a social-democratic tendency, is young, has attended university, holds a management position, and has a liberal political philosophy is likely to be favourable to a transformation of gender relations, be it in supporting the demands of the feminist movement or in rejecting the model of unequal gender relations. These results support those obtained from similar research conducted in Canada (Fletcher and Chalmers 1991; Tremblay and Boivin 1991), in the United States (Cook 1989; Klein 1984: 108-11; Lilie, Handberg, and Lowrey 1982; Welch and Sigelman 1982), and in Europe (Mossuz-Lavau and Sineau 1983: 68-77; Welch and Thomas 1988). I propose the following explanation.

The social-democratic and liberal political philosophies meet in their conception of the state, which they view as an instrument for achieving greater social equality between individuals. Therefore, many of the demands voiced by the feminist movement for the equality of women and men call for a statist solution. Also, the people who are to the left and the centre-left of the political spectrum can support feminist demands because they conform to their vision of the relations between the state and society. In regard to education, university is an institution that favours the criticism of traditional beliefs and the transmission and acquisition of new cultural and ethical standards. It is in this way that attending university can give rise to a new understanding of gender relations and gender roles that is compatible with the feminist creed. Moreover, most universities now offer feminist courses. This value transformation is effected much more readily in people living in a social climate favourable to such a re-examination. Starting in the middle of the 1970s the feminist movement in Quebec has in fact been examining gender relations in so far as they imply segregated and specialized roles according to sex. The female candidates aged between 18 and 49 at the time of my study in 1989 were at most 35 in 1975, an age at which many people re-examine their beliefs and become more receptive to new ideas.

Gender Differences in Support for Feminist Demands

The last part of this research consists in discovering whether women and men react in the same way to feminist demands. Tables 1, 2, 3, and 4 reveal at least two constants. One is that for 17 of the 22 statements the male candidates expressed a point of view that is compatible with feminist goals. The answers from men are similar to those from women, except in respect to affirmative action and systemic discrimination in politics. Whereas a major-ity of the female respondents are in favour of affirmative action programs in politics, almost half the male respondents are opposed. Similarly, whereas a majority of women believe that the rules of the game in politics prevent the full integration of women into the political system, more than 56 per cent of the men do not.

The other constant is that even though the answers of men are less polarized than those of women—only 9 of the 17 statements won the support of at least 75 per cent of the male respondents for any one of the possible answers—men and women are similar in their lack of unanimity regarding certain feminist demands: like their female colleagues, men are divided on the question of freedom of choice for women on matters of reproduction, on the importance of the maternal role, on systemic discrimination, and on affirmative action programs in politics. They are also divided on the conse-quences for the political system of the presence of more women on the polit-ical scene.

Nevertheless, there are statistically significant differences between the answers of the female and male candidates: such a gap is evident in 9 of the 22 statements—where men are more reluctant to support feminist demands. The differences are apparent particularly in the statements concerning poli-tics (all except the one on affirmative action), culture (sports activities and homosexuality), employment (notably affirmative action in employment), and the family and reproduction (freedom of choice for women regarding abortion). In the case of the question about the particular responsibility of female politicians for the portfolios which concern the family and education, and the one about the transformation of the rules of the political game, *it is the men whose answers conform more to the feminist point of view*. In fact, to agree with these propositions implies to endorse a hierarchical division of gender roles unfavourable to women, because they define women primarily as 'pri-vatized' human beings (Sapiro 1983). First, this result can be explained as much by the absence of a consensus between female politicians regarding their responsibility to the female population, as by the refusal of men in pol-itics to recognize for their female colleagues such a specific responsibility, which would signify the end of the myth of neutral (meaning male) political representation (see Tremblay 1991). Second, the result can also be explained by an idealistic conception of the political role of women, and a confidence by men in their traditional style of public management, which is an integral part of the political culture.

CONCLUSION

This chapter set out to explore the idea that the presence of more women in the parliamentary arena could make the political system more receptive to the demands of feminists, and indeed favour a transformation in gender relations. I carried out a survey of opinions of the female and male candidates for the NDPQ, the PLQ, and the PQ in the 1989 Quebec general election, with the intention of answering three questions: (1) What feminist demands do women in politics support? (2) Which variables (age, level of education, occupation, political party, and political philosophy) are associated with favourable (or unfavourable) opinions of feminist demands? (3) Which demands divide the sexes?

A majority of the Quebec female candidates in 1989 expressed opinions compatible with the feminist perspective on most of the questions. These answers consisted as much of support for the feminist creed as of a rejection of the unequal or segregated conception of gender roles. The support of the female candidates was weaker on the questions of homosexuality, the role of women in politics, and the consequences of their presence on the parliamentary scene. In fact, the feminist profile drawn by the factor analysis is one of a young New Democratic or PQ candidate with a university education, who has a management or professional job, and whose view of society is compatible with a liberal philosophy. Men, as a whole, do not express opinions that are contrary to feminist ideals: they agree with their female counterparts, except on the questions of affirmative action in politics and systemic discrimination in the political system. The subject of politics is the one where the female-male gap is widest.

In two respects these results supported the argument that if more women entered Parliament, the political system would become more receptive to the demands of the feminist movement. Firstly, since political women are in favour of feminist demands, if their numbers were greater they could not only call into question the political culture defined by and for men, but could also ensure that their feminist point of view were heard (and perhaps even adopted), as Kanter (1977), Mezey (1978), and Saint-Germain (1989) have demonstrated for the United States. Secondly, female politicians support more than men the central demands of the feminist movement—notably free choice regarding abortion—and that is not insignificant in a context where this right is not recognized by the law. (For more on this subject, see Brodie, Gavigan, and Jenson, 1992: 57-116.)

Nevertheless, following the example of Gotell and Brodie (1991), I think that this relationship between women in politics and the promotion of the feminist demands has no firm basis. As these authors say, 'it ignores the practical obstacles confronting female partisans who attempt to alter male-defined agendas' (p. 60). In my opinion it is important to take into account the conditions that allow female politicians to respond positively to this type of social demand. Many studies have shown that the political environment influences opinions about feminism. In a survey of the members of the United States House of Representatives between 1972 and 1980, Welch (1985) demonstrates that the pressures of conformity could bring these women legislators to stifle their liberal tendencies. In a survey of the

American candidates in the 1976 election, Carroll (1994) found that many of the women have feminist opinions but do not express them publicly for fear that the electorate will think they are interested only in feminist issues. MacManus (1981) has the same opinion: the American female politicians at the local level whom she studied at the end of the 1970s refused to let their feminist convictions appear, to avoid an identification with feminism that might harm their political carriers. It is thus important to determine how much influence the political environment has on female politicians regarding the demands of feminists, notably by research on the influence of political parties, political ambition, and the political culture.

Far from blaming systemic causes for the precariousness of the relationship between the presence of more women in politics and the promotion of feminist demands, this study suggests that some women would be more likely than others (because of their socio-economic and philosophical profiles) to listen to and defend the demands of the feminist movement. And if it is still desirable to increase the number of women in politics—if only to remedy a serious shortcoming in the representativeness of the political system and to answer the demands of the feminist groups—it would be interesting to consider the characteristics of women who aspire to the legislature, since these characteristics are linked to attitudes toward feminism and, in the longer term, influence the possibility of seeing a transformation in gender relations.

NOTES

1 Just consider the symposia of the Association féminine d'éducation et d'action sociale in 1986 (called 'Carrefour sur l'accès des femmes au pouvoir politique'), another by the Fédération des femmes du Québec in 1987 ('Femmes et pouvoir politique: une greffe impossible?'), the one by FRAPPE in 1990 ('First World Summit: Women and the Many Dimensions of Power'), and a last one at the University of Ottawa in 1994 called 'Femmes et représentation politique au Canada/Women and Political Representation in Canada'.

2 The variable for political philosophy was constructed and measured with the help of six questions about general social issues (drugs, the fight against crime, the ordination of women to the priesthood, capital punishment, the defence budget, and jobs for immigrants; see Appendix). I have designated two orientations, either the liberal political philosophy or the conservative one. The liberal orientation is associated with the idea of progress by creating a disposition towards the acceptance of individual rights and obligations. Encompassing the notions of responsibility and of individual freedom, it is characterized notably by tolerance towards others, acceptance of a pluralistic society, a tendency towards compromise, and so on. The conservative outlook, on the other hand, tends to favour restrictions on individual rights and obligations. It is expressed, for example, in strictness and intolerance of others.

3 This technique of descriptive statistics enables us to analyse the relationship between two groups of variables and to extract meaningful relationships. By means of schematics and global visualization on the cartesian axes of chi-square, factor analysis interprets the dispersion cloud of data, examining more particularly the proximities, distances, and relationships between the variables. For more on this statistical technique, see Lebart, Morineau, and Tabard (1977): 59-71, 140-9.

4 It is for readability that I have produced four figures instead of only one, since 33 variables with unequal importance would have had to be represented on a single graph.

5 F corresponds to the Fisher statistic used to make comparisons between groups. The degree of freedom (df) is defined by the minimum number of cells in the table whose values must be known to be able to complete all the cells. The Fisher law involves two degrees of freedom, one for the numerator, the other for the denominator. The P signifies the level observed, that is, the possibility that a relation between variables is not due to chance. According to the number of comparisons made we have corrected this level with the Bonferonni statistic.

BIBLIOGRAPHY

Bashevkin, Sylvia B. (1985), 'Political Participation, Ambition and Feminism: Women in the Ontario Party Elites', *American Review of Canadian Studies* 15 (4): 405-19.

———— (1989), 'Political Parties and the Representation of Women', in Alain Gagnon and Brian Tanguay, eds, *Canadian Parties in Transition* (Toronto: Nelson Canada), 446-60.

Bashevkin, Sylvia B., and Marianne R. Holder (1985), 'The Politics of Female Participation', in Donald C. MacDonald, ed., *Government and Politics of Ontario*, 3rd ed., 275-88 (Scarborough, Ont.: Nelson).

Berkman, Michael B., and Robert E. O'Connor (1993), 'Do Women Legislators Matter? Female Legislators and State Abortion Policy', *American Politics Quarterly* 21 (1): 102-24.

Black, Jerome H., and Nancy E. McGlen (1979), 'Male-Female Political Involvement Differentials in Canada, 1965-1974', *Canadian Journal of Political Science* 12 (3): 471-97.

Brodie, Janine (1987), 'The Gender Factor and National Leadership Conventions in Canada', in George Perlin, ed., *Party Democracy in Canada: The Politics of National Party Conventions*, 172-87 (Scarborough, Ont.: Prentice-Hall).

Brodie, Janine, Shelley A.M. Gavigan, and Jane Jenson (1992), *The Politics of Abortion* (Toronto: Oxford University Press).

Burt, Sandra (1988), 'Legislators, Women, and Public Policy', in Sandra Burt, Lorraine Code, and Lindsay Dorney, eds, *Changing Patterns: Women in Canada*, 129-56 (Toronto: McClelland and Stewart).

Carroll, Susan J. (1994), *Women as Candidates in American Politics*, 2nd ed. (Bloomington, IN: Indiana University Press).

Cook, Elizabeth Adell (1989), 'Measuring Feminist Consciousness', *Women and Politics* 9, (3): 71-88.

Eichler, Margrit (1979), 'Sex Equality and Political Participation of Women in Canada: Some Survey Results', *Revue internationale de sociologie* 15 (7): 49-75.

Elshtain, Jean Bethlee (1974), 'Moral Woman and Immoral Man: A Consideration of Public-Private Split and Its Political Ramifications', *Politics and Society* 4 (4): 453-73.

Fletcher, Joseph F., and Marie-Christine Chalmers (1991), 'Attitudes of Canadians toward Affirmative Action: Opposition, Value Pluralism, and Nonattitudes', *Political Behavior* 13 (1): 67-95.

Gingras, Anne-Marie, Chantal Maillé, and Évelyne Tardy (1989), *Sexes et militantisme* (Montreal: CIDIHCA).

Gotell, Lise, and Janine Brodie (1991), 'Women and Parties: More than an Issue of Numbers', in Hugh G. Thorburn, ed., *Party Politics in Canada*, 6th ed., 53-67 (Scarborough, Ont.: Prentice-Hall).

Kanter, Rosabeth Moss (1977), 'Some Effects of Proportions on Group Life: Skewed Sex Ratios and Responses to Token Women', *American Journal of Sociology* 82 (5): 965-90.

Klein, Ethel (1984), *Gender Politics: From Consciousness to Mass Politics* (Cambridge, Mass.: Harvard University Press).

Leader, Shelah Gilbert (1977), 'The Policy Impact of Elected Women Officials', in Louis Maisel and Joseph Cooper, *The Impact of the Electoral Process*, 265-84 (Beverly Hills, CA: Sage).

Lebart, L., A. Morineau, and N. Tabard (1977), *Techniques de la description statistique: Méthodes et logiciels pour l'analyse des grands tableaux* (Paris: Dunod).

Lilie, Joyce R., Roger Handberg, Jr, and Wanda Lowrey (1982), 'Women State Legislators and the ERA: Dimensions of Support and Opposition', *Women and Politics* 2 (1-2): 23-38.

MacManus, Susan A. (1981), 'A City's First Female Officeholder: "Coattails" for Future Female Officeseekers?' *Western Political Quarterly* 34 (1): 88-99.

McLaughlin, Audrey (1992), *A Woman's Place: My Life and Politics* (Toronto: Macfarlane Walter and Ross).

Mezey, Susan Gluck (1978), 'Support for Women's Rights Policy: An Analysis of Local Politicians', *American Politics Quarterly* 6 (4): 485-97.

Mossuz-Lavau, Janine, and Mariette Sineau (1983), *Enquête sur les femmes et la politique en France* (Paris: PUF).

Norris, Pippa (1986), 'Women in Congress: A Policy Difference?', *Politics* 6 (1): 34-40.

Payette, Lise (1982), *Le pouvoir? Connais pas!* Montreal: Québec/Amérique.

Saint-Germain, Michelle (1989), 'Does Their Difference Make a Difference? The Impact of Women on Public Policy in the Arizona Legislature', *Social Science Quarterly* 70 (4): 956-68.

Sapiro, Virginia (1983), *The Political Integration of Women: Roles, Socialization, and Politics* (Urbana, IL: University of Illinois Press).

Sapiro, Virginia, and Barbara G. Farah (1980), 'New Pride and Old Prejudice: Political Ambition and Role Orientation among Female Partisan Elites', *Women and Politics* 1 (1): 13-36.

Sharpe, Sydney (1994), *The Gilded Ghetto: Women and Political Power in Canada* (Toronto: HarperCollins).

Smith, Lynn, and Eleanor Wachtel (1992), *A Feminist Guide to the Canadian Constitution* (Ottawa: Canadian Advisory Council on the Status of Women).

Thomas, Sue (1991), 'The Impact of Women on State Legislative Policies', *Journal of Politics* 53 (4): 958-76.

Tremblay, Manon (1991), *Les femmes en politique représentent-elles les femmes? De quelques conduites des femmes et des hommes en politique au Québec à l'endroit des demandes exprimées par les mouvements féministes* (Ph.D. dissertation, Université Laval).

—— (1992), 'Quand les femmes se distinguent: féminisme et représentation politique au Québec', *Canadian Journal of Political Science* 25 (1): 55-68.

—— (1993), 'Political Party, Political Philosophy and Feminism: A Case Study of the Female and Male Candidates in the 1989 Quebec General Election', *Canadian Journal of Political Science* 26 (3): 507-22.

Tremblay, Manon, and Guylaine Boivin (1991), 'La question de l'avortement au Parlement canadien: de l'importance du genre dans l'orientation des débats', *Canadian Journal of Women and the Law*, 4 (2): 459-76.

Welch, Susan (1985), 'Are Women More Liberal Than Men on the US Congress?' *Legislative Studies Quarterly* 10 (1): 125-34.

Welch, Susan, and Sue Thomas (1988), 'Explaining the Gender Gap in British Public Opinion', *Women and Politics* 8 (3-4): 25-44.

Welch, Susan, and Lee Sigelman (1982), 'Changes in Public Attitudes toward Women in Politics', *Social Science Quarterly* 63 (2): 312-22.

Appendix

We would like to know your opinion on several questions concerning gender relations. Please indicate your level of agreement or disagreement to *each* of the following statements by circling the appropriate response.

1. It is preferable that mothers with school-age children not work full-time outside the home.

_____ .	_____ .	_____ .	_____ .	_____ .	_____ .
Agree Strongly	Agree	Neither	Disagree	Disagree Strongly	Don't Know

2. Affirmative action (requiring an equal number of women and men) should be introduced so that more women could gain access to the various posts of political responsibility.

_____ .	_____ .	_____ .	_____ .	_____ .	_____ .
Agree Strongly	Agree	Neither	Disagree	Disagree Strongly	Don't Know

3. Abortion should be outlawed under all circumstances, except when the life of the mother is at risk.

_____ .	_____ .	_____ .	_____ .	_____ .	_____ .
Agree Strongly	Agree	Neither	Disagree	Disagree Strongly	Don't Know

4. Women in politics have a primary responsibility for questions concerning the family and education.

_____ .	_____ .	_____ .	_____ .	_____ .	_____ .
Agree Strongly	Agree	Neither	Disagree	Disagree Strongly	Don't Know

5. A woman who works outside the home can have as satisfactory a relationship with her young children as a woman who stays at home.

_____ .	_____ .	_____ .	_____ .	_____ .	_____ .
Agree Strongly	Agree	Neither	Disagree	Disagree Strongly	Don't Know

6. The development of child-care facilities is indispensable to the autonomy of women.

_____ .	_____ .	_____ .	_____ .	_____ .	_____ .
Agree Strongly	Agree	Neither	Disagree	Disagree Strongly	Don't Know

7. It is not suitable for boys to study home economics (cooking, sewing, etc.) at school.

_____ .	_____ .	_____ .	_____ .	_____ .	_____ .
Agree Strongly	Agree	Neither	Disagree	Disagree Strongly	Don't Know

8. On the job, affirmative action for women is a form of discrimination against competent men.

_____ .	_____ .	_____ .	_____ .	_____ .	_____ .
Agree Strongly	Agree	Neither	Disagree	Disagree Strongly	Don't Know

9. An abortion should be available to any woman who desires one.

_____ .	_____ .	_____ .	_____ .	_____ .	_____ .
Agree Strongly	Agree	Neither	Disagree	Disagree Strongly	Don't Know

10. Generally speaking, the financial needs of women are less important than those of men.

_____ .	_____ .	_____ .	_____ .	_____ .	_____ .
Agree Strongly	Agree	Neither	Disagree	Disagree Strongly	Don't Know

11. Both girls *and* boys should be able to practise the same sporting activities (boxing, weight lifting, synchronized swimming . . .).

_____ .	_____ .	_____ .	_____ .	_____ .	_____ .
Agree Strongly	Agree	Neither	Disagree	Disagree Strongly	Don't Know

12. The way politics works precludes the full integration of women into parliamentary life.

_____ .	_____ .	_____ .	_____ .	_____ .	_____ .
Agree Strongly	Agree	Neither	Disagree	Disagree Strongly	Don't Know

13. Women and men doing equivalent jobs should earn an equivalent salary and equal social benefits.

_____ .	_____ .	_____ .	_____ .	_____ .
Agree Strongly	Agree	Neither	Disagree	Disagree Strongly	Don't Know

14. The integration of a greater number of women into politics should improve political life.

_____ .	_____ .	_____ .	_____ .	_____ .	_____ .
Agree Strongly	Agree	Neither	Disagree	Disagree Strongly	Don't Know

15. Women and men should share the tasks related to maintaining a family, according to their respective responsibilities.

_____ .	_____ .	_____ .	_____ .	_____ .
Agree Strongly	Agree	Neither	Disagree	Disagree Strongly	Don't Know

16. Paternity leave should enable men to fully assume their paternal responsibilities, without giving up their work outside the family home.

_____ .	_____ .		_____ .	_____ .
Agree Strongly	Agree	Neither	Disagree	Disagree Strongly	Don't Know

17. Education for girls should be oriented towards the acquisition of domestic and maternal skills.

| _____ . | _____ . | _____ . | _____ . | _____ . | _____ . |
| Agree Strongly | Agree | Neither | Disagree | Disagree Strongly | Don't Know |

18. Women should occupy 50% of decision-making posts in society, that is to say, a proportional place to that which they represent in the population.

| _____ . | _____ . | _____ . | _____ . | _____ . | _____ . |
| Agree Strongly | Agree | Neither | Disagree | Disagree Strongly | Don't Know |

19. It is not suitable for women to occupy jobs traditionally reserved for men, such as fireman, mechanic, garbageman. . .

| _____ . | _____ . | _____ . | _____ . | _____ . | _____ . |
| Agree Strongly | Agree | Neither | Disagree | Disagree Strongly | Don't Know |

20. Sex education should present homosexuality as a normal form of sexuality.

| _____ . | _____ . | _____ . | _____ . | _____ . | _____ . |
| Agree Strongly | Agree | Neither | Disagree | Disagree Strongly | Don't Know |

21. It is more difficult for women than for men to have access to decision-making posts in politics.

| _____ . | _____ . | _____ . | _____ . | _____ . | _____ . |
| Agree Strongly | Agree | Neither | Disagree | Disagree Strongly | Don't Know |

22. School textbooks and teaching should present women and men evolving in roles and functions which are not differentiated and specialized according to gender.

| _____ . | _____ . | _____ . | _____ . | _____ . | _____ . |
| Agree Strongly | Agree | Neither | Disagree | Disagree Strongly | Don't Know |

23. Women MLAs have the specific responsibility to represent not only their own electors, but women throughout Quebec.

| _____ . | _____ . | _____ . | _____ . | _____ . | _____ . |
| Agree Strongly | Agree | Neither | Disagree | Disagree Strongly | Don't Know |

At this point, we would like to know your position on general political questions. Indicate your level of agreement or disagreement for each of the following statements by circling the appropriate response.

24. The use of marijuana and hashish should be decriminalized for consenting adults.

| _____ . | _____ . | _____ . | _____ . | _____ . | _____ . |
| Agree Strongly | Agree | Neither | Disagree | Disagree Strongly | Don't Know |

25. Stronger sentences would enable criminal problems to be kept in check.

_____ .   _____ .   _____ .   _____ .   _____ .   _____ .
Agree   Agree   Neither   Disagree   Disagree   Don't
Strongly   Strongly   Know

26. Women, like men, ought to be permitted to be ordained as priests.

_____ .   _____ .   _____ .   _____ .   _____ .   _____ .
Agree   Agree   Neither   Disagree   Disagree   Don't
Strongly   Strongly   Know

27. The national defence budget should be reduced.

_____ .   _____ .   _____ .   _____ .   _____ .   _____ .
Agree   Agree   Neither   Disagree   Disagree   Don't
Strongly   Strongly   Know

28. Capital punishment should be applied to people found guilty of murder.

_____ .   _____ .   _____ .   _____ .   _____ .   _____ .
Agree   Agree   Neither   Disagree   Disagree   Don't
Strongly   Strongly   Know

29. Job preference should be given to people from Quebec rather than to immigrants.

_____ .   _____ .   _____ .   _____ .   _____ .   _____ .
Agree   Agree   Neither   Disagree   Disagree   Don't
trongly   Strongly   Know

CHAPTER 3

A Job Well Begun . . .

Representation, Electoral Reform, and Women

Jane Arscott

What would a feminist theory of electoral representation look like? No such theory as yet exists, in part because feminists disagree about the general purpose that electoral representation is to serve. For example, were Parliament to be transformed as the result of a general election into a body made up entirely of women, some feminists would maintain that feminist representation had been achieved. Others would argue that feminist representation was not guaranteed simply by electing women; the most credible measure of their attachment to feminism would be their behaviour in office. Still others would be concerned that such a body might fail to reflect the full range of feminist opinion in the nation. Even in a Parliament made up of many women and some men it is conceivable that a large proportion of the women elected would not necessarily be feminist women, or at least not the right kind or kinds of feminist women. There is as yet no single conception of feminist electoral representation. However, several conceptions of its future possibilities have been put forward, not the least of all by Virginia Sapiro, Anna Jónasdóttir, and Iris Marion Young. Others have begun to consider which conceptions best apply to our particular political settings.

This chapter discusses the present condition of theorizing about women and electoral representation in general and the final report of the Royal Commission on Electoral Reform and Party Financing in particular. In order to assess the promise of the Royal Commission's recommendations about women and representation, several explicitly feminist conceptualizations of representation are first compared with the well-established view that representation is best understood as a procedure for sorting out fairly the competing interests of individuals. I then take up the main merits of the work of the Royal Commission as it pertains to women's representation—the acknowledgement of earlier *sex bias*, a recognition of the value of gender-neutral language, and the introduction of 'under-representation' as a catch-phrase and reform slogan.[1] I will then turn to the main shortcoming of the report: its failure to look beyond symbolic numerical equality to the actual results of policy making and resource allocation. The chapter concludes with some thoughts about the second half of the job that has yet to be done. Nothing less than feminist political outcomes will satisfy those of us who do not think that a solution is to be found in half-measures that would increase the proportion of female members of parliament to 20 to 40 per cent. Why work toward an increased number of women unless that is 'also a means to achieve another goal: a change in the policies adopted and implemented through political processes' (Skjeie 1991: 234)?[2]

CONCEPTUALIZATIONS OF REPRESENTATION

The Liberal Theory of Representation and Challenges to It

The procedural theory of interest representation historically is associated with the writings of Mill ([1861] 1977: 448-50); Ward (1950: 3-19); Pitkin (1967: 232); and Birch (1971: 119) among many others. The emphasis of the simple-plurality electoral systems on equality of opportunity, equal conditions of voter eligibility, and equal weight for everyone's vote has long been thought to be the best way to ensure that a government derives its legitimacy from the consent of the governed. In first-past-the-post electoral systems such as we have in Canada, the person with the most votes wins, even if he or she has fewer than half the votes cast. This system helps to create majority governments but may not reflect the actual discontent of the voters with a sitting member or government as expressed in the popular vote. But this theory is less concerned with skewed outcomes and structural bias than with the fairness of the election procedure. For example, skewed outcomes occur when more votes are cast against the party that forms the government than for it, but there is no formal mechanism for transforming the dissenting vote into actual seats. Structural bias makes it necessary for women candidates to be partisan politicians first and feminists second, a phenomenon that has led Skjeie to conclude that the existing party structure continues to give gender only secondary importance in matters concerned with electoral representation (Skjeie 1991: 238). In Canada, Chantal Maillé (1995) in particular has argued that formal political representation by women should no longer be the sole topic of interest to *woman-sensitive* political analysts. Electoral representation in national politics, worthy though it is for a narrow range of purposes, should no longer be treated in isolation from women's participation on school boards and municipal councils, not to mention their involvement in parallel structures associated with women's movements. Feminist arguments in the courts, grassroots protest, networking, education of the media, and lobbying are all ways in which women's movements seek to bring about far-reaching social, political, economic and cultural change, including change to public policy (Lisa Young 1996; Skjeie 1991: 258). The demand that electoral representation be by women and for them in the sense of holding legislators accountable for actively working to reshape the political agenda makes representation a more complex undertaking than before.

Supporters of the liberal theory accept varying degrees of inconsistency between the best possible representation in theory of every eligible person in the community and its realization in practice. From time to time some categories of people have been considered unqualified to be representatives because of their supposed effect on the survival and effectiveness of the political system. For example, there are no openly lesbian women among the federal legislators, even though heterosexuality is not a formal qualification for public office. Nevertheless norms and past practice continue to weigh heavily against broadening the pool of potential women candidates. That kind of inconsistency between theory and practice is accepted for the sake of governability so long as it involves no significant sacrifice of the legitimacy of the political system. However, this attitude helps to justify and perpetuate the existing electoral system with only superficial changes of the sort recommended by the Royal Commission.

The final report of the Royal Commission on Electoral Reform and Party Financing and its other publications are characterized by arguments which affirm this procedural theory of representation (Canada 1991: 1, 8; Smith 1991). Some women's groups, such as the National Action Committee on the Status of Women, had hoped that the Commission would recommend an electoral system such as proportional representation that would make electoral outcomes more in keeping with the popular vote by turning significant numbers of widely dispersed votes into seats. In this they were disappointed.

In recent years the procedural theory of representation has been challenged increasingly by feminist theorists and activists who have identified long-standing sex biases in politics that affect both its practices and its theories, including representation (Pateman 1980 and 1985; Mueller 1988; Clark 1988). Some, Sapiro (1981) in particular, have called for what amounts to a gender-interest theory of representation, which could more accurately take account of the diverse interests of women than before. Women, they argue, have identifiable interests that cannot be represented through existing theories, structures, and practices. The theory of representation, according to Drude Dahlerup (1982: 39), has first to be revised to take account of systemic barriers which prevent many of the issues that most concern many women from being given a high priority on the political agenda and in policy formation (Iris Young 1989: 261-2). Those barriers include exploitation, marginalization, powerlessness, cultural imperialism, and violence (Iris Young 1988: 276-87). They need to be addressed if representation and justice are finally to be free of group oppression. Other theorists of representation, many of them writing about racial and ethnic dysfunction in the United States, would have the theory incorporate greater representativeness of the actual composition of society, especially of visible minorities (Bell 1987; Swain 1992b).

For supporters of the procedural theory the problem of too few women is almost exclusively a matter of numbers to be worked out within the existing system of political parties.[3] To them the problem can be rectified by making it easier for significant numbers of women to get elected. Under this theory, if women have at least some interests distinct from those of men, special provisions to accommodate such interests can be introduced within limits. In general the limits are set by the conviction shared by most liberals that pluralities must continue to be the decisive element in the selection of candidates and that in the legislatures decisions must be made by a majority vote. However, might there be some issues on which the wishes of pluralities and majorities ought to be set aside in favour of the wishes of the minority most affected by the decision? Many feminists think that at least women, aboriginal peoples, and visible minorities are groups that at present have compelling claims to be treated in this way in some instances. To the liberal theory's supporters, the goal of (and strategies for) achieving equity between underrepresented groups and the state can be safely left to the workings of political parties. That is because it is in their interest to accommodate the demand for more women, more aboriginals, or more non-whites rather than to be subjected to additional interference in the form of quotas.

In contrast to the procedural theory of representation, feminist concepts of representation in general consider the under-representation of women to be broader and more intractable than do the liberals. For them it is not only a matter of increasing the number of women elected but, more importantly, of electing representatives who will actually pursue feminist policies (Whip 1991: 18-19; Costain 1988b: 171). Exponents of gender interest and of representativeness tend to see multiple systemic barriers to gender parity in legislatures and to recommend measures that are more intrusive and that require more, not less, government involvement. Such measures are likely to be much more long-term and complex than anything envisaged by the Royal Commission.

The procedural theory of representation has most recently been affirmed (but with significant and perhaps inconsistent modifications) by the Royal Commission (Canada 1991: I, 8). The Commission's final report maintains that 'free and open competition for candidacy and election' will continue to ensure that in future the best people will be selected 'regardless of their sex, ethno-cultural heritage or financial resources'. At the same time, the Commission has acknowledged that one of the main tasks of electoral reform is to 'help reduce the systemic or structural barriers to candidacy' without compromising the competitive selection process. The 'virtual exclusion' of several segments of the Canadian population, especially women, is no longer acceptable because 'the full range of Canada's interests' will remain unrepresented until representation begins to reflect more 'reasonably' the actual composition of society.

Steps toward a Feminist Theory

The preliminary work toward what Jill Vickers calls 'a feminist understanding of representation' has already begun on the international scene in the work of Sapiro (1981), Jónasdóttir (1988), and Iris Young (1989; 1990; 1994). In the last 15 years or so the demands for electoral representation for women have become more radical; that is, they have increasingly rejected the possibility of grafting women's representation onto existing theory. Rather, the call has gradually emerged to rethink politics, including representation, in its entirety (Jones 1988: 25; Vickers 1988: 12-14).

Virginia Sapiro argues that women as women share an identifiable set of interests and that the recognition of these interests as politically significant will go a long way (but not all the way) toward making politics a legitimate activity once again. These unnamed shared interests might provide a basis for future electoral representation once women themselves become socially conscious of these interests. This position generated a good deal of discussion about women as a unifying category of analysis and of the function of interests in theories of politics, including electoral representation (Diamond and Hartsock 1981: 719). Sapiro's view of women as bearers of politically significant interests drew on the already well-established view in political science that the possession of certain sorts of interests, many of them derived historically from property holding and tax paying, also applied to women, although in ways that gave them a distinct interest in political outcomes, owing to their earlier exclusion and different life experiences from men. This view of women's representation was strongly criticized, especially by left-wing writers who contended that Sapiro's conceptualization of 'women' and 'interests' could not withstand close scrutiny. For example, she ignored evidence that women and their interests often worked to benefit women in the privileged classes and that women from those classes could not be counted on to represent all women.

Anna Jónasdóttir (1988: 55) has challenged both the homogeneity and the artificially unified character of Sapiro's category of women and her use of it as an undifferentiated interest group. She has substituted a range of smaller-scale group identities deeply divided along lines of class, race, and ethnicity but with the potential to form alliances for common purposes. She bases women's claims for representation on their status as an oppressed group that has experienced systemic discrimination. Women as a historically mistreated group rather than women as bearers of a shared interest are the philosophic and political justification for this group's claim to representation. Here the claim to representation links some groups to systemic discrimination in a manner that generates an entitlement.

Young takes a step further with this group-based claim grounded in systemic discrimination. Young conceives of a differentiated citizenship based on group identities, which are to be understood in relationship to other groups in particular and to the social processes that created them (Young 1989: 258-67). Most recently Young (1994: 737) has suggested the 'serial' manner in which socially relevant group identities come to be formed, disappear at times, and are formed anew in response to 'a common set of structural constraints and relations' that 'condition action and its meaning'. In contrast to earlier non-feminist theories of representation that award access to representation on the basis of one's possession of the right sorts of interests or recognized capacities as an individual, feminist conceptions of representation have gradually moved toward identity-based representation. This would give historically oppressed groups a stronger claim to actual representation by members of their group than individuals and groups that had not experienced systemic discrimination.

Some theorists have worried that taking group claims seriously threatens to fragment communities rather than unite them (Phillips 1992: 89). Young's oppressed groups include 'women, blacks, Native Americans, Chicanos, Puerto Ricans and other Spanish-speaking Americans, Asian Americans, gay men, lesbians, working-class people, poor people, old people, and mentally and physically disabled people' (Young 1989: 261). Will Kymlicka (1993: 76) estimates that these groups cover about 80 per cent of the American population, excluding only 'relatively well-off, relatively young, able-bodied, heterosexual white males'. Young suggests that a very broad range of people might ultimately benefit from the development of group-rights claims. She stops short of considering as Phillips has done, that it may be impossible to say who legitimately represents a group and how such a group is to be defined. Young also overlooks the important questions of how such groups could be held accountable for their actions. Unlike Young, Phillips and Kymlicka worry less about the existence of oppressed groups than about the possibility that integrating their demands for representation into electoral politics might be unworkable and, worse, unjust. But surely the problem that Young would have us keep in view is the virtual monopoly that some men have on most of the effective instruments of power, especially those related to government. In this light the worries of Phillips and Kymlicka, though real, are less compelling than Young's effort to discover an effective means to continue the historical process of democratization. She seeks to redress the injustices suffered by oppressed groups in the immediate future, even if that weakens some aspects of the integrative function of citizenship as it existed before. Differentiated citizenship of the sort described by Young is not necessarily weaker or less desirable than earlier conceptions of citizenship; it may simply require us to change the way we think about citizenship and how we benefit from it.

Identity-based feminist conceptions of representation need not be divisive, though such conceptualizations probably require thinking about integration differently from the manner associated with the homogeneity of identical values and beliefs. Rather, integration thought about from this new perspective involves a social consciousness of different but equal ways of understanding one's relation to the polity; that is what identity-based feminist representation seeks to promote. Its realization would require members of the previously excluded group to represent themselves. Whereas women's concerns have often been expressed by sympathetic male supporters on the left, identity-based representation will be satisfied with nothing short of self-representation. What men in general cannot represent on behalf of women's identities and interests at present is that group's coming to terms with its own history of discrimination, the process of its empowerment, and the visible evidence that the public through its government and policy formulation is finally committed to a new course for the future (Baines 1991: 213; Costain 1988a: 37-9; Skard and Haavio-Mannila 1985b: 75-6).

The imaginary all-female parliament might be considered inadequate by proponents of an identity-based feminist conception of representation. This is because it would not represent historically significant groups of oppressed males, including men who were gay, disabled, non-white, or aboriginal or had some combination of these attributes. Such attributes might constitute a politically viable identity that would enable them to seek official recognition of their claims on the public through the state. Existing affirmative action legislation makes it clear that women, visible minorities, aboriginals, and people with disabilities are the only oppressed groups in Canada for which some special arrangements might be contemplated at present in order to improve the quality of their political representation. In other important political matters, people of a particular region, language, or ethnicity have at times been treated for some purposes as populations worthy of special consideration. Arguably one of the most important functions of public policy and law is to reassess the groups that are given official status and representation from time to time. If an identity-based theory of electoral representation were to be widely accepted, the electoral system might have to be changed radically to facilitate the representation of group identities. But we are so far from the realization of this theoretical position as to make it irrelevant for the practical purpose of achieving better representation for the handful of groups that the state acknowledges. At present there is little possibility that the public will accept Young's 'oppressed group serial' conceptualization of representation or that men will be excluded from Parliament. Therefore the pragmatic school of identity-based representation measures advances in the representation of women in the same way as do non-feminist students of representation, that is, by tracking their numbers in legislatures.

Non-feminists, feminists, and identity-based feminists all pay attention to the numbers of women in legislatures, but they do so for different reasons. Non-feminists and many feminists other than identity-based feminists track the changes in the number of women in order to decide when there are enough so that no additional measures are needed to cause more of them to be elected. This is the unspoken message behind the notion of a 'critical mass'. Other feminists view tracking as a strategy for realizing the specific short-term goal of getting more women elected. They do so in the hope of changing the political agenda and its outcomes. They would have the allocation of resources to demonstrate the government's commitment to include women as full partners in all aspects of its concerns. Before showing how recent, theoretical considerations of representation play out on the federal scene, let me first summarize the argument that makes up the rest of the present article.

The principal merits of the Royal Commission on Electoral Reform and Party Financing and its discussion of women and representation are its acknowledgement that there was sex bias in previous electoral practices, its support for the use in future of gender-neutral language in the Elections Act, and its introduction of 'under-representation' as a catch-phrase and reform slogan. I contend that the Commission's purpose in tinkering with electoral law and provisions affecting political parties with respect to women's representation was to produce a Parliament with a fairer and more balanced make-up, something approximating sex parity. But sex parity of the sort envisaged by the Royal Commission would be more symbolic than real. That is partly because of the Commission's superficial understanding of what function the presence of elected women is to serve. It is not women as women or as bearers of interests, but women as an oppressed group both experiencing systemic discrimination and having diverse identities and circumstances in relation to the Canadian polity, that needs to be represented more accurately by our elected representatives. Proponents of the idea that there is not yet a critical mass of women Members of Parliament have not made much of this potentially radical approach to women's representation and what it aims to accomplish.

Women's Electoral Representation in Canada

The Continued Absence of a Critical Mass of Women MPs

The expression 'the higher, the fewer' epitomizes the extent to which women have as yet failed to gain access in significant numbers to the political élites in Canada (Bashevkin 1985a: chap. 3; Brodie 1985: chap. 1).[4] Women may have gained a toehold in the House of Commons, the Senate, the Privy Council, and the executive ranks of political parties, but they have not as yet established a secure base from which to attain something approximating sex parity,[5] especially in the country's most important representative institution.[6]

In order to rectify this deficiency, which calls into question the quality of federal political representation, the Royal Commission recommended measures to encourage political parties to nominate more women in winnable ridings and to finance their campaigns.[7] Electing more women is not the same thing as creating a 'critical mass' of women legislators. A 'critical mass' might consist of anywhere between 10 and 60 per cent of the Members of Parliament (Maillé 1990: 3; Randall 1987: 109; cf. Dahlerup and Haavio-Mannila 1985: 166).[8] This level of female representation could reasonably be expected to enable the women Members to promote female interests. Without using the term 'critical mass' the Royal Commission maintained that special temporary measures to cause more women to be elected might be justified, especially if the proportion of woman MPs failed to reach 20 per cent in the natural course of events. Special provisions would be justifiable only until 40 per cent of the MPs were women. In the eye of the Commission, then, a critical mass is anywhere between 20 and 40 per cent. Recent studies of women's representation in provincial legislatures suggest that in addition to percentages, partisanship, and the distribution of women legislators in government, opposition and third parties affect the difference that women legislators make (Arscott and Trimble 1996). While sheer numbers remain important, so too is the particular site where the representation takes place.

The recommendations sought to lower the financial barriers to nomination and the cost of contesting elections by introducing spending limits on nomination campaigns, permitting donations for this purpose to be eligible for tax credits and making child-care expenses an allowable tax deduction for candidates (Dobrowolsky and Jenson 1993: 53). It was further recommended that parties be required to create formal structures and procedures to establish the qualities required for candidates and the pool of prospective candidates. Should those measures not produce the desired results quickly enough, candidates for parties in which women made up a specified minimum percentage of its winning candidates would receive a higher rate of reimbursement on their election expenses. This measure would be necessary only if the percentage of women elected to the House of Commons after adoption of those measures remained below 20 per cent. Political parties would be able to claim the percentage over 20 and under 50 that they had obtained, so if a third of a party's elected candidates were women, the party would be able to claim 133 per cent of the amount to which it would otherwise have been entitled.[9]

If the recommendations of the Royal Commission had been adopted, measures might ultimately have been taken to seek to boost the number of seats in the House of Commons held by women from 13 per cent (39 seats) to something between 20 and 40 per cent (59 to 118 seats). As we know, the 20 per cent level was not reached, in the 1993 federal election, contrary to the predictions of the Commission. If this level had been reached and the Commission's recommendations had been in effect, additional measures would probably not have been needed since a more or less natural integration of women would already have begun and the process would best be left alone to reach its own equilibrium.[10] In the absence of the measures recommended by the Commission, this *laissez-faire* state of affairs will continue for the foreseeable future, and further increases will continue to depend on the willingness of political parties to nominate women in winnable ridings.[11] The special temporary measures proposed would almost certainly have had the desired effect of sharply increasing the number of female MPs: to do so would have served the short-term financial interests of the political parties by making their campaigns less costly as a result of the tax relief for getting women elected. However, the financial measures to reward parties that achieved sex parity would have been the butt of a lot of jokes if the Progressive Conservative Party had been rewarded for its successful election of the two-member caucus of Elsie Wayne and Jean Charest. In fact, the skewed results of the 1993 election cast doubt on the plausibility of a mechanism of the sort proposed by the Commission.

In Norway, Sweden, and Denmark quotas have helped to achieve a critical mass of women legislators. However, as local commentators have noted, those provisions have failed to shift the legislative agenda toward issues such as day care and family violence that largely determine the quality of women's lives.[12] In other words, the election of more women may not have the desired effect in Canada or elsewhere, even if a critical mass in terms of their winning a minimum percentage of seats is achieved. The modest changes envisaged by the Commission on Electoral Reform may well achieve a critical mass as defined by the number of seats held by women but without entirely solving the problem of women's under-representation. Sole attention to the critical mass and its numbers game may appear to affirm an orthodox theory of political representation that takes too narrow a view of the validity of established procedures for selecting candidates and of the range of interests that deserve to be represented.

But attaining a critical mass of female legislators may actually be less important than the inclusion of women's issues on the public agenda: numbers alone are no guarantee that women's issues will become any more significant than before (Phillips 1991: 70). Not only are there too few women in Parliament, but additional measures may have to be taken before issues of importance to many women will appear on the political agenda. It is encouraging that women MPs from all the parties have occasionally worked together closely, most notably to defeat an amendment to Bill C-43 that would have required any woman seeking an abortion to obtain the consent of two doctors in whose opinion the continuance of the pregnancy constituted a danger to the woman's health (Brodie 1992: 88). But such cross-party alliances remain the exception, and small numbers of women in each caucus are left to ensure that women's interests are considered fully on all questions of the day. A larger number of women MPs might begin some wider process of gradual social change as women's interests were brought to bear more directly on the national political agenda than before. But will *numerical* representation completely solve the problem of the under-representation of women?

The present generation of women MPs closely resembles the general population in the percentage that are married (Canada 1991: I, 105-7).[13] Unlike the general population, however, they are likely to have post-secondary education, be in their forties, and have no children. Among women MPs, occupations involving law and business are over-represented while occupations involving the fisheries, agriculture, clerical work, and homemaking are under-represented. In general women MPs are similar in their class background, education, and occupations to male MPs. It is conceivable that the election of more women will simply replace men with women without altering the range of interests and identities being represented. Thus the number of women elected might approach the goal without ending the criticism, especially if the women elected, as is most often the case now, were fortyish, publically heterosexual, able-bodied, white, well-educated, and urban.

In fact the selection of both female and male MPs is open to the criticism that the House of Commons does not reflect the diversity of the population as well as it could. Though the theory of representation does not require Parliament as a body to correspond to the composition of the population, the fact that it remains a bastion of privilege made up of older, white, able-bodied heterosexual men (and a growing number of women) who are already socially advantaged makes it increasingly difficult for the public to identify with its representatives or with the institutions and the issues they consider important (Phillips 1991: 90; Mohanty 1987: 38). The Royal Commission acknowledged this fact, but without giving it a great deal of weight in its assessment of the continued effectiveness of Canada's political representation. All issues are women's issues, from defence policy to day care to taxation and health care, but women legislators have as yet little opportunity to express their concerns as women.

Could it be that the source of the problem is *not* solely the absence of women but the absence in Parliament of a sufficiently broad range of both interests and identities that under other conceptions of representation might more accurately reflect the concerns of the electorate? This is not the way the problem has generally been considered, certainly not by the Commission on Electoral Reform. The main aspects of representation taken up by the Commission were the accountability of representatives to the electorate, the diversity of society's political preferences, and the view in some segments of the public that geographic or partisan representation fails to do justice to the current range of citizens' interests. The relative ease of accountability of the kind provided by the present single-member, simple-plurality voting system was considered in the light of competing opinions about the 'quality' of representation. The quality of the representation of women was acknowledged to be poor but correctable within the existing framework. Thus 'under-representation' was used as a catch-phrase to direct public attention to only one of several possible conceptions of the problem.

An opportunity was missed to undertake such a re-examination of existing practices and well-established theories from a feminist perspective. However, the Royal Commission's recommendations did promise improved representation for women in several important respects.

Prospective Benefits from the Recommendations

The Royal Commission on Electoral Reform and Party Financing deserves high praise both for including sex as an important aspect of analysis and for actively promoting better representation by women. Its final report, *Reforming Electoral Democracy*, contains recommendations that seek to make women genuine full partners in the political life of Canada. Its timely recommendations that any future Elections Act be written in gender-neutral language and that several barriers to the selection of women candidates be removed may eventually prove to have been important. If what can be called a woman-sensitive political culture is to develop—meaning one that acknowledges the historical and continuing structural disadvantages experienced by women by virtue of their sex and gender, and that seeks to redress this imbalance—these recommendations may eventually prove to be as important as the Royal Commission on the Status of Women and section 28 of the *Charter of Rights and Freedoms* (Canada: 1991: I, 93-4; Cairns 1991: 78-9).[14] Despite the regrettable fact that the Royal Commission's recommendations, especially those concerning the representation of women in the House of Commons, are a dead letter, the subject of women and representation remains very much alive, thanks in part to the dissatisfaction with the recommendations and with the fact that next to nothing has come of them. The two aspects of gender analysis taken up in the work of the Commission are a benchmark against which the success of women in future federal elections can be measured; the use of gender analysis, modest though it certainly is, serves notice that sex parity will remain a public issue until the principle is fully incorporated into the selection of politicians not only to the House of Commons but also to provincial and territorial legislatures, and the Senate, not to mention the Supreme Court and the highest elected positions within political parties. The election and appointment of more women to these posts can be expected in the longer term to influence high-ranking appointments in the public service and Crown corporations once the climate of opinion becomes more favourable to women.

Some readers of *Reforming Electoral Democracy* may think the steps taken are a small concession and mostly of symbolic value. But this view overlooks the as yet unrealized potential of the measures. Symbolically, the election of more women demonstrates by example that women in general and not only the all too rare woman of exceptional qualities are eligible more or less on the same basis as men already are. The candidate chosen by the voters may be female or male, but the general expectation would be that, in the absence of systemic discrimination and barriers, women will in fact be elected in about the same numbers as men. The Royal Commission mentioned systemic discrimination but regarded it as an intractable problem. In particular the Commission did not see any point in assigning blame for this unfortunate situation. The report's use of gender-neutral language, in combination with its implicit assumption that equality of access to election will be achieved, fosters the public expectation that women will soon be as visible as men in federal politics.

Acknowledgement of Sex Bias

Reforming Electoral Democracy has thus broken important new ground in publicly recognizing additional obstacles and barriers to women's political participation, sex bias foremost among them. The Commission's discussion of sex bias, though tentative and incomplete, marks an important addition to the understanding of political culture in government circles (Canada 1991: I, 93-4). The Commission found that 'women are the most under-represented segment of Canadian society', being under-represented in relation to their proportion of the electorate by 74 per cent after the 1988 election, that is, fewer than 4 in 10 of the number that under conditions of normal distribution would accrue to them. The percentage fell to 66 per cent after the 1993 election. This statistical evidence lent additional support to the claim, concisely expressed to the Commission in a brief from the Canadian Advisory Council on the Status Women that 'the voice of government' remains 'a man's voice' 20 years after the Royal Commission on the Status of Women. The findings and recommendations of the Royal Commission are clearly one important step toward making Canada's political system officially recognize that biological sex and culturally conditioned gender make a difference to the ways in which women and men relate to politics and public policy.[15]

The Value of Gender-Neutral Language

Whatever other measures to assist the election of more women to the House of Commons are eventually adopted, at the very least the Elections Act has been rewritten in non-sexist language, as recommended by Robinson and Saint-Jean, and as has been done in volume three of the final report (Canada 1991: III; Robinson and Saint-Jean 1991: 161). This attention to gender-neutral language is official acknowledgement that the Government of Canada does not condone the perpetuation of sex bias with regard to the nomination and election of Members of Parliament. In the past, the practices of political parties in general, and of constituency executives in particular, have failed to identify women as persons qualified to seek and win elected office in federal politics; this is no longer the case.

The removal of an established bias, even the minor practice of linguistic bias, though important, does nothing to create a positive climate for women as legislators and prospective legislators. Such a climate will exist only when systemic discrimination has been pulled up by the roots; that will be a much larger and more complex task than the gentle weeding-out of masculine nouns and pronouns begun by the Commission. At stake is the substantive access of half the population to the highest elected offices in the country. The fact that the recommendations of the Commission go beyond gender-neutral language and try to remove two additional obstacles to the successful nomination and candidacy of women is especially encouraging. However, the language of formal equality incorporated into the Elections Act will be without force unless there are also substantial measures to reorient policy making in Parliament. The catch-phrase of under-representation may be the slogan with which to achieve this goal.

Under-Representation: Catch-phrase and Reform Slogan

Despite increases in the number of women elected in the past two federal elections, change for the better has been nearly as slow, indecisive, and difficult in the last two decades as in the previous five, despite a net increase in women MPs to 13 per cent in 1988 and 18 per cent in 1993. While optimists may point out that the electoral representation of women in Canada has increased 1,800 per cent in the last 25 years after 50 years of no increase, on this account, each additional woman elected increases the percentage by a full 100 per cent. However those of us who will be satisfied with nothing less than half of all the seats, posts, and honours that a grateful nation has to bestow on its citizens remain dissatisfied with incremental gains that at current rates will not produce sex parity in our lifetime.

It is conceivable that the electoral success that eluded generations of female aspirants to Parliament can be achieved relatively quickly and easily as the result of natural tendencies in this direction, as predicted by Studlar and Matland (1994: 78-9) and modest tinkering with the electoral system. Lise Gotell and Janine Brodie (1991: 53) use the image of a long-sought-after watershed to describe what many analysts believe to be breakthroughs for women in politics in the federal elections of 1984 and 1988. But the watershed becomes more 'uncertain' in a subsequent piece by Brodie (1991: 5). The wider political culture that has supported sex bias over the years in many other areas of our shared economic, social, political, and legal life has proved to be even more resistant to change. The Commission would have it believed that the electoral system and the function of political parties within it are sufficiently malleable to bring about the desired change at little or no risk to the continued good working of the system.

The word 'under-representation' draws attention to the fact that women make up slightly more than 50 per cent of the adult population but hold only 18 per cent of the seats in the House of Commons (13 per cent at the time the report was tabled in Parliament). Under-representation is a catch-phrase that can be used to bring the public together to support electoral reform in response to an identifiable grievance. As a reform slogan it appeals to the public's sense that the natural mechanism of distributive justice has in this case failed to produce a fair outcome. By tinkering with electoral law and the workings of political parties, supporters of the Electoral Reform Commission's proposals seek to arrive at a representation that is fairer and more balanced, at least in terms of the sex distribution of the elected MPs.

But parity between the sexes in and of itself may have very little at all to do with the qualities and capacities required of elected representatives or with a desirable theory of representation.[16] So long as parity between the sexes in representation is considered to be an end in itself rather than as one index among several that measure the quality of participation of women and men in political life, the opportunity to develop an increasingly sensitive, sophisticated, and evolving measure will be lost to a mechanical, blunt, and static result. In fact, the procedural theory of representation has had nothing to say about sex or sex distribution as a criterion for fair and equitable representation.

The Main Shortcoming: Is Sex Parity Symbolic or Real?

The important question of whether increased numbers of women will represent interests and identities different from those of their male predecessors, the same identities and interests in a different way, or the same interests in the same way requires more careful consideration. Reservations about the possibility that systemic bias may persist despite electoral reform are raised in Brodie's (1991) research paper for the Royal Commission. The proposed reform might succeed only in winning access to high political office for a very select segment of Canadian womanhood that is relatively uniform in age, race, class, education, marital status, and sexual orientation. Their interests might not vary significantly from those of the men they would replace. More generally, a wide range of interests would continue to be unrepresented even after electoral reform. Among the numerous reasons why some interests remain unrepresented, some of the most important are lack of leisure time or of proficiency in one of the country's official languages, inadequate financial resources, unpolished lobbying skills or a politically inexperienced support network, all of which can compound the obstacles faced by newcomers who seek election. In the absence of formal mechanisms to help potential communities of interest to organize themselves into politically effective bodies, candidacies by members of oppressed groups face formidably long odds. Women and other oppressed groups are unlikely to become full partners in federal politics until the excessively narrow selectiveness of candidates ceases *and* formal mechanisms are introduced to enhance the expression of hitherto latent interests.

Should the public expect all politicians to be cut from the same cloth? Can female politicians reasonably be expected to behave like male politicians, the only difference being the style of their suits? Putting an all-important question in this manner both trivializes it and draws attention to the many ways in which the sex of politicians continues to matter in the public's assessment of them (Cantor et al. 1992; Aitken 1958; Robinson et al. 1991).[17]

The problem of making the political behaviour of female prospective MPs more closely resemble that of already successful males was the way in which the question of the future political participation of women as candidates was addressed by a symposium sponsored by the Royal Commission, 'Active Participation of Women in Politics'.[18] Several of the participants argued that the topics addressed were all based on the assumption that what is wanted is female politicians who imitate male norms, a standard of 'success' which was challenged by participants from various regions and backgrounds. Formal political power was but one aspect of political power, noted Carolle Simard of the Université du Québec à Montréal. To consider access to high public office in isolation from other forms of power that Canadian women already skilfully exert, she warned, overemphasizes and even misconstrues their powerlessness, along with the reasons for it (Canada 1991: IV, 149). Rosemary Brown, executive director of Match International and candidate for the NDP leadership in 1975, worried that the papers presented had focused exclusively on women politicians who are white and who live in either Quebec or Ontario, and not on 'women politicians outside the golden triangle'. Important as it certainly is to have *more women*, she said, what is needed is more women who will 'champion *ethnic and geographic diversity*' (Canada 1991: I, 153). The reason for electoral reform, according to Jane Jenson, was 'not just to integrate women into the political system, but also to integrate all under-represented groups' (Canada 1991: IV, 146). In her view representation *for* women and others is at least as important perhaps ultimately more important than, representation *by* women.

Aside from the reservations expressed by Simard, Brown, Jenson and several other speakers whose remarks are summarized in volume four of *Reforming Electoral Democracy*, the reader gets little sense that there is anything really difficult involved in redressing the sex balance—at least not anything that exhortation, election expense write-offs, and formalized nomination procedures will not be able to fix (Canada 1991: IV, 146).[19] The possibility that parity itself might be difficult to achieve was lightly passed over. So, too, was the character of systemic barriers that are neither systemic discrimination in the legal sense nor barriers to entry in the practical sense.[20] This entire middle range remains unexplored. Systemic barriers are by definition more or less intractable, and it may require concerted, interventionist, and even strongly coercive measures to remove them. Such considerations were dismissed with the intellectually unsatisfactory remark in the published summary that women confront similar barriers in other careers. Some of the additional barriers that will continue to keep qualified women on the margins of federal politics involve

- sex stereotyping;
- the difficulty of juggling career, family, and political responsibilities; [including]
- problems of child care;
- jobs that are less flexible for entering politics than those held by men;
- negative attitudes within parties;
- the fact that men tend to have better networks to help them in politics; and
- the question of how female politicians are portrayed in the media (Canada 1991: IV, 146).[21]

The Commission's summary of its proposals that specifically affect the representation of women makes no reference at all to systemic barriers; the only barriers mentioned are financial and 'procedural' (Canada 1992: 1; Copps 1992: 4-5).[22] Both sorts of obstacles can be overcome. 'Particular hurdles . . . include financial barriers' to women's participation and thus deterred them from 'becoming candidates for elected office' in the past. 'Procedural obstacles' involved access to nominations within political parties (Canada 1992: 1).

Among the vital points of information that are not conveyed in the Commission's summary is the fact that the under-representation of women in the House of Commons had prevailed long before the 5 per cent reached in 1980 and that the continued under-representation is due to something of greater consequence than lack of political will, too few friends to show female newcomers the ropes, cumbersome rules governing elections, disregard for women's merits, or insufficiently deep pockets.[23] Whether the goal for the representation of women is 1, 10, 20, or 40 per cent, to think about the representation of women in this way does little to help us understand the reasons for their under-representation in the first place. That subject would have taken the Royal Commission far beyond its mandate. This work is perhaps best left to others in the form of a second Royal Commission on the Status of Women for the twenty-first century.

The 20 per cent level of federal representation by women is within reach, but without some kind of government-sponsored inducements, such as those recommended by the Royal Commission, the next 30 per cent of seats remains elusive. For the first time in the history of the Canadian women's federal franchise, more than 20 per cent of the candidates were female in the 1993 federal election (cf. Brodie 1991: Table 1.1).[24] For a sex parity scenario to play itself out, many more female candidates would have to be nominated than in the last federal contest in 1993, and they would have to be elected in unprecedented numbers. Since it is unlikely that either or both of these conditions will be met in the next few elections, women will continue to be numerically under-represented in Parliament, as they were in the past. Sex 'dis'parity is all too likely to continue for many more decades.

The Commission aimed to improve the representativeness of the House of Commons without interfering with the prerogative of political parties to determine their internal policies and practices. The solution depends for the most part on the goodwill of the national political parties, the same institutions that for so long have been instrumental in keeping out all women but the hand-picked few.

The anticipated changes to the balance between the sexes in the composition of the House of Commons implicitly moves away from the liberal theory of electoral representation by incorporating for the first time the demand for a measure of representativeness based on sex. An increase in the number of women in Parliament may raise the profile of women's issues on the political agenda and in the national legislature. But this remains to be seen. Unless the public agenda is gradually reshaped under a new set of pressures, an increase in the number of female MPs in itself serves no useful purpose other than a symbolic one. And important and promising though symbolic change can be, symbolism without real change can create false expectations that lead to disappointment, disaffection, and even rejection of the legitimacy of the political system. Making politics more responsive to the concerns of women is of greater lasting importance than making more women fit into the partisan corsets used by the political parties to mould women aspirants to public office in their image of political womanhood. The political parties themselves are, in fact, part of the problem of under-representation, and not the solution (Bashevkin 1989: 457-8).

Conclusion: A Job Worth Doing . . .

Some of the Commission's conclusions about whether political parties can continue to provide good representation, and the sanctity of the single-member, simple-plurality voting system may work subtly against the admission of women and their interests to a full partnership in the political system. That is in part because the conclusions hold to an excessively narrow understanding of representation, its shortcomings, and the possible solutions to them. The question of who is to do the representing currently overshadows the all-important questions of what constitutes a legitimate political interest or a politically viable identity and which interests and identities are to be given greater access to the national decision-making processes. For these reasons, the proposed changes will improve sex parity, despite the fact that the numerical under-representation of women is the expression of a more complex complaint. Useful though the concept of under-representation can be for improving on the present situation, this concept in isolation from a broader discussion of the meaning of representation does not adequately address the charge that electoral representation will fail to select the most salient interests and identities of the country's female electorate. Although the government has sought to encourage women candidates and reduce barriers to their success, this two-pronged strategy may be challenged even after a critical mass in the numerical sense has been achieved. Perhaps ideas such as critical mass and under-representation need further refinement. In combination with a feminist conception of representation theorists might be better able than is the case at present to define goals that would both make improvements where possible and work toward large-scale social change. A critical mass of women legislators is certainly more likely to put women's identities and issues on the public agenda, but their mere presence will not necessarily have the desired effect. The goal, after all, is not so much the election of women but the election of enough diverse women (and men) who are committed to changing the public agenda to make it more sensitive to women.

The aspiration to move toward sex parity, though praiseworthy in itself, leaves unanswered equally important questions about the narrow range of identities and interests that find their way into Parliament. The desire to make representation more sensitive to the issue of representativeness will certainly become even more important once sex parity has been achieved. Communities of interest that are dispersed geographically rather than concentrated in particular ridings and others that lack the resources to organize electorally will still be unrepresented after the current round of electoral reform. Although some progress is being made to redress the numerical under-representation of women, the full measure of what it means to be under-represented remains to be addressed. The present concern simply to elect more women perhaps foreshadows the kinds of complaints that some segments of the public can be expected to express before the next round of electoral reform. The election of more women MPs will certainly be an encouraging sign that women do have a place in public life. But whether women's identities and interests will move upward from their low standing on the public agenda as the result of the '20 to 40 per cent solution' is, I have argued, a separate question that has yet to be addressed.

Sex parity that is primarily a symbol does not deserve to be called gender parity because it refers simply to the number of women MPs and not to the range of interests that they are likely to represent.[25] Regardless of the seriousness of this short coming, the recommendations of the Commission, on the whole, have been well received by the public. They have not, however, been acted upon by the government.[26] Some segments of the public, including many women politicians, believe that an easy and workable solution is at hand to remedy under-representation, enhance the quality of representation, and elect more women. The recommendations affecting representation for women deserve wider public support than they have received. The Royal Commission's program of reform faltered because of its combination of innovation and reformism. Neither its natural support among politicians and in political parties nor the supporters of reform among the nation's social movements gave it a strong enough endorsement to enable it to persuade the government to act decisively on the recommendations (Dobrowolsky and Jenson 1993: 45-7). The solution to the under-representation of women is not only the election of more women but also more effective representation of the full range of issues that concern the female electorate as well as more representativeness of the diversity of interests and identities that make up the entire electorate. Much has been accomplished, and much remains to be done. More women? Yes, certainly. More issues of concern to women? Not yet. A job well begun is a job half done.

What will this as yet unrealized vision of woman-sensitive, even feminist, theory of representation be like? Jill Vickers maintains that any such representation must attend to the needs, identities, and interests both of women's diversity and of their commonality (Vickers 1996b: 48). The aim of such a theory must be to transform politics, its programs, processes, and structures in a way that demonstrates that 'all women matter'. Finally, a feminist theory of representation must reach out to its critics, especially those who think effective representation is impossible, to argue for the practical ways in which feminist representation can democratize the institutions and practices of government and civil society to make them more responsive, not only to women, but to other previously under-represented segments of society. Bringing together the already completed and the uncompleted halves of what is admittedly a long, difficult job makes it possible to see at the same time what has already been accomplished and what remains to be done.

NOTES

Caroline Andrew, Peter Aucoin, Herman Bakvis, David Braybrooke, Jane Jenson, Jill Vickers, Daniel Woolf, and François-Pierre Gingras have been immensely helpful to me in clarifying my ideas about the representation of women. Their assistance, valuable though all of it has been, is not to be mistaken for agreement with the author on the point of view expressed here.

1 See the glossary for the meaning of terms such as 'sex bias', 'gender-neutral', and 'under-representation'.

2 Hege Skjeie calls the demand that women politicians transform public policy a 'mandate of "difference"'. In Canada, Lisa Young (1995) has applied this new order of demands to electoral representation in the House of Commons. Because the term used by Skjeie does not translate well from Norwegian into English, another term such as 'transformative politics' or 'demands to reorder public policy' might resonate more strongly among members of the women's movement and the electorate.

3 The Commission took the view that the tradition of responsible government in Canada requires and affirms the continued utility of political parties as 'primary political organizations in a parliamentary system' (Canada 1991: I, 12).

4 Bashevkin also notes that the more competitive the desired positions are, the fewer women succeed in gaining them.

5 The word gender is most often used in place of the word sex in the work of the Commission. For the most part the two words are *not* interchangeable. Therefore it is important to choose the right word for each context. Gender is perhaps the more politically expedient word because it appears to be the less value-laden of the two. Regardless of semantics, sex parity symbolizes the demand to redress long-standing sex bias, and so for the sake of clarity sex and not gender appears to be the more accurate of the two at least for conveying the meaning of the change envisaged. Had the Commission paid greater attention to the inclusion of women's needs and interests in addition to their concern for the numbers of women to be elected in future, 'gender' would be the appropriate term. As nothing of this nature was contemplated, it seems best for the time being to discuss only sex and sex parity with regard to the Commission's work.

6 Rare is the theory of democratic representation that calls for equal numbers of men and women, though this could be achieved through recourse to two-member constituencies as was proposed in discussions about the Charlottetown Accord and has been suggested for the territorial government of Nunavut (Nunavut 1994). The idea of electing equal numbers of female and male Senators was accepted in principle by the premiers of British Columbia, Nova Scotia, and Ontario. Iris Marion Young's suggestions for empowering oppressed groups includes giving government funding to help such groups organize themselves, especially their interest-aggregating activities; holding formal consultations with such groups in policy formulation and program delivery even to the point of having the groups generate policy themselves and requiring the bureaucracy to respond directly to their proposals; and giving such groups a veto on matters that affect primarily those groups (Young 1989: 261; 1990: 184).

7 See recommendations 1.3.19 to 1.3.23 in the Commission's final report (Canada 1991: I, 117-21). In the language used by the Commission, representativeness, lack of 'quality' representation, and under-representation are only loosely related, and are considered for the most part as specific and relatively self-contained problems to different categories of persons and groups within the electorate. Hence, under-representation refers primarily to the 'woman problem', and quality is discussed primarily in connection with the 'interests problem', especially as it relates to aboriginal peoples dispersed over a wide geographical area. Representativeness, which is the broadest of the three, addresses mainly the 'minorities and disadvantaged groups problem', which affects both women and aboriginal peoples. Representativeness is considered primarily in relation to the public's confidence in the electoral process and representative government. The connections between the three concepts and their related problems require more attention than the Commission's public summary of its findings and conclusions has given to each of them separately.

8 Randall refers to the 'contagion effect' in Northern Europe, where the large number of women in parties of the left impelled other parties to begin recruiting more women candidates. In the 1970s a number of left-wing parties in Sweden,

Norway, and Denmark adopted the principle that at least 40 per cent of representation at all levels of these parties was to be female (Skard and Haavio-Mannila 1985a). In Norway and Sweden those left-wing parties proposed that all political parties should adopt the 40 per cent rule for their electoral lists (Skard and Haavio-Mannila 1985b: 51-80). When the measure failed, the Norwegian Labour Party adopted the rule for its own candidates in local and national elections. Norway was used by the Commission as an example of how quotas can affect numerical representation (Canada 1991: I, 112-13). But contributors to *Unfinished Democracy* (Skard and Haavio-Mannila 1985a) maintain that the political representation of women in Nordic countries remains more symbolic than real. The Commission discussed the possibility of recommending proportional representation and quotas as a way to increase the proportion of women elected to the House of Commons. In the end, however, it opted for a more conventional approach that relies in the first instance on the political parties to identify their interests with the advancement of women within their ranks.

9 Once the proportion of women in the House of Commons reached 40 per cent the plan would be discontinued. The plan would also lapse regardless of its success after three federal elections. If quotas proved to be ineffective, the report of the Commission implies, additional measures to achieve the desired effect would then be necessary.

10 A high turnover of MPs gives women politicians more frequent and realistic opportunities for election (Lisa Young 1992: 100). But this may also make women politicians more vulnerable to being removed without having gained sufficient experience to move very far up the ladder within their caucuses (Randall 1987: 104). Pearson's exclusion of Pauline Jewett from Cabinet in the 1960s on the grounds that there was already one woman minister would no longer be accepted, though there may be other bits of biased 'conventional wisdom' about the sorts of posts for which women MPs are best suited (Anderson 1987: 44).

11 A winnable seat in general terms is a seat in which no more than 10 per cent of the vote separated the first- and second-place finisher. Other factors to take into account include voter volatility, turnover rates, and levels of spending in marginal seats. For further information on more sophisticated measures of these factors see Blake 1992.

12 But see *Unfinished Democracy* as in note 8 above, especially 79-80, 160-3, 166.

13 Many more male MPs than men in the general population are married.

14 The writing of the Charter and the efforts of women to have it include equality between the sexes have provided a banner under which under-represented categories of persons, especially women, are demanding additional status and recognition for themselves and their concerns.

15 The mandate of the Commission permitted it to consider fundamental changes to the electoral system, but the Commission decided to restrict its activities to the established 'first-past-the-post' single-member, simple-plurality voting system (Canada 1991: I, 18-21). Many analysts agree women candidates would fare at

least somewhat better under proportional representation than they will after electoral reform (Norris 1985: 93-5; Canada 1991: I, 111-12). NAC favoured the introduction of proportional representation in its presentation to the Beaudoin-Dobbie Committee on constitutional renewal and to the Royal Commission. Comparisons made by the Commission show that Canada's present electoral system places it in the middle of the list of countries that have adopted proportional representation. Its use in federal elections in Canada would probably help women make marginal gains in their percentage of representation, but discussions about which electoral system elects more women ignores the more important question of which interests, groups, and issues women legislators represent. Proportional representation is no substitute for effective group and issue representation (Young 1991: 187).

16 In the fortunate circumstance in which there are many equally well-qualified applicants, choices might reasonably be made on the basis of a characteristic such as sex or type of hair. Sapiro (1981) gives the example of equally well qualified candidates in which one is a woman and a redhead. The prospective voter (whose sex is not identified) is also a redhead. Under what conditions is it rational to select the redheaded female candidate? Unfortunately, this argument has yet to be used effectively in public discussion of why we ought to have more women and more diverse representatives of many sorts.

17 Dorothy Cantor's *Women in Power* is full of examples of this unfortunate phenomenon. Closer to home Audrey McLaughlin has wryly recounted the advice on comportment that she was given when first elected leader of the NDP. Wearing dark blue, she was told, would give her an added aura of authority by making her look the part of a national leader. She reports having made it her policy *not* to wear blue. The many hats of Ellen Fairclough, the domestic life of Judy LaMarsh, and Sheila Copps's control of the pitch of her voice have been examined by several different generations of journalists. On the subject of the typecasting of women politicians, the article by Kate Aitken (1958) in *Maclean's* remains current.

18 The Commission sponsored five symposia in order to prepare public opinion and public opinion makers for the Commission's recommendations. The symposium was held in Montreal from 31 October to 2 November 1990. The National Action Committee on the Status of Women was not invited to participate because women politicians were considered to be the women most knowledgeable about women's future in the electoral life of the country. Jane Jenson describes royal commissions as a means of representation in which voices continue to be heard selectively, despite the opportunity they provide for opening access to a broader public than usually influences government policy making (Jenson 1994: 52-4).

19 Regulating the process by which constituency associations select their candidate may open up the process to more women. The lack of fairness and the financial cost of the unreformed processes continue to place prospective women candidates at a considerable disadvantage (Matas 1992: A1, A7; Howard 1992: A4).

Much more could be said about the negative effects of control by riding associations over the selection of candidates.

20 One former Conservative MP, Dorothy Dobbie, suggested that women have few, if any, systemic barriers to overcome. But there was general disagreement with her comments. Much less was reported about the range of activities undertaken by women that might be affected by systemic barriers. It would be interesting to know whether the transcripts of presentations made to the Commission bear out this generalization. Janine Brodie's work points out most consistently that there are additional obstacles, including systemic barriers.

21 In addition to the already established 'barriers research' that treats obstacles to nominations and financing as easily remedied, attention needs to be paid to systemic barriers and to a critical review of the theory of representation itself.

22 The deputy leader of the federal Liberal Party, Sheila Copps, draws her analysis from work done by the Commission, but she does not mention the possibility of systemic barriers that might prevent the removal of minor obstacles from having the desired effect.

23 The seriousness of this oversight extends to the Commission's final report, in which the legal concept of 'systemic discrimination' is treated entirely separately from 'barriers to entry' and the two sources of disability are not related to each other. See Canada 1991: I, 97-8, 107-13.

24 In the 1993 general election 22 per cent of candidates were female, up from 19 per cent in 1988 and 14 per cent in the previous three elections.

25 I agree with Anne Phillips that proponents of sex parity need to consider the possibility that the best way to represent women is as a group, but not for the reasons she gives (Phillips 1992: 89). Sex parity is a worthy short-term goal but not the ultimate aim. The political aspiration of groups, at least of some groups in some circumstances, might be better achieved through collective representation. Such a system would not have to replace entirely the one-person, one-vote system of interest aggregation, by which the quantity of support is registered but not the intensity with which the preference is held. For example, one can imagine an elected Senate that would reflect group interests and identities better than it does under the current system of government patronage.

26 In February 1992 the report of the Royal Commission was referred to the House of Commons Special Committee on Electoral Reform, which considered mainly changes to the voting process. In one of its two reports the committee said that it would consider measures to increase the number of female candidates and the establishment of aboriginal constituencies in a third phase. But nothing further happened on this score before the 1993 election. However, the committee had recommended that the child-care expenses of a person seeking election or nomination as a candidate become deductible under the Income Tax Act; this recommendation was not included in the amendments to the 1993 Canada Elections Act (Seidle 1994: 76). I am grateful to Leslie Seidle for giving me this information.

BIBLIOGRAPHY

Aitken, Kate (1958), 'For the Sake of Argument: Women Are Misfits in Politics', *Maclean's*, 4 Jan.

Anderson, Doris (1987), *To Change the World: A Biography of Pauline Jewett* (Richmond Hill: Irwin).

Arscott, Jane, and Linda Trimbley, eds (1996), *In the Presence of Women: Representation in Canadian Governments* (Toronto: Harcourt Brace, forthcoming).

Baines, Beverley (1991), 'After Meech Lake: The Ms/Representation of Gender in Scholarly Spaces'. In *After Meech Lake: Lessons for the Future*, eds David E. Smith, Peter MacKinnon, and John C. Courtney (Saskatoon: Fifth House), 205-18.

Bashevkin, Sylvia (1985), *Toeing the Lines: Women and Party Politics in English Canada* (Toronto: University of Toronto Press).

———— (1989), 'Political Parties and the Representation of Women'. In *Canadian Parties in Transition: Discourse/Organization/Representation*, eds Alain G. Gagnon and A. Brian Tanguay (Scarborough: Nelson), 446-60.

Bell, Derek (1987), *And We Are Not Saved: The Elusive Quest for Racial Justice* (New York: Basic).

Birch, Anthony (1971), *Representation* (London: Pall Mall).

Blake, Donald E. (1992), 'Party Competition and Electoral Volatility: Canada in Comparative Perspective'. In *Representation, Integration and Political Parties in Canada*, vol. 14 of the research studies of the Royal Commission on Electoral Reform and Party Financing (Ottawa and Toronto: RCERPF/ Dundurn) 253-73.

Brodie, Janine (1985), *Women and Politics in Canada* (Toronto: McGraw-Hill Ryerson).

———— (1991), with Celia Chandler, 'Women in Canadian Politics'. In Megyery (1991): 3-59.

———— (1992), 'Choice and No Choice in the House'. In *Politics of Abortion*, ed. Janine Brodie et al. (Toronto: Oxford University Press), 57-116.

Cairns, Alan (1991), 'Constitutional Change and the Three Equalities'. In *Options for a New Canada*, ed. Ronald L. Watts and Douglas M. Brown (Toronto: University of Toronto Press), 77-102.

Canada (1970), Royal Commission on the Status of Women. *Report* (Ottawa: Information Canada).

———— (1991), Royal Commission on Electoral Reform and Party Financing. *Reforming Electoral Democracy: Final Report*, 4 vols (Ottawa: Supply and Services Canada).

———— (1992), Royal Commission on Electoral Reform and Party Financing. 'Royal Commission Recommends Steps to Increase Women's Political Participation', *Communiqué*, no. 13 (Ottawa: RCERPF).

Cantor, Dorothy W., and Toni Bernay (1992), with Jean Stoess, *Women in Power: The Secrets of Leadership* (Boston: Houghton Mifflin).

Clark, Lorenne (1988), 'Liberty, Equality, Fraternity—and Sorority'. In *Legal Theory Meets Legal Practice*, ed. Anne Bayefsky (Edmonton: Academic), 261-81.

Copps, Sheila (1992), 'To Encourage Women, Members of Visible Minorities and Aboriginal Persons to Run for Office: Reflections on Obstacles and Solutions to Fair Liberal Electoral Representation'. Paper delivered to Biennial Convention of the Liberal Party of Canada, Hull, Quebec, 22 Feb. 1992.

Costain, Anne N. (1988a), 'Representing Women: The Transition from Social Movement to Interest Groups'. In *Women, Power and Policy: Toward the Year 2000*, ed. Ellen Boneparth and Emily Stoper, 2nd edn (New York: Pergamon), 26-47.

———— (1988b), 'Women's Claims as a Special Interest'. In Mueller (1988): 150-73.

Dahlerup, Drude (1982), 'Overcoming the Barriers: An Approach to the Study of How Women's Issues Are Kept from the Political Agenda'. In *Women's Views of the Political World of Men*, ed. Judith Stiehm (New York: Transitional), 33-66.

Dahlerup, Drude , and Elina Haavio-Mannila (1985), 'Summary'. In *Unfinished Democracy Women in Nordic Politics*, trans. Christine Babcock (Toronto: Pergamon), 160-9.

Diamond, Irene, and Nancy Hartsock (1981), 'Beyond Interests in Politics: A Comment on Virginia Sapiro's "When Are Interests Interesting? The Problem of Political Representation of Women"', *American Political Science Review* 75 (1981): 717-23.

Dobrowolsky, Alexandra, and Jane Jenson (1993), 'Reforming the Parties: Prescriptions for Democracy'. In *How Ottawa Spends, 1993-1994* ed. Susan D. Phillips (Ottawa: Carleton University Press), 43-81.

Gotell, Lise, and Janine Brodie (1991), 'Women and Parties: More than an Issue of Numbers'. In *Political Parties in Canada, 6th edn*, ed. Hugh Thorburn (Toronto: Prentice-Hall), 53-67.

Haavio-Mannila, Elina, et al. (1985), *Unfinished Democracy: Women in Nordic Politics*, trans. Christine Badcock (Toronto: Pergamon).

Howard, Ross (1992), 'Liberal MPs resent Chrétien's Choices', *Globe and Mail*, 14 Nov.

Jenson, Jane (1994), 'Commissioning Ideas: Representation and Royal Commissions'. In *How Ottawa Spends, 1994-1995: Making Change*, ed. Susan D. Phillips (Ottawa: Carleton University Press), 39-69.

Jónasdóttir, Anna (1988), 'On the Concept of Interest, Women's Interests and Limitations of Interest Theory'. In Jones and Jónasdóttir (1988): 32-65.

———— (1994), *Why Women Are Oppressed* (Philadelphia: Temple University Press).

Jones, Kathleen (1988), 'Toward the Revision of Politics'. In Jones and Jónasdóttir (1988): 11-32.

Jones, Kathleen, and Anna Jónasdóttir, eds (1988), *The Political Interests of Gender* (Beverly Hills: Sage).

Kymlicka, Will (1993), 'Group Representation in Canadian Politics'. In *Equity and Community: The Charter, Interest Advocacy and Representation*, ed. F. Leslie Seidle (Montreal: Institute for Research on Public Policy), 61-89.

Maillé, Chantal (1990), with Valentine Pollon, *Primed for Power: Women in Canadian Politics* (Ottawa: Canadian Advisory Council on the Status of Women).

────── (1996), 'Political Representation and Women in Quebec'. In Arscott and Trimble (1996, forthcoming).

Matas, Robert (1992), 'B.C. Catching Election Fever', *Globe and Mail*, 11 Nov.

Megyery, Kathy, ed. (1991), *Women in Canadian Politics: Toward Equity in Representation*, vol. 6 of the research studies of the Royal Commission on Electoral Reform and Party Financing (Ottawa and Toronto: RCERPF/Dundurn).

Mill, John Stuart ([1861] 1977), *Considerations on Representative Government* (1861). In *Collected Works of John Stuart Mill*, ed. John M. Robson, vol. 19 (Toronto: University of Toronto Press), 371-577.

Mohanty, Chandra Talpade (1987), 'Feminist Encounters: Locating the Politics of Experience', *Copyright* 1: 30-44.

Mueller, Carol, ed. (1988), *The Politics of the Gender Gap: The Social Construction of Political Influence* (Beverly Hills: Sage).

Norris, Pippa (1985), 'Women's Legislative Participation in Western Europe'. In *Women and Politics in Western Europe*, ed. Sylvia Bashevkin (Ottawa: F. Cass), 90-101.

Nunavut Implementation Commission (1996), 'Two Member Constituencies and Gender Equality: A "Made in Nunavut Solution"'. In Arscott and Trimble (forthcoming, 1996).

Pateman, Carol (1980), 'Women, Nature and Suffrage', *Ethics* 90: 564-75.

Phillips, Anne (1991), *Engendering Democracy* (University Park, PA: Pennsylvania State University).

────── (1992), 'Democracy and Difference: Some Problems for Feminist Theory', *Political Quarterly* 63: 79-91.

Pitkin, Hannah Fenichel (1967), *The Concept of Representation* (Los Angeles: University of California Press).

Randall, Vicky (1987), *Women and Politics: An International Perspective*, 2nd edn (London: Macmillan).

Robinson, Gertrude, and Armande Saint-Jean (1991), with Christine Rioux. 'Women Politicians and Their Media Coverage: A Generational Analysis'. In Megyery (1991): 127-62.

Sapiro, Virginia (1981), 'Research Frontier Essay: When Are Interests Interesting? The Problem of Political Representation of Women', *American Political Science Review* 75: 701-16.

Seidle, F. Leslie (1994), 'The Angry Citizenry: Examining Representation and Responsiveness in Government', *Policy Options* 15 (July-Aug.): 75-80.

Skard, Torild, and Elina Haavio-Mannila (1985a), 'Mobilization of Women at Elections'. In Haavio-Mannila et al. (1985), 37-50.

——— (1985b), 'Women in Parliament'. In Haavio-Mannila et al. (1985): 51-80.

Skjeie, Hege (1991), 'The Rhetoric of Difference: On Women's Inclusion into Political Elites', *Politics & Society* 19: 209-32.

Smith, Jennifer (1991), 'The Franchise and Theories of Representative Government'. In *Democratic Rights and Electoral Reform in Canada*, ed. Michael Cassidy, vol. 10 of the research studies of the Royal Commission on Electoral Reform and Party Financing (Ottawa and Toronto: RCFERPF/Dundurn), 3-28.

Studlar, Donley T., and Richard E. Matland (1994), 'The Growth of Women's Representation in the Canadian House of Commons and the Election of 1984: A Reappraisal', *Canadian Journal of Political Science* 27: 53-79.

Swain, Carol M. (1992a), *Black Faces, Black Interests: The Representation of African Americans in Congress* (Cambridge, MA: Harvard University Press).

——— (1992b), 'Some Consequences of the Voting Rights Act'. *Controversies in Minority Voting: The Voting Rights Act in Perspective*, eds Bernard Grofman and Chandler Davidson (Washington: Brookings Institution), 292-96.

Vickers, Jill, ed. (1988), *Getting Things Done: Women's Views of Their Involvement in Political Life* (Ottawa: UNESCO, Division of Human Rights and Peace, and CRIAW).

——— (1996a), *Re-engineering Political Science: A Feminist Account* (Halifax: Fernwood), forthcoming.

——— (1996b), 'Toward A Feminist Understanding of Representation'. In Arscott and Trimble (1996, forthcoming).

Ward, Norman (1950), *The Canadian House of Commons: Representation*, 2nd edn (Toronto: University of Toronto Press).

Whip, Rosemary (1991), 'Representing Women: Australian Female Parliamentarians on the Horns of a Dilemma', *Women and Politics* 11: 1-22.

Young, Iris Marion (1988), 'Five Faces of Oppression', *Philosophical Forum* 19: 270-90.

——— (1989), 'Polity and Group Difference: A Critique of the Idea of Universal Citizenship', *Ethics* 99: 250-74.

——— (1990), *Justice and the Politics of Difference* (New Haven, CT: Yale University Press).

——— (1992), 'Together in Difference: Transforming the Logic of Group Political Conflict', *Political Theory Newsletter* 4: 11-26.

——— (1994), 'Gender as Seriality: Thinking about Women as a Social Collective', *Signs: Journal of Women in Culture and Society* 19: 713-38.

Young, Lisa (1991), 'Legislative Turnover and the Election of Women to the Canadian House of Commons'. In Megyery (1991): 81-100.

——— (1996), 'Fulfilling the Mandate of Difference'. In Arscott and Trimble (1996, forthcoming).

GLOSSARY

Formal equality—A situation in which 'the state will accord equal rights under the law without discrimination to all who qualify (usually citizens or residents)'. (Vickers 1996a)

Gender analysis—A type of analysis used in public policy analysis to emphasize the fact that 'men and women are both differently related to the state and, potentially at least, differently affected by government policies, programs and changes in entitlements'. (Vickers 1996a)

Gender-neutral—Having no effect 'on a society's (or group's) socially constructed gender conceptions'. Describes 'policies, programs or changes in entitlement'. (Vickers 1996a)

Gender parity—A distribution of seats in Parliament that would accord approximately equal importance, time and resources to the issues, interests and concerns of women and of men.

Representation by women—A system in which the person elected would have to be a woman, but not necessarily a feminist.

Representation for women—A system in which the person selected could be of either sex but would take women's concerns as a guiding point in her or his activities.

Representativeness—Selection based on the aim of representing the widest possible range of people having salient differences in their attributes, identities, and interests.

Sex bias—Methods, attitudes, and behaviour that view the world from a male perspective. Its multiple forms include androcentrism, gynopia, gender-insensitivity, over-generalization, under-generalization, and the use of double standards. (Vickers 1996a)

Sex parity—A distribution of seats in Parliament that would award approximately equal numbers to 'men' and 'women'.

Systemic barriers—Barriers that 'form part of a system of structural discrimination.' The barriers prevent some people from 'realizing opportunities or receiving equal protection or benefit of the law. Barriers are understood to be both *systemic* and *structural*, that is, endemic to the social, economic, political and cultural arrangements in a society.' (Vickers 1996a)

Systemic discrimination—'Practices and attitudes that have, whether by design or impact, the effect of limiting an individual's or group's right to the opportunities generally available because of attributed rather than actual characteristics.' (See Vickers 1996a for elaboration.)

Under-representation—The extent to which the proportion of women in Parliament is less than their proportion of the population. Women make up half the population but hold only 18 per cent of the seats in the House of Commons. (Aboriginal peoples, visible minorities, and people with disabilities are also under-represented.)

Woman-sensitive—Conscious of the 'possible sex/gender implications of proposed policy, program and entitlement changes', especially with a view to its effect on women. (Vickers 1996a)

PART II

Gender and Public Policy

CHAPTER 4

Gender and Public Policy

Making Some Difference in Ottawa

Sandra Burt

Groups seeking to further women's interests have been active in Canada since at least the late 1800s. During the past 20 years in particular researchers have uncovered some of the contributions these groups have made to Canadian life. Many community activist groups are trying to build support for feminist positions at the local level and have rejected involvement in organized politics. Other groups have chosen to work within existing organizations, such as trade unions or professional associations, in order to change women's material conditions without necessarily lobbying governments. The most visible groups are the advocacy organizations that have accepted the challenge of working for change from within the political system. These advocacy groups have achieved heightened visibility since the early 1970s, primarily as a result of their proliferation and stronger voices, especially at the national level. In this chapter I examine the range of policy issues that the national organizations committed to political action have addressed during this period of high visibility, in particular during the past 10 years. I examine as well the response of federal governments since the early 1980s to the demands of feminist groups and explore the future implications of current trends.

For this analysis the state is viewed as a set of sectors or arenas, with differentiated patterns of authority and interaction, but united by a common general framework or boundary limits of action.[1] The groups examined here in their interactions with the state describe themselves as feminist or committed to some form of role changes or equality for women. Their goals are situated within the various streams of feminist thought. Carole Pateman (1986: 7) proposes that either feminist claims can be accommodated within existing political structures or they can pose a radical challenge to both the policies and the policy-making process. She calls this a distinction between 'domesticated' and 'distinctive' feminism. Proponents of the domesticated version of feminism argue that traditional world-views can be modified to accept the presence of women. Distinctive feminism, on the other hand, is predicated on the assumption that patriarchy is at the heart of these existing world-views. A distinctive feminist approach asks new questions and establishes new categories in the quest for women's autonomy as opposed to women's equality. Pateman herself rejects the possibility that women can be brought into the public world of liberal theory, characterized by a presumably genderless individual, and made to fit 'into a unitary, undifferentiated framework that assumes that there is only one—universal—sex' (Pateman 1986: 7). She argues that the so-called universal individual of the liberal public world has been created with male characteristics and 'constructed on the basis of male attributes, capacities and modes of activity' (p. 7). So for Pateman, domesticated feminists have accepted the dominant male-inspired boundaries of social, economic, and political action and seek ways to improve women's opportunities for achievement within these boundaries.

In the first section of this chapter I examine the recent feminist agenda of the national women's lobby groups as reflected in their policy proposals, and assess those proposals within the context of Pateman's dichotomy. While it would be misleading to catagorize the numerous opinions held by these groups as expressions of either one view or the other, a review of their proposals does suggest some trends.

THE AGENDA OF THE NATIONAL GROUPS

Since second-wave feminist groups first emerged in the 1970s, they have been engaged in a continuing process of self-identification. In the early days of the second-wave women's movement these identities were forged partly in response to federal government initiatives. The 1970 report of the Royal Commission on the Status of Women was an early blueprint for action, and the 'Strategy for Change' conference, the organizing session for the National Action Committee on the Status of Women (NAC) that was convened in Toronto in 1972, was primarily a forum for addressing the commission's recommendations. The meeting was opened by Florence Bird (the chair of the commission), addressed by Elsie Gregory McGill (a member of the commission), and supported with a $15,000 grant from the federal government. The list of recommendations generated by that conference included government funding for action as well as legislated measures for equality rights.

This early call for government financial assistance set the tone for relations between feminist groups and the government in subsequent years. In the Secretary of State alone, the budget for women's groups grew from $223,000 in 1973 to $12.5 million in 1985, although there have been yearly reductions since then, as a result of the Conservative government's policy, between 1989 and 1993, of removing funding for advocacy groups. This reliance on government support has undoubtedly affected the goals and strategies of women's groups in the sense that project grants (almost half of the total grant packages) had to conform to government guidelines. But there is little evidence that women's groups were co-opted in this process. Rather, the government funds, relatively secure for at least the first 10 years of the movement, provided the groups with the resources for organizing, research, and action. And relatively little control was exercised over the groups' activities. In his review of federally funded organizations, including multicultural and linguistic groups as well as women's groups, Leslie Pal (1993: 275-6) argues that the program descriptions and control mechanisms within the Secretary of State have been vague and applied loosely. Indeed, groups like NAC that have received both project and operational funding became increasingly confrontational with the federal government in the mid-1980s, especially on the issues of free trade and constitutional reform. So government funding was important because it gave women's groups a measure of legitimacy, guaranteed them a voice in the federal government's policy deliberations, and provided the groups with the means to survive. Moreover, government control over the spending of this money was restricted primarily to the establishment of guidelines for proposals for project or core funding. As well, time constraints were imposed by application deadlines.[2] In the short term, this funding provided thousands of groups with the necessary basis for political action.

In 1984 I administered a questionnaire to women's groups across Canada in order to determine their goals and organizing practices. There were thousands of such groups in existence at the time, but most were local, short-lived, and difficult to find. For that survey I used a list drawn up by the Women's Program, Secretary of State, which included all women's groups that had inquired about group funding. The list, which was prepared in 1982 and updated in 1983, contained 612 functioning groups. Only 144 of these groups completed the questionnaire, but their responses do suggest some trends. The results of that survey confirmed that there was a wide diversity of goals among feminist groups. This was expected, for women have never been a single-interest group. The organizations participating in the 1984 survey concentrated primarily on the reform of the abortion law, sexual equality in the workplace, an end to violence against women, and a national child-care strategy (Burt 1990: 17-28). Although a small number of the groups were working for fundamental shifts in the social and economic roles of women and men, most limited their activities to trying to improve the status of women in the existing system. They set their goals within the context of equal rights—improving women's access to jobs, economic security, and political power. In Pateman's terms, they were committed primarily to domesticated feminism, with less visible but nonetheless significant visions of distinctive feminism. And sometimes the two streams could be found co-existing within the same organizations.

Nine of the approximately 20 national groups in existence at the time took part in the survey. All nine were engaged in political advocacy work; that is, they were seeking to change government policy by applying pressure to policy makers. In the survey the groups were asked, in an open-ended question, to name the one issue that was most important for them at that time. The answers ranged widely from improving opportunities for women in sport to assisting female prisoners. For the most part, the goals were woman-centred and focused on breaking down barriers to the fair and equal treatment of women in the home or the workplace (see Table 1). This is not surprising, given the groups' commitment to incremental change from within the political system. But the goals also included world peace and empowering women on issues of health and well-being. These issues, expressed as demands for better access to safe abortions, reproductive health, and an end to male violence are either exclusively or primarily female-specific. They do not fit easily into the category of equal rights, although some feminists (in particular in the United States) have developed complicated arguments for establishing the hypothetical equal right of men to maternity benefits (Pateman 1986: 8). While these issues are not nearly as far-reaching in their implications as the transformative goals of Pateman's distinctive feminism, they bring women's bodies into discussions in the presumably genderless public sphere and are grounded in a belief in the need for women's autonomy. In other words, they draw attention to gender differences.

In 1984 NAC was the national voice for many of the smaller groups. NAC describes itself as an umbrella organization representing other women's groups. In 1980 it had established 10 regional representatives in order to improve its contact with member groups across the country; this number was later increased to 13. According to Susan Phillips (1991), who has mapped the network of relationships among women's groups, NAC serves as a co-ordinator rather than a controller of the activities of other groups. However, it has had some difficulties speaking for the multiplicity of views represented

TABLE 1 GOALS OF THE NATIONAL FEMINIST GROUPS, 1984

Equal Rights
> Pensions for women
> Increased tax allowance for children
> Good-quality child care
> Spousal half-interest in matrimonial property
> Salary with CPP benefits for farm wives
> Equal access of men and women to all sports

The Social Order
> Promotion of the value of agriculture
> Arms control and disarmament

Women's Autonomy and Health
> Censorship of pornographic movies
> Access to abortion
> Occupational health of women

in its member groups. In 1982, for example the francophone Fédération des femmes du Québec left the organization briefly when it disagreed with NAC's position on the Constitution bill. In 1991 the Association for Women's Equity in the Armed Forces (1993) withdrew from NAC on the grounds that 'the National Action Committee executive and some of the members continue to mistakenly relate working toward equal career choices and conditions of service for military women, to being anti-peace.' The letter of cancellation also noted that 'verbal abuse' and 'heckling' had greeted the group's delegates at NAC's annual meeting.

In 1984 NAC's vision was for the improved status of women in Canada, with greater power for women in politics and business. The members attending the annual general meeting passed a women's agenda that included a call for quality child care; attention to women's issues in the 1984 federal election; the legalization of midwifery; representation of Native women at the first-ministers' conference on aboriginal rights, as well as the repeal of provisions in the Indian Act that discriminated against women; and free-standing abortion clinics. In addition, members addressed the broader issues of non-profit housing, Canadian intervention in Central America, and nuclear disarmament and peacemaking, both nationally and internationally. Indeed, 7 of the 37 resolutions passed at that meeting (19 per cent of the total) were related to peace.

Among the national groups generally, the prime goal of advocacy work in 1984 was the attainment of equal rights for women. But the quest for equal status was part of a commitment to building a different political system. There was as well a poorly expressed but nonetheless pervasive commitment to a politics of sharing rather than a politics of manipulation,[3] coupled with concern about women's personal autonomy and the building of a safe society and a peaceful world.

In 1993 when I mailed a second survey to national women's groups, the number had doubled, and 22 of them participated in the study. As in the 1980s, there was strong emphasis generally on equal rights for women. Fourteen of the 22 groups noted equal rights as their primary goal. But equal rights was a more inclusive concept in 1993 than in 1984. In this second survey some respondents noted their specific concern with the rights of immigrant and minority women. In 1981 the federal government held the first national conference on immigrant women, and this was followed in 1986 by the founding of the National Organization of Immigrant and Visible Minority Women. This group is concerned primarily with equity for its members. Its perspective is contained in a 1988 speech by Glenda Simms (1989: 16) delivered at a conference on equity: 'We want equity in all the efforts that are made on behalf of Canadian women. We have been very dissatisfied with the efforts so far. We know that there is employment equity for women. . . . But we know that the women who have benefited are not our women, and we want questions answered.'

The groups in the 1993 study were asked to explain their understanding of feminism, and 19 of the 22 respondents did so. Of these, 12 (63 per cent) referred to some variation of the equal rights theme.[4] For them, feminism meant the full equality of women, equal opportunity for women, or the attainment of women's legal equality. An additional three respondents defined feminism as promoting and valuing women's work. Only two respondents offered definitions that were not woman-centred (one was humanist, the other, inclusive). As in 1984, there was an overwhelming commitment (from 15 of the 22 groups) to equal-rights feminism in the stated goals (see Table 2). In addition, most of the goals were group-specific. For example, the Women's Committee of the Canadian Ethnocultural Council (Ethno Canada 1988: 9) lobbies the federal government for the provision of adequate language training, including child care and a transportation allowance, to all immigrant women. It also wants to see an increase in the number of appointments of women from minority ethnic groups to federal boards and commissions. The Elizabeth Fry Society concentrates on helping women in prison. The women's committees in the unions are interested in pay equity for their members.

As a co-ordinating group, NAC is more general in its orientation but is similarly preoccupied with equal rights. In 1993 it concentrated even more on rights than in 1984. This may be due in part to its attempt to accommodate the immigrant and racial-minority women it now seeks to represent (Ethno Canada 1988: 9). At the 1993 annual general meeting the resolutions passed were more inclusive of minority and immigrant women (although demonstrating surprisingly little interest in the issues or views of Native or Inuit women) and less concerned than in the past with world peace. In its

---

TABLE 2 GOALS OF THE NATIONAL FEMINIST GROUPS, 1993

Equal Rights
      Improve the economic status of women
      Integrate women in all aspects of the armed forces
      Advance economic status of unionized women
      Work for equality of women in the law
      Advance professional women
      Work for affordable, accessible child care
      Promote the status of women

Research
      Improve women's education and training
      Feminist research and networking

Women's Autonomy, Health, and Safety
      Improve access to abortions
      End violence against women
      Provide services to women

resolutions extending beyond the status of women, NAC was concerned primarily with ending racism and homophobia. This emphasis on equal rights was reflected in NAC's slogan in the 1993 federal election campaign: 'Equality is the bottom line.'

The concentration on equal rights is consistent with a growing preoccupation generally in Canada with the language of the Charter of Rights and Freedoms, which is grounded in liberal equal rights thinking. If interests 'emerge out of political action itself and are variable' (Brodie et al. 1992: 6), then the Charter ought to make a difference to the articulation of interests by groups in the system. Sixteen of the 22 national groups in the 1993 study viewed the Charter as a positive force in Canadian women's lives. The reasons given generally included some elements of specific rights, for example, the affirmation of lesbian rights, better rights for women in prison, or more access to abortions. Two respondents were unsure about the effect of the Charter, and the remaining four felt that women's lives were about the same after the Charter as before. So there is substantial support for the document, and this support is seen in the kinds of goals the groups have set for the 1990s. The arguments of feminist legal groups (for example, the National Association of Women and the Law and the Legal Education and Action Fund) have been important in the development of rights thinking. Most significant has been the argument that the implementation of equal rights laws sometimes requires consideration of the history of the subjugation of women and their exclusion from some rights.

This call by feminist advocacy groups for equal rights is primarily a call for government action, in the form either of social programs or of funding for women's groups. In the early years of funding from the Women's Program in the Secretary of State, there was little discussion about the implications of state support. Government money was accepted so that the groups could carry out what they saw as essential functions. But when the federal government began to reduce the size of the budget for 'women's issues' in 1989 (and for the first time funded groups with explicitly anti-feminist goals), there was more discussion of the groups' relationship with the state. For most of these groups the call for state funding is part of a larger strategy of opposing the exclusive reliance on market forces for social justice. Others consider it a fair return for women's unwaged work, which is seen as an essential part of the existing economic system.[5]

Overall, the period from 1984 to 1993 saw more emphasis by national women's groups on equal rights and less on world peace. Women's health and safety, however, remained a constant objective. For the most part the equal-rights argument was framed in traditional liberal terms—as a demand by 'domesticated feminists' for access to the already existing worlds of business and politics. At the same time NAC claimed special status at the constitutional bargaining table in 1992 in the deliberations that led up to the referendum on the amending of the Constitution. Again in the federal elections of 1984, 1988, and 1993 NAC led the way in demanding a special leaders' debate on women's issues. But these were relatively minor variations on the dominant theme of equal rights. The argument for special status was never fully developed by the national feminist groups lobbying governments for change. Instead, the groups concentrated on winning some of the already scarce resources in the market system—jobs and higher status. With the addition of the call from immigrant and minority women for an equal place in the economy, the emphasis on rights was further strengthened.

GOVERNMENT POLICIES FOR WOMEN DURING THE SECOND WAVE

Progressively from the early 1970s to the mid-1980s, the federal government has endorsed the equal-rights principle, expressed either as legal equality or equality of opportunity, and gradually but less enthusiastically in the early 1980s as substantive equality or equality in outcome. For the most part it has rejected the call for special status. But there are some important exceptions. Since the publication of the report of the Royal Commission on the Status of Women, the federal government has been committed, in varying degrees, to the principle of equality as the right to be treated the same. It has rejected the argument that women have an equal right to be different, except as it relates to women's health and safety. The government also demonstrated an early willingness to expand the size of the public sphere, moving issues like domestic violence and child care into the realm of public policy; recently, however, there have been reversals of this trend. Even during the period of Conservative rule from 1984 to 1993, when the power of a pro-family and anti-feminist group was strong within the government caucus, the legal equality guidelines were maintained.

The Framework

The federal government's first summary declaration of its 'women's policy' was published in 1979 as the National Plan of Action. This plan named five policy areas of concern: rape, wife battering, sexual harassment, women in the media, and pensions. But the early emphasis on women's safety was short-lived, for in subsequent policies there has been a shift away from personal safety and well-being to economic equality. From the time of its election in 1984 the Conservative government was prepared to treat women's issues as legal-equality issues but was less committed than its Liberal predecessor to redistributive programs such as child care or pensions for housewives. The shift was most apparent in 1986 with the publication of a new work plan for ministers responsible for the provincial status of women, called *Dimensions of Equality*. In this blueprint the newly elected Conservative government reaffirmed the established principle of working toward women's equality. Equality was defined in that document as the equal sharing in the benefits of, and participation in, all federal programs and initiatives. This was an equal-opportunity document, underlining the principle of treating women the same as men. Justice and fairness were defined as equality of opportunity as well as of outcome. For according to the government, these two principles are not served 'if the law results in differential effects, has detrimental consequences for certain individuals or groups, or excludes an individual or group from the protection and benefits of the law' (Canada 1986: 12). The federal government's commitment to action was expressed as a determination 'to create the conditions that will enable Canadian women to pursue their ambitions on an equal footing with men and to realize their full potential in all spheres of society' (p. 31). The 1989 update of *Dimensions of Equality* reaffirms the principles of the earlier documents and calls for a partnership of government, business, labour, and women's groups in the struggle to achieve such equality. More recently, a 1993 program of Status of Women Canada combines the earlier concerns for women's safety with the more recent emphasis on equality in the Framework for Women's Equality and Safety (Canada 1993b: 1).

A review of government policies in the same period shows that there has been considerable progress toward the formal legal equality of women and men and some, although less substantial movement toward equality of outcome. It reveals as well that there are significant differences in the ways in which issues relevant to women's lives have been treated by different departments of the federal government.

Justice

The federal government has been most active in the area of formal legal equality. This has been the easiest issue to deal with, since what it requires primarily is agreement in principle with the concept of legal equality, while placing the burden of proof and compliance on the individual. In the first instance this was interpreted as the removal of discriminatory provisions from existing laws. In the years that have followed the implementation of the equality provisions of the Charter, there has been an additional focus on the equal treatment of women in the legal system. In 1985 the Charter of Rights and Freedoms made it illegal to discriminate on the basis of sex. In that same year the federal government passed the Statute Law Amendment Bill to correct obvious cases of sex discrimination in federal laws. At the same time, the Department of Justice published a working paper, *Equality Issues in Federal Law* (Canada 1985) in an attempt to generate discussion and action on the so-called grey areas in legislative provisions that might be subject to the sex equality rule. The government's position at that time was that some situations (such as maternity, combat duty in the armed forces, and family allowance payments) might require sex-specific regulations. But subsequently this list of special cases was shortened to reproductive issues and violence against women. The Charter is portrayed as a people's document, and questions about its interpretation 'must be answered by Canadians themselves before government formulates plans for carrying out the consensus that emerges' (p. 20).

The mechanisms for developing or acting on that consensus were not put in place. The equality issues fall into a variety of departmental categories, and departmental norms and personalities have been important influences on the interpretation of the Charter.

For example, the changing of the 1869 Indian Act involved band councils but failed to include the affected constituency of Native women. The new provisions ameliorate but do not remove the unequal treatment of Native women who marry non-Indians as they are defined in the Act. Bill C-31 restored Indian status to these women and granted first-time status, but not band membership, to their children. Grandchildren were denied such legal status. Sally Weaver (1993: 128) has concluded that the bill did much more to enhance the power of Native band councils (usually controlled by men) than to ensure Native women's legal equality. Here, the special rights demanded by the bands conflicted with the legal equality rights of Native women. Women's equality rights took second place. According to Weaver (1993: 128), 'the new Indian Act [1985], once again, legitimizes discrimination against Indian women.'

Through its Court Challenges Program, which originally budgeted $9 million for equal-rights cases, the federal government has actively encouraged women, as well as other groups affected by the Charter, to develop their positions on equal rights. The program was established in 1985, cancelled in 1993, and then reinstated at the beginning of the 1993 election campaign. The Court Challenges Program has made it possible for the Legal Education and Action Fund (LEAF) either to represent one of the parties or to serve as intervenor (that is, to offer an opinion on the possible effect of the case on women's interests) in test cases related to women's equality rights. The program has also reinforced the principle that women's rights are just one part of the larger package of equal rights that the government is prepared to consider.

In June 1991 Kim Campbell, the Conservative Minister of Justice, convened a symposium on women, law, and the administration of justice. It was an attempt to facilitate the development of a justice system that was more reflective of the realities of women's lives. The recommendations of the participants included improved representation of women on judicial bodies, a code of ethics for judges, and guarantees that women's voices would be heard in Supreme Court cases. Contained within the demands was a developing argument for interpreting equal rights as the right to be different. The federal government's response, published in the fall of 1993, was a rejection of this argument for 'special treatment' for women. For example, in their recommendations the groups asked the Minister of Justice to 'ensure that in future, positions taken by the federal government in all constitutional litigation are consistent with her expressed commitment to overcoming the inequality of women' (Canada 1993a: 3). The government responded that a thorough review was already under way. 'The Attorney General's ultimate decision therefore reflects a balancing of wide-ranging and sometimes competing policy, fiscal and legal considerations' (p. 4). In its response the government was sympathetic to the need for improved training of judges and law enforcement officials on gender issues but did not agree to establish new programs. Nor did it revisit the criteria applied in existing programs.

The Employment Sector

Although the principle of equal opportunity for women has informed this sector, the work-force continues to be segregated by sex. Federal government sponsorship of organizations of immigrant and racial-minority women in the 1980s helped to ensure that equal opportunity in the workplace would remain a primary goal of advocacy groups into the 1990s. There have been some significant improvements in the employment opportunities and conditions of work for women since the early 1970s. Most dramatic has been the shift from the idea of equality as the right to be paid equally for the same job to the right to equal pay for work of similar value. Pay equity is the most explicit statement of the government's willingness to treat people engaged in different forms of labour as if they were the same. However, this concept of difference is firmly contained within a value system developed primarily by white, affluent, and propertied men.

In 1986 the federal government, guided by the recommendations of the Parliamentary Sub-Committee on Equality Rights, declared its intention to pursue pay equity, and had already begun to do so. In 1984, for example, the government established the national Equal Pay Program for employees under federal jurisdiction, based on the principle of equal value. A pay equity settlement for about 70,000 federal civil servants was reached in June 1990, which provided retroactive and continuing pay increases of 4 to 7 per cent for affected workers. While these increases were criticized by the public service unions as too little, too late, they nonetheless provide evidence of some shifts in the thinking of legislators about policies for women.

The federal government's employment equity strategy was also designed within equal opportunity guidelines. Employment equity became the popular term for affirmative action programs in 1984 following the publication of the report of the federal Royal Commission on Equality in Employment (Canada 1984). Unlike pay equity, which is intended specifically to remove discriminatory pay policies, employment equity is seen as a mechanism to facilitate the movement of specifically targeted groups into all sectors of the labour force. It was created as a response to exclusionary hiring practices that have resulted in the concentration of the targeted groups in particular (and frequently low-status and poorly paid) job categories. Federal employment equity legislation has been in place since August 1986; it targets women, aboriginal peoples, persons with disabilities, and racial minorities. This earliest legislation applies to federally regulated employers and Crown corporations with 100 or more employees. The terms of the legislation require employers to prepare work plans for increasing the representation of the designated groups to match their availability in the external work-force. The legislation also stipulates that employers must file annual progress reports with the Minister of Employment and Immigration. A second plan, for businesses doing work with the federal government, was put in place in October 1986. These federal contractors are not required to submit annual reports but may be reviewed by the Department of Employment and Immigration.

These federal programs have not succeeded in removing the targeted inequalities in employment patterns. For example, in 1990 women were still over-represented in clerical, sales, and service occupations (57 per cent of women in the paid labour force versus 26 per cent of men) (Canada 1992b: 4-5). At the same time women remain under-represented in managerial positions. Some of the designated groups have fared more poorly than others. Women who also have one or more of the other targeted characteristics have been the most seriously disadvantaged. Aboriginal women, for example, have not benefited from the legislation. By 1990 'their representation in the work force covered by the Act remained well below their known availability in the Canadian labour force' (Canada 1992b: 9). At first glance one might conclude that women who are members of one of the other targeted groups should be doubly advantaged by the terms of the legislation. On the contrary, however, employers have tended to treat women as a separate group and to assume that the other targeted groups are predominantly male. Nicole Morgan explains this apparent contradiction as a situation where the needs of one group are played off 'against the needs of another'. She noted this response to the employment equity legislation during a conference on the subject, when one director said, ' "I think we should pay more attention to the disabled now." His remark was met with applause, but one woman pointed out that 50 per cent of the disabled were women. There was a silence' (Morgan 1988: 40-1).

Employment equity efforts in the federal civil service have been similarly ineffectual. In September 1988 the federal government established a task force to identify barriers to the advancement of women within the federal public service. In the report, published in 1990, managers were encouraged to 'pursue the objectives of employment equity' (Canada 1990). Even before the task force reported, there was apparent evidence of some recent progress for women. The federal public service had about 90,000 female employees in 1987, an increase of 15 per cent from 1976. Increasingly, these women were moving into managerial positions. 'In 1985 there were three times as many female managers as in 1976.' They were younger than their male counterparts: 39 per cent of women were under 40, compared to 15 per cent of the men. And the promotion rate between 1985 and 1987 was 29 per cent for women, and 13 per cent for men (Morgan 1988: 52-3).

But Morgan's clear and perceptive analysis of career patterns in the federal civil service reveals that men also have advanced in the job hierarchy. In 1976 only 7.7 per cent of male civil servants were in senior management jobs, compared to 10 per cent in 1985. For there was a net increase in senior management positions in this period, and women's increases did not even keep pace with men's increases. 'Because women have lagged behind in the past, they will never catch up to men unless their advancement is more rapid, which does not seem to be the case' (p. 54). The new world of gender segregation may be one in which the non-management levels are largely the preserve of women, 'while the management levels will be divided between men and women, with men always managing to stay one step ahead' (p. 55). There are several explanations for the failure of the employment equity laws. The federal government's decision to use the pool of qualified applicants as the reference point avoids the issue of socialization patterns among young girls and boys. Also, the compliance mechanisms are weak. And the reliance on employers to establish targets and, in effect, to regulate their own plans of action has contributed to the disappointing record.

There has been some progress in the designation of jobs in the Canadian Armed Forces, primarily as a result of judicial decisions. In 1989 the Canadian Human Rights Tribunal 'ruled that all military occupations (except submariner) were to be opened to women within ten years' (Association for Women's Equity 1993: 1). In February 1990 the government established a Minister's Advisory Board to pursue this issue.

In an attempt to have some influence on the socialization of girls and women, and to challenge the stereotypes of the appropriate roles for men and women, one-half of the 2,500 Canada Scholarships awarded annually by the Natural Sciences and Engineering Research Council for graduate study in engineering and the natural sciences are given to women. That program was established in 1988. In addition, in 1990 the National Research Council began to provide financial assistance ($37,000 over three years) to about 75 female undergraduates enrolled in these subjects.

Overall the programs have been most effective in establishing women's legal right to access to employment. Equality of outcome, however, has been less apparent. In 1993, for example, it was still the case that 72 per cent of workers in the lowest-paying jobs were women. In that same year, 62 per cent of single mothers lived below the poverty line. While women have won access to jobs formerly designated as male only, they are frequently subjected to sexual harassment on these jobs. Women's occupational health and safety continue to be peripheral to governments' concerns. And the impact of free trade has been disproportionately severe for women.

Social Services

In 1970 the members of the Royal Commission on the Status of Women proposed that child care should be a major legislative concern of governments committed to improving women's access to the labour force. Since 1970 the federal government has followed an erratic program, constrained by constitutional limits on its jurisdiction, budget constraints, and increasingly a desire to return the issue to the private sphere.

Since child-care services fall under provincial jurisdiction (much like health care), the federal government has been restricted to providing funding in some shared-cost arrangements. Since the 1940s and into the 1980s both levels of government gradually came to see themselves less as regulators and more as service providers. Throughout the 1970s the federal government matched provincial spending on child care, with no upper limit. By the early 1980s, the problems with this formula were apparent. There were too few spaces, yet the federal costs were rising each year. In 1984 the Conservatives campaigned with a promise of improved child-care services. By 1987 that promise was expressed as the National Strategy on Child Care. This new initiative, which reflected the Conservative government's commitment to free enterprise, might be viewed as the first step of a program to return child care to the private sphere. The plan included funding for 200,000 new child-care spaces in either public or private facilities, and allocated $6.4 billion to the program over seven years. In addition, the yearly child-care tax deduction would be increased from $2,000 to $4,000 per child. In its 1994 Budget, the Liberal government reaffirmed the principle of mixed public-private child-care services, and allocated a modest $360 million over two years to new child-care spaces.

That plan failed to obtain Senate approval before the 1988 federal election, and subsequent proposals in 1992 deleted the creation of new child-care spaces. The government's explanation for this deletion was the growing federal deficit. Instead, tax deductions were increased to $5,000 per child, and the ceiling of $8,000 was removed. 'The 1992 proposals reflect a shift away from providing support for services towards income relief for families. But critics of the plan note that with these changes the average increase in benefits for families with combined incomes of less than $50,000 a year will be only $250' (Burt 1993: 226-7). Its main effect was to extend the life of the private care systems, which had been facing increased restrictions as a result of the work of public care advocacy groups.

With its 1995 budget the federal Liberal government dismantled the 1966 Canada Assistance Plan and substituted block funding to the provinces. The new plan was justified as a means of cutting federal costs while at the same time increasing provincial/territorial autonomy. It will eventually remove the existing cost-sharing agreements for welfare and social services, and replace them with what the government calls a set of shared principles and objectives. This could be the end of national standards for social services, and will reduce the transfer payments to the provinces. The plan will force provincial and territorial governments to choose between scarce dollars for health care and scarce dollars for welfare. Welfare appears to be the obvious loser.

Women's Health and Safety

For women's groups, reproductive issues (including abortion and sexual harassment) and male violence have increasingly been viewed as matters of autonomy and self-control. For the federal government, they have been viewed primarily as matters of health and safety. Whereas policies in other areas have been characterized by an equal rights mentality, issues related to women's bodies have been characterized by a protective mentality similar to that which informed the legislation on women's issues in the late nineteenth century. Between 1969 and 1988 abortion was regulated by section 251 of the Criminal Code, which labelled abortion a crime but permitted it when the mother's health was in jeopardy. Control over the decision lay with a panel of doctors rather than with the mother herself. When this provision was struck down by the Supreme Court in 1988, the federal government grappled with alternative legislation, which finally emerged in 1989 as Bill C-43. Although this bill, which passed narrowly in the House of Commons, failed to gain Senate approval, it is nonetheless significant for the insight it offers into government thinking in this area. Like the earlier provisions in the Criminal Code, Bill C-43 also labelled abortion a crime. Abortions 'were legal if done by or under the direction of a physician who believed that the pregnancy threatened the health or life of the mother' (Pal 1991: 42). The therapeutic abortion committees were gone, but the physician 'expert' remained.

The issue of male violence against women has received similar treatment. In the third report of the federal government on the compliance of Canada with the UNs Convention on the Elimination of All Forms of Discrimination against Women (Canada 1992a), violent crimes are categorized as 'lifestyle health risks'. Since the mid-1980s the government has undertaken a series of measures to provide some protection for women who have suffered physical abuse.

Here, the work of researchers investigating the problem of violence was instrumental in pushing the issue to the top of the legislative agenda. These researchers were working within the federal government's advisory bodies as well as in sexual assault centres across the country. For in the early 1980s violence was not an issue for the government. It was not on the list of subjects addressed by the Royal Commission on the Status of Women and cannot even be found in the index! There, the discussion of women and justice focused on female offenders and their situation. In 1987 Linda MacLeod summarized the history of government action this way:

Just a few years ago, wife battering was still a laughing matter for some of Canada's political leaders. . . . Government officials rallied in response to . . . public outcry. The results have been impressive. Canada became the first country to adopt a nationwide charging policy, encouraging police to lay charges in wife-battering cases. Several provincial/territorial governments launched large-scale public education programs. National task forces were created. More money was allocated to services to help battered women and their children. . . . Wife battering was identified as a priority concern in the two most recent Throne speeches (1984 and 1986) and Canada has participated in spreading awareness of wife battering in the international community. (MacLeod 1987: 3)

Most of the policies have been developed by the Department of Health and Welfare. In 1988, for example, the department introduced a program on family violence which included funding for 500 additional shelter spaces. Again in 1988 the issue was integrated into the new Family Violence Initiative involving six federal departments and agencies: Health and Welfare, Justice, the Solicitor General, the Secretary of State, Indian Affairs and Northern Development, and the Canada Mortgage and Housing Corporation. This program also deals with prevention and incorporates many of the recommendations made by women's groups and the government's own Advisory Council on the Status of Women.

In addition, the federal government, through Status of Women Canada, in August 1991 sponsored a $10 million study to be carried out by the Canadian Panel on Violence against Women. This study was in keeping with Status of Women's mandate to participate in the Family Violence Project as an advocate on behalf of women affected by family violence. The panel brought feminists into the policy advisory capacity yet again, in the tradition begun in the Women's Program of the Secretary of State over a decade earlier. And the interaction among the panel members, feminist groups, and the government reveals much about the current state of movement politics. In their report, the panel members talked about several problems they encountered. They had most difficulty selecting appropriate mechanisms for carrying out their work in the 15 months allotted to them. They noted the problem of adding members of cultural and racial minorities to the advisory board after the process of consultation was well underway. They had to deal with the question of how best to integrate aboriginal concerns without imposing constraints on the aboriginal process. Finally, over one-half of the members of the advisory committee had strong ties with feminist organizations, and they were forced to deal with the question of whom they represented on the panel (Canada 1993c: App. B).

The panel was criticized by some feminist groups, including the NAC, for excluding immigrant and racial-minority women from the advisory committee. The groups argued as well that the advisory committee should consist solely of representatives of women's groups. They also objected to the government's continued insistence on studying the problem of violence when the shelters were in desperate need of additional funds. The discussion which followed the creation of the panel brought to the foreground the differences among feminists, and between feminist and government views of an appropriate process for change. At issue was the central question of who would have control over the development of new policies.

But the panel was important for bringing feminist discourse to the public table in this policy sector of health and safety. As the members noted, the 'Panel's legal and political situation was such that it had no identity separate from government' (Canada 1993c: B4). Some panel members and most women's groups saw this as a serious flaw in the process. But it had some unintended consequences. For in reflecting on the problems with the process, the panel members articulated a feminist interpretation of violence. They rejected the government label of family violence, with its focus on individuals, and defined violence as a socially structured problem of abuse against women and children. They provided an important opportunity for women's voices to reach the policy makers. The language of the report is clear and uncompromisingly feminist. The authors' purpose was to demonstrate 'how looking through a feminist lens enables us to see how gender, race and class oppress women and how these forms of oppression are interrelated or interconnected' (Canada 1993c: 13).

But the publication of the panel's report has not solved the problem of male violence—and no solution appears imminent. The questions of resolving gender differences and removing social oppression remain unanswered.

CONCLUSIONS

In 1986 I concluded a review of the influence of the women's movement on Canadian public policy since 1970 as follows:

> Women's groups in Canada have taken a leading role in working out a program of adjustment to the new realities [of the 1980s]. In the early 1970s they focused on equal rights for women in the public world. As women assumed new responsibilities in the labour force and politics, the emphasis shifted from equal rights legislation to role changes for both men and women. (Burt 1986: 183)

To date, that shift has not been sustained by the national feminist groups, which have become increasingly preoccupied in the 1990s with an equal rights agenda. There are several reasons for this preoccupation. Certainly the 1982 Charter of Rights and Freedoms, with its rights-based discourse, has been a significant factor in the acceleration of interest in equal rights reforms. In addition, the federal government's poor record on equal rights has forced feminist groups to persist in the call for substantive gender equality. Equity gains in employment or legal status that seemed imminent in the early 1980s became improbable by the early 1990s, primarily as a result of a shift in federal policies away from the 'just society' initiatives of the Trudeau Liberals toward the 'competitive edge' position of the Mulroney Conservatives. Federal policies between 1984 and 1993 were informed by a neo-conservative political philosophy that offered competitiveness 'as the rationale for deficit reduction, controlling inflation rates, cuts to social programs, plans for expansion of training and labour force programs, downsizing and enhancing productivity within the public service' (Phillips 1994: 12). In this 'competitive' environment there was little room for measures that would result in substantive economic equality for women and men. For while there were some improvements in some women's wages as a result of pay equity legislation, many women's jobs have been lost as a consequence of free trade, economic restructuring, and civil service downsizing. Repeatedly, studies of the effects of such measures have underscored the particular vulnerability of women to the consequences of a 'competitive' policy package. Furthermore, in the wake of fairly ineffectual initiatives such as employment equity, the focus of legislators has shifted away from women to other disadvantaged groups, on the assumption that the 'woman problem' has been solved.

In October 1993 the Liberals were elected with the promise of new policy directions. There are early indications that the language of competitiveness has been replaced by the language of citizen responsibility (or self-help). But the new rhetoric masks some continuities with the earlier Conservative agenda. For 'responsibility' will also have 'the long-term effect of reducing the size and the role of the state, although this is more a consequence, rather than a central objective' (Phillips: 13). Some of the implications of this rhetoric for women became clear in the February 1995 budget. Paul Martin, the Minister of Finance, stressed the principles of down-home wisdom, getting government right, and exercising prudence and caution. In terms of program delivery, getting it right means reducing social programs, especially unemployment benefits, and further reducing the size of the public service, initiatives that affect women disproportionately. According to the 1995 budget projections, approximately 16 per cent of departmental savings will be realized by cut-backs in human resource development, compared to about 10 per cent in defence. In 1997-8, spending on social programs will be reduced by 8 per cent from 1994-5 levels (Canada 1995).

In these terms, 'getting government right' does not include a comprehensive child-care strategy. It can't accommodate increased spending on job training and retraining for women. It includes a reinstatement of the principle of family versus individual income for old age security benefits. And the decision to institute a new block grant to the provinces for social programs, to be reduced by $2.5 billion in 1996-7, will make it more difficult for provincial governments to maintain income security programs for single mothers, and adequate social services for older women.

Historically in Canada, feminist groups have relied on government funding for their organizing base and have called for governments delivery of services for women. Federally, governments for the past ten years have been
rejecting these demands. In the new Liberal climate of self-help and individual
responsibility feminist groups must rethink their relationship with the state.

NOTES

1 For a good discussion of some of the theoretical issues within this perspective, see
   Coleman and Skogstad (1989), Intro. and Chap. 1.

2 This constraint proved to be significant, especially for the National Action
   Committee on the Status of Women, in the lobbying that preceded the passage of
   the 1982 Charter of Rights and Freedoms. See Burt (1988).

3 This commitment to a different political vision in a world in which women have a
   more significant role in decision-making was expressed repeatedly by the presidents of the national women's groups in interviews conducted from 1984 to 1986.

4 This question was not included in the 1984 questionnaire.

5 See for example the 1993 campaign literature of the NAC.

BIBLIOGRAPHY

Association for Women's Equity in the Canadian Forces (1993), *Newsletter* 3, no. 3
(Feb.), Annex A.

Brodie, Janine, Shelley A.M. Gavigan, and Jane Jenson (1992), *The Politics of Abortion*
(Toronto: Oxford University Press).

Burt, Sandra (1986), 'Women's Issues and the Women's Movement in Canada Since
1970.' In *The Politics of Gender, Ethnicity and Language in Canada*, ed. Alan Cairns
and Cynthia Williams (Toronto: University of Toronto Press).

———— (1988), 'The Charter of Rights and the Ad Hoc Lobby: The Limits of
Success', *Atlantis* 14: 74-81.

———— (1990), 'The Institutionalization of Women's Groups', *Canadian Public Policy*
16, no. 1 (Mar.): 17-28.

———— (1993), 'Changing Patterns of Public Policy'. In *Changing Patterns*, 2nd edn,
eds S. Burt, L. Code, and L. Dorney (Toronto: McClelland and Stewart).

Canada (1984), Royal Commission on Equality in Employment, *Report* (Ottawa:
Minister of Supply and Services).

———— (1985), Dept. of Justice, *Equality Issues in Federal Law: A Discussion Paper*
(Ottawa: Minister of Supply and Services).

———— (1986), *Dimensions of Equality: A Federal Government Work Plan for Women*.
Proceedings of Annual Conference of First Ministers, Nov. 20-1 (Ottawa:
Minister of Supply and Services).

—— (1990), Task Force on Barriers to Women in the Public Service, *Report* (Ottawa: Minister of Supply and Services).

—— (1992a), Dept. of Multiculturalism and Citizenship, *Convention of the Elimination of All Forms of Discrimination Against Women: Third Report* (Ottawa: Minister of Supply and Services).

—— (1992b), Advisory Council on the Status of Women 'Re-Evaluating Employment Equity: A Brief to the Special House of Commons Committee on a Review of the Employment Equity Act' (Ottawa).

—— (1993a), Dept. of Justice, *Department of Justice Response to the Recommendations from the Symposium* (Ottawa: Minister of Supply and Services).

—— (1993b), Status of Women Canada, *Perspectives* 6, no. 3 (Fall).

—— (1993c), Canadian Panel on Violence against Women, *Changing the Landscape: Ending Violence, Achieving Equality* (Ottawa: Minister of Supply and Services).

—— (1995), Dept. of Finance, *Budget* (Ottawa: Minister of Supply and Services).

Coleman, William D., and Grace Skogstad (1989), *Policy Communities and Public Policy in Canada: A Structural Approach* (Mississauga, Ont.: Copp Clark), Intro., Chap. 1.

Ethno Canada (1988), (published by Canadian Ethnocultural Council), 8, no. 3 (Fall).

MacLeod, Linda (1987), *Battered but Not Beaten: Preventing Wife Battering in Canada* (Ottawa: Canadian Advisory Council on the Status of Women).

Morgan, Nicole (1988), *The Equality Game: Women in the Federal Public Service (1908-1987)* (Ottawa: Canadian Advisory Council on the Status of Women).

Pateman, Carole (1986), 'Introduction'. In *Feminist Challenges*, eds Carole Pateman and Elizabeth Gross (Sydney: Allen and Unwin).

Pal, Leslie (1991), 'Courts, Politics, and Morality: Canada's Abortion Saga'. In *The Real Worlds of Canadian Politics*, 2nd edn, eds Robert M. Campbell and Leslie Pal (Peterborough, Ont.: Broadview).

—— (1993), *Interests of State: The Politics of Language, Multiculturalism, and Feminism in Canada* (Montreal and Kingston: McGill-Queen's University Press).

Phillips, Susan D. (1991), 'Meaning and Structure in Social Movements: Mapping the Network of National Canadian Women's Organizations', *Canadian Journal of Political Science* 24, no. 4 (Dec.).

—— (1994), 'Making Change: the Potential for Innovation under the Liberals'. In *How Ottawa Spends 1994-95: Making Change*, ed. Susan D. Phillips (Ottawa: Carleton University Press).

Simms, Glenda (1989), 'Double Vision Equity'. Paper presented at the conference of the National Organization of Immigrant and Visible Minority Women of Canada, *Equity: Myth or Reality*.

Weaver, Sally (1993), 'First Nations Women'. In *Changing Patterns*, 2nd edn, eds S. Burt, L. Code, and L. Dorney (Toronto: McClelland and Stewart).

CHAPTER 5

Equity and Opportunity

Lesley A. Jacobs

Within the brief history of legislative measures that address gender inequalities in the workplace, the 1986 federal Employment Equity Act and the 1987 Ontario Pay Equity Act both appeared to be of monumental significance when they were introduced.[1] Together with the federal Contractor's Program, the Employment Equity Act promised to be the most extensive affirmative action program yet embraced by a Canadian government, affecting at present more than 1.5 million employees (Redway 1992: 1). It required Crown corporations and federally regulated industries to set goals and timetables for the employment of visible minorities and women. In a similar spirit, the Ontario Pay Equity Act, which institutionalized the principle of equal pay for work of equal value, was viewed at the time it was passed as the most far-reaching attempt ever made anywhere in the world to legislate on women's wages. That was because it applied the principle of comparable worth to both the public and private sectors of the Ontario economy (Egri and Stanbury 1989: 274; Fudge and McDermott 1991: 8). While much of the critical discussion of these two pieces of legislation has concentrated on their scope and design, this chapter discusses the underlying rationale for this type of legislation, for it is my view that much of that more technical discussion rests on confusion about the purpose of such legislation.

The source of this confusion is the failure to distinguish between the intended effects of this legislation and its basic rationale and justification. The tendency has been to assess this legislation in terms of whether it has indeed had specific results rather than whether it measures up to its basic rationale. In particular, the tendency has been to focus on the effect of pay equity and employment equity on the wage gap between men and women. Initially, there was considerable optimism about the potential of both of these pieces of legislation to reduce the wage gap. For example, in 1987 one economist predicted that the Ontario Pay Equity Act would reduce the wage gap in Ontario by 10 to 15 percentage points (Robb 1987: 455). Similar optimism greeted the Employment Equity Act, which, it was predicted, would increase significantly the number of women in upper management jobs and consequently raise the average wage of working women

(Gunderson 1990: 46-72). Certainly, this seems to have happened in the United States (Hacker 1992: 37-42; Aaron and Lougy 1986: 1-15).[2] But half a decade later it is clear that these original expectations about the effect of pay equity and employment equity on the wages of Canadian women were blindly optimistic.[3] It is now very doubtful that the affirmative action and pay equity measures of the federal and Ontario governments will have a large enough effect on the gender wage gap to justify their existence.[4] For that reason the following questions are now frequently being asked more seriously: Is their existence warranted, and should other governments adopt similar policies?[5]

The aim of this chapter is to resurrect the now unfashionable view that the policies of affirmative action and equal pay for work of equal value that underlie the federal Employment Equity Act and the Ontario Pay Equity Act respectively can be defended on the grounds that they contribute to the realization of an ideal of equality of opportunity between men and women in Canadian society. This view, although once prevalent among those concerned with gender issues, has been pushed aside, largely because of doubts about the visionary depth of the ideal of equality of opportunity. It has been replaced instead by an ideal of equality of results, which emphasizes the goal of reducing the wage gap. But recent feminist legal and political theory allows us to formulate a principle of equality of opportunity that offers a promising way to analyse issues posed by gender inequalities in the workplace and, as a result, to provide a clear rationale for the recent employment equity and pay equity measures. The idea is that even if pay equity and employment equity legislation do not have the effect on the wage gap that has sometimes been expected, they should nevertheless be embraced because they enhance equal opportunities for women.

EQUALITY: RESULTS OR OPPORTUNITIES

Egalitarians today disagree over the kind of equality that institutions and public policy should promote. The fundamental question they ask is, equality of what? for there is no consensus about the ways which individuals should be made equal (Sen 1992: 12-30). There is an elementary distinction to be made among the competing answers to this question between the theories of distributional equality that embrace equal opportunities and those that embrace equal results. Equality of opportunity, as a broad class of theories of distributional equality, holds that everyone should have an equal opportunity to enjoy a certain set of goods. Within this broad class, various theories differ principally in how they answer two questions: (1) Which goods are to be subject to the principle of equality of opportunity? (2) What are the necessary conditions for there to be equality of opportunity? Equality of results, as a broad class of theories of distributional equality, holds that a distributional process should result in everyone's enjoying a certain set of goods in roughly equal proportion. Theories of equality of results differ principally about which goods should be enjoyed in equal proportions.

Among those concerned with gender inequality in the workplace, the tendency has been to assess the federal Employment Equity program and the Ontario Pay Equity Act from the perspective of how much effect they have had on the wage gap between men and women. This perspective assumes that government policy on gender inequalities in the workplace should seek some ideal of equality of results. Judged by that criterion neither pay equity nor employment equity in Canada appears to be a very desirable policy. It seems doubtful that even significant alterations to the present legislation will produce equal results for men and women. It is my view that equality of results is the wrong standard for judging employment equity and pay equity legislation in Canada. Instead, we must judge this legislation for its contribution to equality of opportunity.

This suggestion in itself is neither original nor innovative. Indeed, it is on the basis of equality of opportunity that policies of this sort were recommended in the influential 1970 report of the Royal Commission on the Status of Women in Canada (Canada 1970: 76-7, 80, 90, 114, 121, 124, 142). The terms of reference of that Royal Commission were to 'inquire into . . . the status of women in Canada . . . to ensure for women equal opportunities with men in all aspects of Canadian society.' This was interpreted by the commissioners to mean that 'equality of opportunity for everyone should be the goal of Canadian society. . . . [It] is our duty to ensure for women equal opportunities with men' (Canada 1970: ix, xi). A similar, albeit more ambiguous, concern for equality of opportunity can be found in the subsequent reports that gave rise to the specific legislation in question. The 1984 Royal Commission report on equality in employment offers the following interpretation of its mandate:

> Equality in employment is not a concept that produces the same results for everyone. It is a concept that seeks to identify and remove, barrier by barrier, discriminatory disadvantages. Equality in employment is access to the fullest opportunity to exercise individual potential. . . . Ignoring differences and refusing to accommodate them is a denial of equal access and opportunity. It is discrimination. People are disadvantaged for many reasons and may be disadvantaged in a variety of ways—economically, socially, politically, or educationally. Not all disadvantages derive from discrimination. Those that do demand their own particular policy responses. (Canada 1984: 3)

A similar emphasis on equality of opportunity, as opposed to equality of results, can be found in the Ontario *Green Paper on Pay Equity*, tabled in 1985. It offers the following explanation for why pay equity is an important policy issue:

The achievement of equal opportunity and social justice for all Ontarians is a fundamental and unalterable commitment of the Ontario Government. For women, this must include employment equity in all its aspects. Therefore, implementation of pay equity, or equal pay for work of equal value, is not at issue; only the method and timing of its achievements are open for discussion and ultimate decision. (Ontario 1985: 1)

The puzzle for us is why, despite these explicit public attempts to link pay equity and employment equity to equality of opportunity, there has been a widespread and persistent inclination among those concerned with gender inequalities in the workplace to evaluate and judge these legislative measures according to a theory of equality of result. The answer probably lies in certain deep reservations that many people have about the very concept of equality of opportunity. These reservations have two likely sources. The first is that equality of opportunity is frequently thought to be an extremely weak sort of egalitarian principle of justice. For some, it amounts simply to the idea that everyone has an equal opportunity to be unequal (Baker 1987: 46). For the women's movement in Canada, the relevant point is that the rhetoric of equal opportunity in the 1960s and 1970s seems not to have made a great deal of difference to the lives of ordinary Canadian women. The emphasis on equality of opportunity appears not to recognize the systemic nature of many of the disadvantages experienced by Canadian women.

The second difficulty with equality of opportunity is that at first glance it appears incompatible with pay equity and employment equity. It is now, for example, a common view in the United States, even among those sympathetic to affirmative action, that these programs compromise equality of opportunity in that they favour members of disadvantaged groups over others in the competition for scarce offices and positions (cf. Hacker 1992: 30). Similarly, critics of pay equity argue that, because such programs interfere with the market that determines wages, they too involve a compromise of equality of opportunity (Paul 1989: 121-2; Flanagan 1987: 439-40). Such programs appear to be more easily justified by an equalitarian emphasis on equality of results.

FAIR EQUALITY OF OPPORTUNITY

Both of these reservations about equality of opportunity can be shown to be misplaced. A theory of equality of opportunity can recognize gender as a form of systemic disadvantage and can be a basis for legislative attempts to address this form of disadvantage. The particular theory of equality of opportunity I have in mind here is an extension of what John Rawls calls *fair* equality of opportunity.

Fair equality of opportunity can be best understood in comparison to what can be described as *formal* equality of opportunity. Formal equality of opportunity requires that everyone have the same legal rights of access to all desirable social positions and offices and that these positions and offices be open to talents in the sense that they are to be distributed to those able and willing to strive for them (Rawls 1971: 66). Equality of opportunity in this formal sense is the one that has most often received recognition in Canadian legislation. But formal equality of opportunity as a theory of equality of opportunity ignores the initial starting positions of different people. With formal equality of opportunity, similarly motivated and endowed individuals may differ in their success because they come from different socio-economic backgrounds. Is this fair? The principle of *fair* equality of opportunity was formulated by Rawls in response to this flaw in the principle of formal equality of opportunity. It maintains that 'those who are at the same level of talent and ability, and have the same willingness to use them, should have the same prospects of success regardless of their initial place in the social system, that is, irrespective of the income class into which they are born' (Rawls 1971: 73).

In *A Theory of Justice* Rawls emphasizes two principal ways to approximate fair equality of opportunity. The first is to avoid excessive concentrations of wealth. This lays the foundations for Rawls's (1971) advocacy of what he calls a property-owning democracy (pp. 274 ff). The second is to design an education system to minimize the effects of socio-economic class on a person's ambitions and the development of his or her natural abilities. As Rawls puts it, 'Chances to acquire cultural knowledge and skills should not depend upon one's class position, and so the school system, whether public or private, should be designed to even out class barriers' (p. 73).

It is a commonplace criticism of Rawls to say that while he is sensitive to race and class as forms of disadvantage that can have a disparate impact on opportunities, he fails to recognize gender as a similar form of disadvantage (Okin 1987: 42-72; 1989: chaps. 1 and 5) The more interesting issue is whether his theory of fair equality of opportunity can be extended to cover gender issues. An obvious starting point is to consider how formal equality of opportunity might be extended to cover gender issues. At first glance this is not a difficult task: formal equality of opportunity can be interpreted to forbid people who are similarly motivated and talented from being denied access to offices and positions on the basis of sex in the same way that it forbids denial of access on the basis of race or social background. And of course, formal equality of opportunity in this sense has received legal status in Canada in various human rights bills and in the United States in the 1964 Civil Rights Act. (It is this formal sense of equality of opportunity that dominated the public debate about sexual equality in the 1960s and 1970s.) But since this level of formal equality of opportunity among men and women has proved not to be enough, it is logical to turn to fair equality of opportunity.

Proponents of fair equality of opportunity are motivated by a belief that similarly endowed and motivated individuals should begin from roughly equal starting positions. For Rawls, it is obvious that the most important influence on people's initial starting position is family background. The truth is that people come from a wide range of family backgrounds, some of them very privileged, others profoundly disadvantaged. Fair equality of opportunity, in contrast to formal equality of opportunity, raises then the issue of justice *between* families. From a policy perspective, justice between families is a central aim of much current social policy and progressive taxation, for the tendency is to redistribute income between families or households rather than between individuals. On the whole, it might make sense to direct policies principally at injustices between families if the concern is only with the effect of race and class on equal opportunities.

But if fair equality of opportunity is to be extended to cover the effect of gender on the opportunities of women, then this raises the issue not only of justice between families but also justice *within* families. It is largely undisputed that Canadian women, even those in the labour market, continue to bear a much greater responsibility for domestic labour and primary care for children than men. And women rarely have access to an equal share of a household's income and financial resources. This injustice within families becomes especially apparent when a marriage breaks down, for a striking feature of divorce and separation is the different economic effects it has on men and women. Whereas divorce or separation usually entails a significant reduction in the standard of living for the woman, it usually translates into a significant improvement for the man (Gunderson et al. 1989: 20). Indeed, one controversial study found in California that in the first year after a divorce the woman's standard of living dropped by 73 per cent while the man's rose by 42 per cent (Weitzman 1985). The important point is that in order to achieve a standard of fair equality of opportunity that is sensitive to gender, government policy must be directed not only at injustices *between* families but also injustices *within* families.

Policies directed at injustices within families can be divided into home-based policies (see Jacobs 1993: chap. 8) and workplace-based policies. Canadian home-based policies include the recently abolished program in Saskatchewan that included housewives in existing public pension schemes and the British Columbia program that collects child-support payments from absent fathers and forwards them to the mothers. The federal Employment Equity Act and the Ontario Pay Equity Act, however, should be regarded as workplace policies that are directed at injustices within families and have the goal of achieving fair equality of opportunity. For this reason, the rest of my discussion will deal with workplace-based policies.

GENDER DISADVANTAGE IN THE WORKPLACE

As we have just seen, the purpose of workplace-based policies is to remedy injustices in families that affect adversely the starting position of women under a scheme of fair equality of opportunity. This purpose distinguishes

these kinds of policies from those designed to eradicate directly discriminatory practices in the workplace, such as sexual harassment. But we need to be
clearer about which injustices within families are to be remedied; this presupposes an account of sexual discrimination.

Before turning to such an account, it is worth emphasizing the radical
character of fair equality of opportunity that has now become apparent
(Jacobs 1994). The extension of Rawls's notion of fair equality of opportunity
to gender issues rests on seeing the continuity between the family and the
workplace. Injustices that exist in the family are translated into injustices in
the workplace. By emphasizing the importance of initial starting positions,
the theory of fair equality of opportunity, unlike that of formal equality of
opportunity, challenges the conventional distinction between public and private. Unfortunately, though, this is frequently overlooked in feminist analyses of equality of opportunity. The denial of the public-private distinction,
neatly captured by the slogan 'The personal is political', has been a mainstay
of feminist thought. Political philosophers such as Rawls are generally considered to have left this distinction intact, and as a result their work is often
regarded with suspicion (Okin 1991a: 71). But this suspicion is misplaced,
and fair equality of opportunity should be regarded as challenging the public-private distinction, not reinforcing it.

An answer to the question of which injustices within families should be
remedied by workplace-based policies requires an account of sexual discrimination because the issue turns fundamentally on how those injustices come to
be manifested in the workplace. The development of an adequate theory of
sexual discrimination has been the goal of much recent feminist legal and
political theory. By and large, the tendency has been to reject the received
approach to sexual discrimination, which holds that sexual discrimination
occurs when women are treated differently from men on the basis of some
arbitrary or socially constructed difference between men and women.
Following convention, I shall refer to this approach as the sex-based *difference*
view (MacKinnon 1979: 107-16; Rhode 1989: 2-3). While the difference view
is widely criticized by feminists for its limitations, it is nevertheless superior
to the view that in the workplace men and women should invariably be treated
the same.[6] The latter view is deeply problematic because it seems to imply
that measures such as maternity leave and job security for pregnant women
discriminate against men. What is worrisome here is that the emphasis on
sameness as the standard for identifying sexual discrimination may be used to
harm women, rather than benefit them. The virtue of the difference view is
that it can say that maternity leaves and job security for pregnant women are
not instances of sexual discrimination against men because the differential
treatment rests on a difference between men and women that is not arbitrary.

The principal objection to the difference view of sexual discrimination
concerns the question of what differences between men and women warrant
different treatment. A nice illustration of this question was provided in the

US Supreme Court's *Manhart* decision in 1978.[7] At issue was a provision in the pension scheme of the Los Angeles Department of Water and Power requiring women employees to contribute approximately 15 per cent more in premiums to obtain the same pension coverage as men. The logic for this requirement, based on actuarial findings, was that women as a group live longer and therefore are a greater liability in a pension scheme. After all, without this requirement, it might seem that male employees are suffering sexual discrimination because they are subsidizing the pensions of female employees. Though the Supreme Court struck down this requirement, a parallel can undeniably be drawn with the claim that maternity leaves rest on biological differences between men and women. It seems that from the sex-based difference view there is no distinction between these two cases. Either they are both instances of sexual discrimination or neither is. Yet an adequate account of sexual discrimination needs to identify grounds for distinguishing between them.

The most persuasive response to this problem is, in my view, to say that the difference view mistakenly assumes that men can suffer from sexual discrimination in our society. There are two competing views about why only women can suffer sexual discrimination. One view—the sex-based *dominance* view—says that men cannot in general suffer sexual discrimination because we live in a society in which institutional power relations between men and women are hierarchical with men at the top. The idea is that the sexual discrimination suffered by women is a result of this male order; and since there is no such parallel in the case of men, they cannot suffer sexual discrimination. As Catherine MacKinnon has put it,

> the gender-neutral approach to sex discrimination obscures . . . the fact that women's poverty and consequent financial dependence on men (whether in marriage, welfare, the workplace, or prostitution), forced motherhood, and sexual vulnerability substantively constitute their social status *as women*, as members of their gender. That some men at times find themselves in similar situations does not mean that they occupy that status as men, as members of their gender. They do so as exceptions, both in norms and in numbers. Unlike women, men are not poor or primary caretakers of children on the basis of sex. (MacKinnon 1989, 228)

The other view—the sex-based *disadvantage* view—says more moderately that in general only women can suffer sexual discrimination because unlike men their sex is a form of disadvantage in our society. A parallel can be made to racism by saying that White people in North America cannot suffer racism, *pace* the claims of white supremacist groups, because for them their race is not a form of disadvantage in our society. Deborah Rhode (1989: 83) explains this view of sexual discrimination: 'A disadvantage framework is concerned not with difference but with its consequences. The legitimacy of

sex-based treatment does not depend on whether the sexes are differently situated. Rather, analysis turns on whether legal recognition of gender distinctions is more likely to reduce or to reinforce gender disparities in political
power, social status, and economic security.'

In both the dominance analysis and the disadvantage analysis of sexual
discrimination, sex currently functions to limit the opportunities for women.
It is difficult, however, to judge which of these two views is more accurate in
its account of why that happens. My inclination is to think that each has
explanatory power in certain domains (Rhode 1989: 85). While rape and
domestic violence raise questions about dominance and the hierarchical
nature of gender, low wages and the segregation of women in certain types of
jobs better exemplify the idea of gender as a form of disadvantage. For our
purposes, it is adequate to work within the sex-based disadvantage framework.

The significance of the disadvantage view, from the perspective of fair
equality of opportunity, is that it concentrates on how differences—biological
or socially constructed—between men and women affect their success under
a scheme of equality of opportunity. This view presupposes, according to
Rhode (1989: 4), 'a substantive commitment to gender equality—to a society
in which women as a group are not disadvantaged in the control of their own
destiny.' This view fits with the concern with starting positions that differen-
tiates fair from formal equality of opportunity. My thought is that the disadvantage framework of sexual discrimination explains how gender as a form of
systemic discrimination effects the equal opportunities of women.

To be more specific, it explains why 'disparate impact' is a violation of a
standard of equality of opportunity, and not simply of equality of results. A
regulation, law, or practice has a 'disparate impact' when it affects a particular
group in society in a disproportionate and adverse manner (Black 1986: 120).
The classic example of disparate impact was provided by the nineteenth-
century French writer Anatole France, who cites laws that forbid the rich as
well as the poor from sleeping under bridges.[8] Ordinarily, disparate impact is
taken as the standard test for systemic discrimination against a particular
group in society (Canada 1984: 193). The central question raised by the existence of disparate impact in this context is whether or not it violates some
standard of equality when it occurs unintentionally. While gender as disadvantage undeniably generates intentional discrimination against women, it
is also generally considered to generate systemic discrimination in the sense
that many laws and employment practices have a disparate impact on women.

Taking disparate impact and systemic discrimination seriously may seem
to lead logically to some ideal of equality of results. The reasoning is that
disparate impact is wrong because it indicates an unequal result. Indeed, it is
sometimes suggested that the only way to take systemic discrimination seriously is through an ideal of equality of results. This way of thinking explains
in all likelihood, why it has become common to judge legislation purely by
its effectiveness in reducing the gendered wage gap. But the adoption of an

ideal of equality of results makes arguments against systemic discrimination an easy target for criticism. Rainer Knopf (1990), for example, argues that measures designed to combat systemic discrimination against women and visible minorities run counter to Canada's liberal democratic tradition. His argument is that those who object to disparate impact and systemic discrimination are committed to an ideal of equality of results and that this ideal is fundamentally 'illiberal' (Knopf 1990: 10-11, 157-77, 183 ff). While there may be some debate about Knopf's understanding of liberalism, he is on firm ground when he says that equality of results does not enjoy widespread acceptance in Canada and that any legislation based on it will be hard to defend. The attraction of taking disparate impact seriously within the framework of fair equality of opportunity is that the prospects are better for the successful adoption of public policy to combat it.[9]

From the perspective of fair equality of opportunity, then, the effect of a labour law or workplace practice on women is discriminatory when the disproportionate and adverse effects of such a law or practice are due to the initial starting position of women. The most striking instance of discrimination of this sort is the practice of paying low wages in certain female-dominated occupations. This practice has a disparate impact in the sense that it results in women employed in such jobs having low incomes. It is frequently said that this disparate impact is not discriminatory because the practice of paying low wages in those sectors of the economy is not directed at disadvantaging women but rather is due to the large supply of workers capable of doing those jobs. Moreover, the fact that these low wages affect women more than men is said to be a result of women's choices—they choose these careers despite knowing they are poorly paid (Paul 1989: 40-6, 51-2). But my view is that neither of these two considerations disqualifies this practice from the charge of sexual discrimination. The question to be asked is why so many women pursue job prospects that have such low wages and consequently further contribute to driving down wages. The answer has to lie, at least partially, in some consideration of the injustices within family. The sexual division of labour in the family as well as the unequal access to family financial resources make it necessary for many women to pursue occupations that can accommodate their domestic responsibilities. The starting position of women in the labour market does, therefore, come to be reflected in the disparate impact of low wages in female-dominated occupations. This workplace practice is, then, discriminatory under fair equality of opportunity, and policies should be designed to remedy it.

POLICY RESPONSES

It has just been argued that the fact that in Canada many women work in female-dominated occupations that are low paid is a striking case of sexual discrimination in the Canadian labour market. The reason is that it is a result of the influence of injustices within the family on Canadian labour practices. The starting position of women in the labour market is adversely affected by the disproportionate burden of child care and domestic labour that they carry at home. What would constitute an adequate policy response to this case of sexual discrimination? It is my view that pay equity and employment equity legislation should be understood precisely as workplace-based policy responses to this widespread discriminatory labour practice.

In general, pay equity ideally functions to correct market-determined wages in female-dominated occupations so that they are consistent with fair equality of opportunity. The problem with relying solely on the market to determine wages in female-dominated occupations is that those wages inevitably reflect the unequal starting positions of women in the workplace. (By its very nature the market is unable to correct for unequal starting positions.) These occupations have low wages in part because so many women are willing to perform the tasks in question; but this large supply of female workers is due to the fact that these women do not have other opportunities for employment that readily accommodate the demands made on them at home. Pay equity approaches this problem by making wages in female-dominated occupations equal to market-determined wages earned by men in occupations of comparable worth. In this sense, pay equity is predicated on the notion that the market should determine wages. All any pay equity policy purports to do, then, is correct in some cases market outcomes that have been tainted by sexual discrimination.

The Ontario Pay Equity Act conforms to this analysis. The uniqueness of this act is that it applies the principle of equal pay for work of equal value not only to the entire public sector of the economy, but also to all private-sector employees with 10 or more employees. The instrument for achieving pay equity under this statute is the 'gender-neutral' job evaluation that compares certain jobs performed predominately by women in terms of skill, effort, responsibility, and work conditions to certain jobs performed predominantly by men. When jobs receive the same evaluation score, the potential then arises for a wage adjustment.

While pay equity legislation targets the workplace practice of paying low wages in female-dominated occupations by raising those wages to the level of those in other occupations of comparable worth, the federal employment equity legislation gives women more opportunities to pursue job prospects in occupations other than those traditionally dominated by women. The disadvantage of gender suffered by women is one of the main reasons why so many women go into female-segregated occupations. Employment equity seeks to ensure that hiring and promotion practices mitigate gender disadvantage. Timetables and quotas for the hiring of women serve this function by compensating women for the disadvantage that gender places on their starting position in a system of competitive equality of opportunity. The issue is, of course, trickier than this because the starting position of individual women is also influenced by class and race. Inevitably an employment equity program that looks only at gender as a form of disadvantage is likely to benefit principally white women from well-off families. For this reason, it makes sense to have an integrated employment equity program such as the federal Employment Equity Plan which addresses both gender and race as a form of disadvantage.

Conclusion

In this chapter I have argued that the rationale for employment equity and pay equity legislation is to promote fair equality of opportunity by remedying the disadvantages that gender has on the starting position of women in the competition for scarce offices and positions. It is against this rationale rather than their contribution to reducing the gender-wage gap that we should judge the 1986 federal Employment Equity Act and the 1987 Ontario Pay Equity Act. But changing the measure for evaluating these two pieces of legislation does not mean that they are not the failures that they are so often said to be. It may well be that neither successfully addresses the adverse effects that injustices in families have on the opportunities for women in the workplace. But that raises questions for research that are very different from ones raised by an emphasis on the wage gap.

Notes

This paper has benefited from a major research grant from the Social Sciences and Humanities Research Council of Canada and a British Columbia Challenge Grant. I am grateful to Meredith Wadman and Doug Simpson for research assistance.

1 Both acts show the influence of American legislation on Canadian public policy. This pattern has a long history. For example, the setting up of the Royal Commission on the Status of Women in Canada in 1967 largely followed the lead of the Kennedy Commission on the Status of Women set up in the early 1960s.

2 For more sceptical views about the effect of affirmative action and comparable-worth legislation on the wage gap in the United States, see respectively Blum (1991: 28-34) and Kelly and Baynes (1988: 244-5).

3 Indeed, it has even been suggested that the Ontario Pay Equity Act will widen the wage gap. See Armstrong and Armstrong (1990: 52).

4 For a more neutral pronouncement, see Gunderson, Muszynski, and Keck (1990: 159-61). One reason for this less optimistic pronouncement is the difficulty of understanding how the rationale for pay equity can be to reduce the gendered wage gap: 'While the wage gap bas been an important factor in the identification of the need for pay equity, it will be less useful in assessing its *impact*. The wage gap is based on the earnings of *individual* men and women. Pay equity will equalize the salaries of female *jobs* with equally valued male jobs that are of equal value' (Weiner and Gunderson 1990: 11).

5 See, for example, McDermott (1991: 31); McDermott (1990: 407); and Burt (1988: 142-3). A similar emphasis can be found in the popular press: 'Women See Small Gain in Pay Equity', *Vancouver Sun*, 17 Jan. 1990, A8; 'Equity Act a Failure, Group Says', *Globe and Mail*, 26 Feb. 1990; 'Job Equity Moves at a Snail's Pace', *Calgary Herald*, 5 Dec. 1990.

6 For an account of this view in Canada at the turn of the century, see Backhouse (1991: 276-88).

7 I draw here on Rhode (1989: 103-7) and MacKinnon (1979: 116). MacKinnon appears now to deny the significance of the *Manhart* case as a challenge to the difference view. See MacKinnon (1990: 220).

8 Interestingly, the same comment by France is quoted at the outset of the *Report of the Royal Commission on Equality in Employment* (Canada 1984: 1).

9 This may, however, undermine the cohesiveness of the women's movement. See Brenner (1987: 447-65).

Bibliography

Aaron, Henry J., and Cameron M. Lougy (1986), *The Comparable Worth Controversy* (Washington: Brookings Institution).

Armstrong, Pat, and Hugh Armstrong (1990), 'Lessons from Pay Equity', *Studies in Political Economy* 32.

Baker, John (1987), *Arguing for Equality* (London: Verso).

Backhouse, Constance (1991), *Petticoats and Prejudice* (Toronto: Osgoode Society by the Women's Press).

Black, William W. (1986), 'Intent or Effects: Section 15 of the Charter of Rights and Freedoms'. In *Litigating the Values of a Nation: The Canadian Charter of Rights and Freedoms*, eds Josephy M. Weiler and Robin M. Elliot (Toronto: Carswell).

Blum, Linda M. (1991), *Between Feminism and Labor* (Berkeley: University of California Press).

Brenner, Johanna (1987), 'Feminist Political Discourses: Radical Versus Liberal Approaches to the Feminization of Poverty and Comparable Worth', *Gender and Society* 1: 447-65.

Burt, Sandra (1988), 'Legislators, Women, and Public Policy'. In *Changing Patterns: Women in Canada*, eds Sandra Burt, Lorraine Code, and Lindsay Dorney (Toronto: McClelland & Stewart).

Canada (1970), *Report of the Royal Commission on the Status of Women in Canada* (Ottawa: Information Canada).

——— (1984), *Report of the Royal Commission on Equality in Employment* (Ottawa: Minister of Supply and Services).

——— (1992), *A Matter of Fairness: Report of the Special Committee on the Review of the Employment Equity Act* (Ottawa: House of Commons).

Egri, Carolyn P., and W.T. Stanbury (1989), 'How Pay Equity Came to Ontario', *Canadian Public Administration* 32.

Eichler, Margrit (1985), 'The Pro-Family Movement: Are They for or against Families?' CRIAW (Sept.).

Fishkin, James S. (1993), *Justice, Equal Opportunity, and the Family* (New Haven: Yale University Press).

Flanagan, Thomas (1987), 'Equal Pay for Work of Equal Value: Some Theoretical Criticisms', *Canadian Public Policy* 13.

Fudge, Judy, and Patricia McDermott (1991), 'Introduction: Putting Feminism to Work'. In *Just Wages: A Feminist Assessment of Pay Equity*, eds J. Fudge and P. McDermott (Toronto: University of Toronto Press).

Gunderson, Morley (1989), 'Male-Female Wage Differentials and Policy Responses', *Journal of Economic Literature* 27.

Gunderson, Morley, Leon Muszynski, and Jennifer Keck (1990), *Women and Labour Market Poverty* (Ottawa: Canadian Advisory Council on the Status of Women).

Hacker, Andrew (1992), 'The New Civil War', *New York Review of Books*, 23 Apr.

——— (1985), ' "Welfare": The Future of an Illusion', *New York Review of Books*, 28 Feb.

Jacobs, Lesley (1993), *Rights and Deprivation* (Oxford: Oxford University Press).

——— (1994), 'Equal Opportunity and Gender Disadvantage', *Canadian Journal of Law and Jurisprudence* (Jan.): 61-71.

Kelly, Rita Mae, and Jane Baynes (1988), 'Conclusion'. In *Comparable Worth, Pay Equity, and Public Policy*, eds Rita Mae Kelly and Jane Baynes (Westport, CT: Greenwood Press).

Knopf, Rainer (1990), with Thomas Flanagan, *Human Rights and Social Technology: The New War on Discrimination* (Ottawa: Carlton University Press).

MacKinnon, Catherine A. (1979), *Sexual Harassment of Working Women* (New Haven: Yale University Press).

——— (1989) *Towards a Feminist Theory of the State* (Cambridge, MA: Harvard University Press).

——— (1990) 'Legal Perspectives on Sexual Difference'. In *Theoretical Perspectives on Sexual Difference*, ed. Deborah Rhode (Cambridge, MA: Harvard University Press).

McDermott, Patricia (1991), 'Pay Equity in Canada: Assessing the Commitment to Reducing the Wage Gap'. In *Just Wages: A Feminist Assessment of Pay Equity*, eds Judy Fudge and Patricia McDermott (Toronto: University of Toronto Press).

——— (1990), 'Pay Equity in Ontario: A Critical Legal Analysis', *Osgoode Hall Law Journal* 28.

Okin, Susan Moller (1987), 'Justice and Gender', *Philosophy and Public Affairs* 16: 42-72.

—— (1989), *Justice, Gender, and the Family* (New York: Basic Books).

—— (1991a), 'Gender, the Public, and the Private'. In *Political Theory Today*, ed. David Held (Stanford: Stanford University Press).

—— (1991b), 'Economic Equality after Divorce', *Dissent* (Summer): 384-6.

Ontario (1985), *Green Paper on Pay Equity* (Toronto: Government of Ontario).

Paul, Ellen Frankel (1989), *Equity and Gender: The Comparable Worth Debate* (New Brunswick, NJ: Transaction).

Rawls, John (1971), *A Theory of Justice* (Cambridge, MA: Harvard University Press).

Rhode, Deborah (1989), *Justice and Gender* (Cambridge, MA: Harvard University Press).

Robb, Roberta Edgecombe (1987), 'Equal Pay for Work of Equal Value: Issues and Policies', *Canadian Public Policy* 13.

Sen, Amartya (1992), *Inequality Re-examined* (Cambridge, MA: Harvard University Press).

Weiner, Nan, and Morley Gunderson (1990), *Pay Equity: Issues, Options, and Experiences* (Toronto: Butterworths).

Weitzman, Lenore (1985), *The Divorce Revolution* (New York: Free Press).

CHAPTER 6

Homeless Women and the New Right

Meredith Ralston

Feminism and feminist methodologies can be viewed in a number of ways: as critiques of traditional research and patriarchal ideology, generally; as a way of doing research; or as a feminist standpoint that takes women as the main subject of research. Feminist methodology can be a mode of analysis, a means of approaching experience, or a way of asking questions (Hartsock 1984; Harding 1987). Feminism can be seen as a response to the fact that women's voices have been left out of traditional theories and research (Lugones and Spelman 1986). Some feminist methodologies assume that women's experiences and ideas are valid in their own right, are not the same as men's experiences, and cannot merely be added to existing theories (Bowles and Klein 1983). To some feminists, the hallmark of feminist social science is the attention to personal, lived experience, expressed by the slogan 'the personal is political', which points out the political nature of everyday life (Stanley and Wise 1983). Dorothy Smith (1987), for instance, argues that women's daily experiences generate 'problems' that require explanation. The answers to these questions can be found in the political, social, and economic orders.

This paper attempts to meet several of these feminist methodological objectives by rendering women visible in research, by allowing women's voices to be heard, and by taking seriously the analysis given by the women interviewed. To that end, the political theory of the New Right will be examined from the perspective of 20 homeless women addicted to cocaine or alcohol. Can neo-conservatism explain the women's situations? Does the theory propose adequate solutions for these women's problems? Since neo-conservatives propose a general theory of society that includes an analysis of the family as well as the political and economic system, they can and should be evaluated according to their ability to account for the women's experiences.

METHODOLOGY

I interviewed 20 women in Halifax who were, or had recently been, homeless and addicted to either cocaine or alcohol. Twelve of the women were recovering from drug abuse; eight were still using drugs or alcohol. Fifteen of the women were European-Canadian, three were African-Canadian, and two belonged to the Micmac nation. Over the course of these long, open-ended interviews we discussed their experiences of being on welfare, being homeless, and having addictions. The women were asked why they thought they were addicted and how or why they came to be homeless and on welfare.

Each of the interviews took from two to four hours. The interview questionnaire was followed quite loosely, allowing for the women's comments, additions, and anecdotes. In order not to ask leading questions, some topics were not brought up until mentioned by the women. For instance, when the women were first asked why they thought they were addicted and homeless, they responded in one of four ways. First, some of the women said simply family background without elaborating:

> *Anne*: The family background is the most important because I was addicted long before I picked up my first drug. I had an addictive personality that was developed. That was the first thing for what it did to my sense of self. Being a female when I moved out of the house and into the workforce was the second thing. All kinds of sexual harassment and everything. I got real pissed off and I decided if I'm going to be harassed, I might as well be paid for it.

If a woman, as in the case above, said that family background was a factor in her addiction, I proceeded to ask about her family so that she could specify what it was about her family that might have caused her to be addicted and homeless.

Other women were very specific about why they were addicted and immediately told me about the sexual abuse they had experienced:

> *Christine*: I was sexually abused by my babysitter's husband. That was when I was 10 or 11. I didn't tell my parents till I was 13 and Mom didn't believe me. I guess I got really unmanageable after that. Before, I was just a normal kid, who didn't like school and wasn't going to study, and was late for curfew sometimes and liked to argue. No one put two and two together. It just got worse. It wasn't just the one thing with him. It went on for months.

In these cases, we would then discuss how this experience had affected her and talk more about her family background.

Still other women answered in the third person, not specifying at first whether these issues had contributed to their own addiction:

Nicole: There are several reasons why people drink and are on the streets. Because of their family background, genetically. They don't feel loved. They don't get what they need in their childhood. They don't get the nurturing. They're always searching for something.

I would then ask if any of the factors she mentioned applied to her, and, depending upon her response, we would discuss family, sexism, or racism.

Finally, the first response of two of the women was to blame themselves and the choices they had made:

Jane: The onus in our life is the choices we make and taking responsibility for them because we have to live with the consequences.

Both women, however, stated what factors, if changed, might have made their lives different. When these elements were explored, Jane and Terri revealed that they had both been victims of sexual abuse when they were children.

As much as possible in this paper, then, I have taken the perspective or standpoint of the doubly or triply oppressed women interviewed. In this way, the perspective of the poor and disempowered will show what, if anything, is wrong with the theory rather than the traditional methods of using the perspective of the abstract individual, the ideal person, a 'veil of ignorance', or objective observer to show what is wrong with the poor or disempowered.

The words of the women are presented largely unedited. Marjorie DeVault (1990) argues that it is important to listen to the women's words and the meaning behind what may seem at first glance inarticulate speech. As she says, many women know what they mean, but are not used to expressing it (p. 102). For instance, the women interviewed had never been interviewed before, and this was one of the first times they had had a chance to gather their thoughts and relate their painful experiences. It was the first time, for example, that many of them had made connections between their experiences in their families of origin and their experiences with men in their adult lives. The interviews were a disturbing discovery process, then, for the women interviewed and also for me as the researcher (in my 'discovery' of self-esteem issues and sexual abuse of children). To me, the interviews were a valuable lesson in the benefits of using feminist methodology to uncover topics that would otherwise have remained hidden.

NEO-CONSERVATISM

Neo-conservatives are most often associated, in Canada, with the Reform Party, REAL Women, and various anti-abortion groups; in the United States, with groups such as the Conservative Caucus, the Conservative Political Action Committee, the Moral Majority, Eagle Forum, and Morality in the Media; and with individuals such as George Gilder (1984, 1981, 1978, 1975,

1974), Charles Murray (1984), Richard Viguerie (1980), Phyllis Schlafly (1977), and Jerry Falwell (1981). They are against big government, big business, and big labour and are pro-family and pro-defence. Neo-conservatives combine classical economic liberalism with social authoritarianism, advocating freedom and liberty of the market, on the one hand, and restrictive social policies regarding morality, family and sexual relations, and law and order, on the other (Levitas 1985; Belsey 1985: 173).

Neo-conservatives claim that the welfare state is in crisis because of the moral decay of society, the loss of the authority of the family, and the intrusion of the state into private life (Klatch 1987; Eisenstein 1984; Gilder 1981; Murray 1984). They believe that government has gone beyond its legitimate functions of rule making and national defence and that the welfare state, in particular, has encouraged women to work, families to rely on day care, and citizens to become dependent upon the state. They argue that increased taxation, caused by the enormous expenditures of the welfare state, has drawn women into the labour force, destroying the traditional family and therefore the moral fabric of society (Eisenstein 1984: 46-9). The dismantling of the welfare state, according to neo-conservatives, will place the burden back on families to care for their members, and this, so it is argued, will regenerate the traditional family.

The problems of the women interviewed, however, would not be solved by dismantling the mechanisms of the welfare state. On a basic level the women would not be able to provide for themselves or their children since they have few marketable skills, except maybe prostitution, and it is unlikely that the fathers of their children would simply come forward and start supporting them. Consequently, if we scrap the welfare state without fully understanding the women's problems, or without attempting to do something about them, then those problems will not be solved. It seems plausible that the women propose different remedies than neo-conservatives, not from laziness or self-interest, but from self-knowledge. They are aware of the problems that have led them to be on welfare and what it took or would take to get them off.

THE WOMEN'S EXPLANATIONS

The women's explanations for their circumstances suggest that there are underlying problems that have created their need for welfare in the first place. Primarily, the women explained their homelessness and addiction by relating their experiences of abuse in their families of origin. Seventeen of the 20 women interviewed (85 per cent) were abused as children, the majority (14) of the 17 having been victims of sexual abuse. The women stated that the abuse and neglect they had suffered as children, in particular the sexual abuse, had been devastating and had resulted in a complete lack of self-esteem and deep-seated self-hatred. They attributed their prostitution, homelessness, and addiction to sexual abuse by their uncles, grandfathers, and fathers. There is ample psychological, sociological, and medical evidence that abuse in their families will damage children and can explain their addiction and problems as adults (see Herman 1981; Russell 1978; Kasl 1989; Ohims 1978; Briere and Runtz 1988; Finkelhor 1978, 1982; Finkelhor and Korbin 1988).

Second, the women believed they had been discriminated against as women and as women of colour. Sexism and racism, then, were also seen as causes of their homelessness and addictions and of their relative inability to get off welfare after recovering from their addictions. The accuracy of the women's observations are attested to by empirical studies showing the disparities in jobs, education, and wages between men and women, and between whites and minorities, as well as the extent of violence against women and children (Amott and Matthaei 1991; Waring 1988; Goldberg and Kremen 1990; Rodgers 1979, 1986; Gordon 1990; Malson 1988; Barry 1979).

Since the women's experiences of welfare have been influenced by abuse in their families and sexual and racial discrimination, it is necessary for the New Right to be able to explain these experiences of childhood physical and sexual abuse, sexism and racism, in order to prescribe adequate solutions and to understand why women are homeless, addicted, and on welfare. Ironically, though the neo-conservative critique of the welfare state does not recognize the women's critique, the concepts of family, women's roles, and race, which are a prominent feature of the women's explanations, are central to neo-conservatism. As the next two sections will show, however, the neo-conservative positions on the family and sexism distort the experiences of addicted, homeless women.

NEO-CONSERVATISM AND THE FAMILY

The family is defined by neo-conservatives as a natural institution and the basic unit of society (Scruton 1984). The family, according to Scruton, is the 'prime focus of leisure and the origin of self-respect, being the first institution through which the social world is perceived' (p. 144). Neo-conservatives, then, recognize the importance of the family in personal development and wish to preserve its traditional form, believing as they do that 'what is achieved through family union could not be achieved in some other way' (p. 144).

The neo-conservative view of the family is, however, problematic. First, neo-conservatives tend not to have an entirely realistic picture of domestic life and write only of an ideal. As Scruton argues, since the family is non-contractual, there is 'no contract of distribution: sharing is simply the essence of family life. Hence everything important is "ours"' (p. 101). Violence against family members is not discussed, and therefore the violence against women and children is obscured, as are the different interests of men and women within the traditional family.

Seen from the point of view of women generally, the family can be a hostile institution that does not protect their interests, privacy, or safety. For these women in particular, the family was a violent place that did not guard their interests or their security.

> *Dana*: I was sexually molested starting when I was five, as I said, but I've seen a lot of physical abuse. I've seen so much abuse. I'll tell you about the time my father beat my brother. He thought my brother stole $20 from him. He took my brother and stripped him naked. He made all of us little kids stand in a row and he tied my brother to the woodshed wall, which was splintered and everything. He put these great big nails in the wall and tied him spread eagle right on the wall and he made us all stand there and watch him get whipped with a bull-whip. 'If you guys ever steal. That's what's going to happen to you.' He made my brother an example. I was five. My brother was seven.

> *Jane*: My father was extremely abusive, he was sexually abusive, physically abusive, mentally abusive. He was an incredibly sick man. He was sick. Our house was like a house of horrors. None of us have a clear picture of what went on in the house. My father gave me nothing do you understand, nothing. So, he came up to the bedroom, and he started talking to me in that nice, that syrupy sick whiny voice he used on the telephone and I never understood but I knew I didn't like it. So he started talking to me like that. He looks at me and says, 'Can I touch you?' And I tell you, I froze from the neck down and the only thing that moved were my lips and I said no. He walked away. And then I knew something. He did so much to my sisters in the attic and basement—out of sight—that one of my sisters had herself put into the home on Quinpool Road. You couldn't invite people to the house. He'd offer them money and make a sexual ploy. He made my life hell.

Feminist theory supplies backing for the women's words. The family is seen by feminists as the primary site of hierarchical power relations between men and women (Okin 1989; Barrett and McIntosh, 1982; Dale and Foster 1986). Historically, women have been considered the property of men, and men could legally control their wives and children as they saw fit. Women had few legal rights within the family, and their union was represented legally by the husband as head of the household (Elshtain 1982; Miles 1988). The traditional family, even today, is characterized by hierarchical relations that give husbands power over wives and parents power over children. According to feminists, then, neo-conservatives ignore the imbalance of power in the family and the economic power of the head of household, who historically has been male. As Hartmann (1987) states, such a traditional view 'assumes the unity of interests among family members; it stresses the role of the family as a unit and tends to downplay conflicts or differences of interests' (p. 111).

Second, though Scruton (1984: 31) argues that the family bond is not a voluntary association, as argued by neo-liberals, he assumes that it is a place removed from the public sphere and outside the realm of justice. The family, then, is assumed to be in a private sphere, separated ideologically and structurally from the public domain. The public-private split of home and work is seen by neo-conservatives as a protection of individual freedom since the private sphere is supposedly a place that is unaffected by others and that does not need regulation from outside. Neo-conservatives do not want to argue, however, that the family cannot be regulated from within. In matters of sexuality and control over children, for instance, neo-conservatives assume that it is imperative for parents, particularly fathers, to regain their control over the family unit (Gilder 1981; Schlafly 1977; Klatch 1987).

The women interviewed did not consider their families safe or just. In particular, they believed that the family needs to be regulated by society. They felt that if society had been more willing to see the problems in families generally and help the more vulnerable members, they would not have suffered so much because of their families. More regulation, according to the women, is absolutely necessary to prevent violence and abuse in homes:

> *Anne*: My life might have been different if more adults hadn't of turned their backs on what was going on. People just don't want to get involved. If people had stepped in a lot earlier and said, 'Hey, you're messing this kid up. Let's take her away.' I just think that especially in case of child abuse or physical abuse, I mean holy shit, fines and jail sentences for people who know what's going on and it's not being reported.

Feminists also believe that this public-private separation is problematic for women and children. They argue that private arenas can be sites of power, dominance, and struggle (Hartmann 1987). In particular, the family needs to be seen as a site of power relations. Feminists argue that the ideological and structural separation of the spheres conceals the power relations within the family and the different interests of the individual family members. Eisenstein (1984) contends that feminists

> do not wish to collapse personal and political life. Rather, they argue that personal (sexual) and political life are interrelated. Feminists do not argue that politics should be based on family life. They argue that the relations of the family are political and should not be. The intent of the feminist argument is to depoliticize its patriarchal aspects—not to conflate it with the state realm. Radical feminists want to destroy the ideology of public and private life in order to uncover the reality of the sexual politics of the family and the state. (p. 215)

Third, neo-conservatives advocate a traditional sexual division of labour in the family, that is, the father as the primary breadwinner and the mother as economically dependent and responsible for looking after the family. All of the women interviewed, except two of the three black women, came from traditional families, and all felt that the sexual division of labour in their families had had deleterious effects on their development:

> *Christine*: Mom did the cooking, cleaning, laundry and we pitched in sometimes. Dad worked in the garage and worked to pay for the clothes and food. It was very traditional. My mother did all the housework. It drove me crazy. Why couldn't he pick up after himself? Or do the dishes?

> *Megan*: My father didn't do anything around the house. I don't think I even seen him pick anything up or hold a mop. The boys didn't do anything either. See, back home [Cape Breton], it's an old-fashioned place down there, you know.

Feminists argue that the traditional family perpetuates the sexual division of labour through socialization and rigid gender roles for men and women. Gendered roles create economically dependent women and thus help to keep women vulnerable and dependent on men. Since looking after family is designated women's work and seen as a labour of love (that is, unpaid), women are either economically dependent upon men in the home or discriminated against in the workplace. Feminists argue that women who work outside the home are still seen to be responsible for the care of their children and for the housework and are therefore considered to be less mobile and committed to working than men (Okin 1989).

Finally, neo-conservatives believe that the nuclear family consisting of working father and home-making, economically dependent mother is natural, widespread, and superior to other (deviant) family forms (Mount 1982). This was not the experience of two of the three black women interviewed, who came from single-parent families and had had good experiences in their family homes. Black feminists argue that the neo-conservative family ideal has never fitted the experiences of black women, and therefore the model of the nuclear family is not natural or universal but instead arises out of particular political and economic circumstances. As Collins (1991) argues, 'the family life of poor people challenges these assumptions about universal family forms because poor families do not exhibit the radical split equating private with home and public with work. In order to survive, the family network must share the costs of providing for children' (p. 47).

The neo-conservative account of the family is inadequate for the women interviewed because it does not consider the violence experienced within their families, the problems with the sexual division of labour, or the prevalence of other family forms.

NEO-CONSERVATISM AND SEXISM

Neo-conservatives argue that the traditional family and women's role within it have developed because of the biological differences between women and men. These differences are natural, pre-determined, and unchanging. Men are instinctively aggressive and dominant; women are passive and nurturing. These differences are reflected in family roles when the father provides for the family and the mother nurtures and cares for the members of the family. Neo-conservatives argue that men should be given back the power that they have lost in the family because of government interference in the private sphere, and women should be encouraged to go back to the home.

There are two reason why neo-conservatives wish to preserve these differences and retain women's place in the so-called private sphere. The first is their fear of men. Gilder argues that men, particularly single men, are a danger to themselves and others. He claims that most of our social problems are created by single men and that the only way to tame their natural instincts is to ensure that marriage and family are attractive to them. Men need to be taken care of, they need stability, and they need to be economically needed by a family. If these conditions are not met, then the sense of obligation and importance needed by men will be lost, men will not be able to harness their natural passions, and they will release their destructive energy elsewhere, usually at the expense of the society at large (Gilder 1975: 6-7). Women, he argues, are the big losers since they, together with children and other vulnerable members of the population fear the naturally aggressive male and need protection from him.

The women interviewed, however, gave chilling testimony to the power that married fathers had in their families and of how they were not protected from the aggressive male. As sociologists and psychologists also suggest, the abuse of children is a result of the amount of control and power fathers already have over their families. None of the women advocated giving fathers any more authority within the family than they already had. Jane and her sisters and mother suffered years of sexual, physical, and emotional abuse at the hands of her father:

> My father is dead, and if he wasn't I would have killed him. . . . He ran over my first dog, thought it was going to break me, the son of a bitch. Never broke me, I spent $500 getting that dog fixed, took me three years. I was a kid, I was 13 years old and he purposely ran over my dog. He was a very, very sick man.

Rather than rely on biology, feminists suggest that men are violent because they have been allowed to be violent. Studies of domestic violence have shown that men can control their anger and violence against other men outside of the home because their hostility is socially unacceptable (Roy 1977).

The second fear implicit in the assumptions of the neo-conservative is that if men are not allowed a dominant role in the home, women will lose the right to be supported. This is the argument of Phyllis Schlafly and others of the so-called 'pro-family' movement.[1] According to Schlafly (1977), women and men have completely different natures and roles and if women would just fulfil their role by staying in the home, then men would live up to their obligations. Women, so it is argued, need protection from working in the labour market in exchange for their services as wives and mothers.

The women interviewed believe it is just as dangerous to be dependent on individual men as on the state itself, and that in some cases it is preferable to be dependent on the state. Their experiences of traditional family life had not been positive and had demonstrated the perils of depending economically on a man, whether it is a father, husband, or boyfriend.

> *Alison*: We lived in the country, really isolated from everything. My father dominated everybody in the family, economically and physically, and we were all scared to death of him. I was sexually abused, emotionally abused, and physically abused by him and my grandfather, and nobody could do anything about it.

White feminists also argue that, however appealing the image of the nuclear family is to some women, the dangers of being financially dependent on a man cannot be overlooked. Being financially responsible for a family has not deterred men from seeking divorces, and women, once widowed, often have no support at all (Eichler 1985: 26). Depending on men for support, no matter how benevolent the particular husband happens to be, makes women vulnerable and more liable to end up living in poverty. Though neo-conservatives tend to assume that any man is better than no man at all, feminists have shown the hardships, not only of single mothers, but also of women living in traditional two-parent families and dependent upon husbands who support them but are abusive. As Gordon (1990: 23) and Piven (1990: 250-64) point out, control by the state may indeed be preferable to dependence on individual men, partly because women do not live with the state.

Black feminists argue that the right of black women to be supported has never been protected or indeed even advocated. Black women have always had to work, and this undermines any argument that women's natural abilities are suited to the home or that they have a right to be maintained in a nuclear family in exchange for sexual, child-care, and home-making services. Collins (1991) argues that black women are socialized for survival and girls are expected to work to support themselves and their children. Work is not and should not be incompatible with black womanhood, as it is in the 'cult of true [white] womanhood' (p. 124).

The neo-conservative account of the roles of men and women did not fit the experiences of the women interviewed. They believed that making women economically dependent on men or giving men more power in the family or society would increase the hardships they already faced and would not have alleviated any of them.

CHALLENGING THE NEW RIGHT

Neo-conservatives are quite explicit about the role of women and the family in their explanatory schema. They believe that the independence of women threatens men and therefore undermines the traditional family, which is the foundation of any healthy society. In order to reverse the breakdown of the family, they believe that women should be induced to return to the home and that men will then fulfil their part of the bargain. Neo-conservatives want to carry out this strategy by dismantling the welfare state and reconstituting the patriarchal family by encouraging women to return to the home.

Feminists argue that neo-conservative policy is ill-conceived and harmful to women both on and off welfare for two reasons. First, they contend that dismantling the welfare state will merely increase women's burden in the home, principally because of the increased caring work that the family, and therefore women, will be expected to do. Second, they argue that dismantling welfare services will not in fact re-create the traditional family. As Eisenstein (1984) argues, to assume that the caring work now done by the state will be taken over by the family ignores the historical development of the welfare state and raises the question of causation. Did the welfare state cause the breakdown of the traditional family, as neo-conservatives claim, or did the gradual disintegration of the traditional family (due in large part to capitalism's need for labour) create the need for the welfare state in the first place? Eisenstein (1984) argues that getting rid of the welfare state will not get rid of the needs that created it and will only serve to worsen the conditions of non-workers within the welfare state. She claims that the welfare state

> is as much a consequence as a cause of changes in the economy and the family (for example, women's entrance into the labor force, new sexual mores and higher divorce rates). If this is true, the traditional (white) patriarchal family cannot be re-stabilized by dismantling the welfare state, because the welfare state developed out of the dissolution of the traditional patriarchal family. (p. 47)

The women's explanations for their experiences agree with the feminist critique of neo-conservatism and show clearly the second set of problems with neo-conservative prescriptions. The white and native women's experiences of childhood abuse show the dangers of giving men more power in families. Feminists argue that traditional families undermine women's security and independence by making them economically dependent on men. They believe that men should not be given more power in families, but should take more responsibility for their violence against women and children. As long as men can abuse members of their families with impunity, families, and hence society in general, will be potentially dangerous places for women and children.

Finally, the study illustrates the importance of listening to the experiences of women; in particular, of women whom Lugones and Spelman (1986) define as the most silenced, that is, women who are not 'white, middle-class, heterosexual, Christian women' (p. 21). The value of listening to these women's voices is the value of their testimony and experiences that have been ignored and dismissed. The women know why they are homeless. They know why they are addicts. No one has thought to ask them what they need or what would help them, because it is assumed either that they do not know, or that they are stupid and lazy and have no potential anyway; or because people think that welfare recipients do not deserve any choices or special treatment because it is their own fault they are on welfare in the first place. The words of the women refute all of the above beliefs and demonstrate the consequences for society of not listening to the needs of the recipients of welfare services.

NOTE

1 Margrit Eichler (1985) argues that the 'pro-family' movement is in fact not consistently pro-family at all, but anti-abortion, anti-homosexuality, anti-contraception, and anti-sex education. It does not promote advances for women in the family or protest against violence against women. Eichler found that the 'pro-family' movement was pro-patriarchal family, promoting the right of women to stay home and to be supported by their husbands.

BIBLIOGRAPHY

Amott, Teresa, and Julie Matthaei (1991), *Race, Gender and Work: A Multi-cultural Economic History of Women in the United States* (Montreal: Black Rose).

Barrett, Michele, and Mary McIntosh (1982), *The Anti-social Family* (London: Verso/NLB).

Barry, Kathleen (1979), *Female Sexual Slavery* (New York: Avon).

Belsey, Andrew (1985), 'The New Right, Social Order and Civil Liberties'. In *The Ideology of the New Right*, ed. Ruth Levitas (Cambridge: Polity).

Bowles, Gloria, and Renate Duelli Klein, eds (1983), *Theories of Women's Studies* (London: Routledge and Kegan Paul).

Briere, John, and Marsha Runtz (1988), 'Symptomatology Associated with Childhood Sexual Victimization in a Nonclinical Adult Sample', *Child Abuse and Neglect* 12: 51-9.

Collins, Patricia Hill (1991), *Black Feminist Thought* (New York: Routledge).

Dale, Jennifer, and Peggy Foster (1986), *Feminists and State Welfare* (London: Routledge and Kegan Paul).

DeVault, Marjorie L. (1990), 'Talking and Listening from Women's Standpoint: Feminist Strategies for Interviewing and Analysis', *Social Problems* 37, no. 1 (Feb.).

Eichler, Margrit (1985), 'The Pro-Family Movement: Are They For or Against Families?' CRIAW, (Sept.).

Eisenstein, Zillah R. (1984), *Feminism and Sexual Equality: Crisis in Liberal America* (New York: Monthly Review Press).

Elshtain, Jean Bethke, ed. (1982), *The Family in Political Thought* (Amherst: University of Massachusetts Press).

Falwell, Jerry (1981), *Listen America!* (New York: Basic).

Finkelhor, David (1978), 'Psychological, Cultural and Family Factors in Incest and Family Sexual Abuse', *Journal of Marriage and Family Counselling*, Oct.

———— (1982), 'Sexual Abuse: A Sociological Perspective', *Child Abuse and Neglect* 6: 95-102.

Finkelhor, David, and Jill Korbin (1988), 'Child Abuse as an International Issue', *Child Abuse and Neglect* 12: 3-23.

Gilder, George (1974), *Sexual Suicide* (New York: Bantam).

———— (1975), *Naked Nomads: Unmarried Men in America* (New York: Quadrangle/ New York Times Book Co.).

———— (1978), *Visible Man: A True Story of Post-Racist America* (New York: Basic).

———— (1981), *Wealth and Poverty* (New York: Basic).

———— (1984), *The Spirit of Enterprise* (New York: Simon and Schuster).

Goldberg, Gertrude Schaffner, and Eleanor Kremen, eds (1990), *The Feminization of Poverty: Only in America?* (New York: Praeger).

Gordon, Linda, ed. (1990), *Women, the State, and Welfare* (Madison, WI: University of Wisconsin Press).

Harding, Sandra, ed. (1987), *Feminism and Methodology* (Bloomington: Indiana University Press).

Hartmann, Heidi I. (1987), 'The Family as the Locus of Gender, Class and Political Struggle'. In *Feminism and Methodology* ed. Sandra Harding (Bloomington, IN: Indiana University Press).

Hartsock, Nancy (1984), *Money, Sex and Power* (Boston: Northeastern University Press).

Herman, Judith Lewis (1981), *Father-Daughter Incest* (Cambridge, MA: Harvard University Press).

Kasl, Charlotte Davis (1989), *Women, Sex and Addiction* (New York: Harper and Row).

Klatch, Rebecca E. (1987), *Women of the New Right* (Philadelphia: Temple University Press).

Levitas, Ruth, ed. (1985), *The Ideology of the New Right* (Cambridge, MA: Polity).

Lugones, Maria, and Elizabeth Spelman (1986), 'Have We Got a Theory for You! Feminist Theory, Cultural Imperialism and the Demand for "The Woman's Voice"'. In *Women and Values: Readings in Recent Feminist Philosophy*, ed. Marilyn Pearsall (Belmont, CA: Wadsworth).

Malson, Micheline R., ed. (1988), *Black Women in America: Social Science Perspectives* (Chicago: University of Chicago Press).

Miles, Rosalind (1988), *The Women's History of the World* (London: Paladin).

Mount, Ferdinand (1982), *The Subversive Family* (London: Jonathan Cape).

Murray, Charles (1984), *Losing Ground: American Social Policy, 1950-1980* (New York: Basic).

Ohims, David (1978), 'The Disease Concept of Alcoholism', *Alcoholism: Clinical and Experimental Research* 2, 2 (Apr.).

Okin, Susan Moller (1989), *Justice, Gender and the Family* (New York: Basic).

Piven, Frances Fox (1990), 'Ideology and the State: Women, Power and the Welfare State'. In Linda Gordon (1990).

Rodgers, Jr, Harrell R. (1979), *Poverty amid Plenty: A Political and Economic Analysis* (Reading, MA: Addison-Wesley).

—— (1986), *Poor Women, Poor Families* (New York: M.E. Sharpe).

Roy, Maria, ed. (1977), *Battered Women: A Psychosociological Study of Domestic Violence* (New York: Van Nostrand Reinhold).

Russell, Diana (1978), *The Secret Trauma: Incest in the Lives of Girls and Women* (New York: Basic).

Schlafly, Phyllis (1977), *The Power of the Positive Woman* (New York: Jove/HBJ).

Scruton, Roger (1984), *The Meaning of Conservatism*, 2nd edn (London: Macmillan).

Smith, Dorothy E. (1987), *The Everyday World as Problematic: A Feminist Sociology* (Toronto: University of Toronto Press).

Stanley, Liz, and Sue Wise (1983), '"Back into the Personal" or: Our Attempt to Construct "Feminist Research"'. In Bowles and Klein (1983).

Viguerie, Richard (1980), *The New Right: We're Ready to Lead* (Falls Church, VA: Viguerie).

Waring, Marilyn (1988), *If Women Counted: A New Feminist Economics* (San Francisco: Harper Collins).

CHAPTER 7

Pro-natalism, Feminism, and Nationalism

Roberta Hamilton

In any system of structured inequality—whether animated by racism, sexual hierarchy, or class—the people on top develop a set of ideas about what those below are 'like'. These ideas help explain why the people who control the resources are in control, and why those below them are destined to serve. That is, they legitimate this inequality and help its beneficiaries feel comfortable with it, since they themselves certainly would not want to be in the other people's shoes. So blacks in the *ante bellum* South were happy, childlike, and docile, and those in Los Angeles fatherless and lacking self-control. Similarly, women are nurturing, passive, and emotional, the poor lazy and untalented. When those on the bottom become publicly and collectively discontented with their lot in life and begin organizing and protesting, those above feel threatened in many ways: economically, politically, socially, and psychologically. They owe their privileges, after all, to the deprivations being protested. But they also feel betrayed. They have always treated those below with the kind condescension that befits their nature, and they ask the question now often heard: what do these people—the French, the blacks, the women—*really* want? The question is important both for its disingenuousness and because of its assumption that there is a quintessential Québécois, woman, or person of colour. What is also interesting is that a social movement created to challenge one of these hierarchal relationships will not necessarily coexist happily with movements created to take on other sets of hierarchical arrangements.

So, in Quebec, the relations of dominance and subordination between English and French have been challenged by the nationalist movement, while the feminist movement has confronted the hierarchical relations between men and women. Both movements intend to transform society, but the relationship between nationalism and feminism has more often been hostile than friendly. Indeed, nationalists, assuming that feminism would cause a disastrous drop in the birth rate, targeted feminists as their particular enemy. For Quebec's high birth rate has been viewed by many—

French and English—as an important reason for the survival of the French nation in Canada. In trying to allay the anxieties of the nationalists, Quebec feminists adopted different, sometimes competing, strategies: placating that form of nationalism, forging a nationalism inclusive of feminist demands, and rejecting nationalist agendas. It has been a complex history, not the least because these different forms of nationalism and feminism have had their own intense and quiescent periods. So the underlying question remains: will feminist and nationalist agendas in Quebec inevitably conflict? And, equally important, will a major site of that conflict continue to be their different positions on pro-natalism?

Clerico-Nationalism and Pro-natalism

With the resurgence of Quebec nationalism in the 1960s, anglophones asked (not for the first time in their history), 'What do French Canadians really want?' As demands by Quebeckers for autonomy grew stronger, culminating in the 1976 victory of the Parti Québécois, many English Canadians became indignant, even outraged: 'How *dare* they consider breaking up our country?'

To understand both the rise of Quebec nationalism and the demands for independence, on the one hand, and the reaction in English Canada, on the other, one needs to understand the history of the relations between French and English in this country and the nature of the contract that created the Canadian Confederation. For this was not a partnership between equals as many English Canadians believe. Rather, Confederation embodied, systematized, and perpetuated the military, and subsequent economic, defeat of the French by the English on the northern half of this continent and their confinement to the geographical area of Quebec (Brunet 1964; Guindon 1988; Hamilton 1988).

Such views, expressed by Quebec intellectuals over the decades, provided the political rationale for a challenge to the legitimacy of Canada itself. How could this state claim to embody the aspirations of the French people if its very creation confirmed their subordination?[1] A state may maintain itself through force, but unless that state develops into a full-scale, full-time military and police operation, it requires the consent of the governed. Patriotism, fear, apathy, or a genuine belief that those who rule are entitled to rule may all translate into such consent. But by the mid-1970s, many Québécois had overcome their fear and apathy and publicly directed their allegiance to the founding of a new national state that would rule in their interests.

English Canada reacted in shock.[2] Until the Quiet Revolution of the 1960s, most anglophones had defined the French as a church-ridden, superstitious, backward, inward-looking (after all, they resisted enlisting in both world wars), and very *prolific* people (McLaren and McLaren 1986). Most important, if the French continued to reproduce at the current rate, they would eventually overrun the country. The victory on the Plains of Abraham would turn out to be hollow.[3] For having won the battle, the English would lose the war that was being waged, not on battlefields, but in bedrooms throughout Quebec. This fear was encapsulated in the phrase 'revenge of the cradle'. Most explanations of Québécois fecundity attributed a large part of it to the influence of the Church, with its well-known injunctions against birth control and its presumed domination of the people of this 'priest-ridden' society (McLaren and McLaren 1986).

Not surprisingly, French intellectuals in Quebec rejected this francophobic and anti-Catholic evaluation of the high birth rate. In 1918 in an article in *L'Action française*, Father Louis Lalande excoriated the *Manitoba Free Press*, which described 'our [French Canadian] large families as a diabolical ruse perpetrated by the "rabbits of Quebec".' Lalande argued that the high birth rate in Quebec represented the happy convergence of female virtue and national destiny. This fecundity, in fact, had saved French Canada from annihilation, and this was to be applauded and sustained.

Lalande gave credit where credit was due: the survival of the nation had been masterminded and executed by the *women* of Quebec, fertile mothers, conscious defenders of the nation. Embedded within these prevailing ideas about the French, then, were assumptions about Quebec women: they were fertile, obedient to the Church, loyal to the nation, and, except for the nuns, absorbed in the tasks of bearing and rearing children. All those children, of course, also 'explained' to the English why the families were poor and uneducated. Yet for the clerical nationalists, the explanation was different: unlike the crassly materialistic and godless English, the French were spiritual, devoted to family and faith (Groulx 1960; Trofimenkoff 1983).

Quebec nationalists have struggled in different ways for well over 150 years to overturn the unequal relations between French and English. Part of that struggle has involved formulating and promoting a belief in the necessity of a high birth rate. Women were encouraged to have children; ideas and information about birth control were suppressed (Clio Collective 1987); large families were eulogized and the mother-child relationship was extolled above all others (Laflèche 1886; Trofimenkoff 1977). Hence, the struggle for national justice often seemed to require that women bear and rear many children. Yet in Quebec, as elsewhere, feminists have challenged the status quo throughout this century. Everywhere they have met resistance, and they continue to do so. But a careful look at these struggles in Quebec suggests that here (in addition to all the constraints faced by feminists in English Canada) loomed that aspect of nationalist ideology which linked survival to a high birth rate—that is, to women exploiting their reproductive potential in the service of the nation.

NATIONALISM AND THE FIRST WAVE OF FEMINISM

Given the link between nationalism and a high birth rate, feminism was a particularly acute threat to Quebec intellectuals during the early decades of this century. For men like Henri Bourassa, influential writer and editor of *Le Devoir*, feminism was yet another insidious foreign doctrine intent on sabotaging French survival (Trofimenkoff 1977). While men everywhere, and many women too, believed that a woman in a ballot box was an unseemly sight that would lead only to neglected and even abused children, as well as to general social decay, French nationalists in Quebec—clerical and lay— harboured, expressed, and organized around their own special dilemma. For national survival itself, it seemed, depended upon women's devoting themselves to motherhood—sublimely undistracted by activities best left to men. Feminists like Marie Gérin-Lajoie responded with a strong Christian feminist argument: that women wanted only the opportunity to do their special tasks with intelligence and in dignity (Lavigne, Pinard, and Stoddart 1979). Such a position—sometimes called maternal feminism—was prevalent in English Canada, England, and the United States. But there some women expressed publicly more radical critiques of their subordinate position in society (Eisenstein 1981; Gorham 1979).

French feminists, meanwhile, met with concerted opposition from lay and Church leaders. In response they left the Montreal Council of Women (MCW) but, in 1907, founded the Fédération Nationale Saint-Jean-Baptiste (Lavigne, Pinard, and Stoddart 1979). However, the Church's injunctions against participating in the MCW were not the only reason for the withdrawal; for the national hierarchy of English and French created second-class places for French feminists, even in these movements dedicated to sexual equality. Yet given the prevailing discourse among nationalists, could women be feminists without betraying the Church and the nation that it embodied? To answer yes was to step onto a minefield where few were prepared to venture. The first wave of feminist movement in Quebec, then, was shaped and informed—some might say 'cabined, cribbed and contained'—by the entire package of clerical nationalist ideology with its emphasis on nation, family, mothers, children and birth rates (Trifiro 1978; Trofimenkoff 1977).

First-wave feminism also coincided with a declining urban birth rate. In retrospect, it can be seen that in cities women born between 1906 and 1921 and still alive in 1961 had an average of three to four children, while their rural counterparts had an average of seven or eight (Henripin 1972). This disparity fuelled anxiety among Quebec intellectuals—lay and clerical—who warned that the family must be defended against urbanization, industrialization, poverty, unemployment, bad housing, and the decline in religious observance (La Semaine Sociale 1923; Trofimenkoff 1983).

Whether from conviction or opportunism, feminists emphasized their own commitment to the family and women's proper sphere (Cleverdon 1950;

Casgrain 1972). But their public enemies remained unconvinced, and many women indifferent, if not actively hostile, even to the most muted feminist pressure. A feminist delegation that petitioned the Legislative Assembly for the vote in 1922—the same year that the last of the other Canadian provinces granted suffrage to its female citizens—received a stern rebuke from Premier Louis-Alexandre Taschereau, who held true to his promise not to grant suffrage during his dispensation (Casgrain 1972; Stoddart 1973). After a five-year hiatus, women from the newly formed League of Women Voters, led by Thérèse Casgrain, and Idola St Jean's more radical Alliance Canadienne pour le Vote des Femmes du Québec, among others, began to make annual pilgrimages to Quebec City to witness their parliamentary supporters introduce bills granting suffrage. In 1940 the feminists' long campaign, which included weekly radio broadcasts, meetings, lectures, and fund-raising events (the Alliance raffled off a brand new Ford sedan in 1931) paid off. Against strong clerical opposition, the Liberal government under Premier Adélard Godbout gave women the vote (Casgrain 1972).

Until the late 1960s the suffragist heroine was Thérèse Casgrain, whose broadcasts in French, unlike those in English, stressed the centrality of the family to Quebec society. When she adapted a poster from the feminist committee of the Montreal Women's Club for the League of Women, she omitted the words 'equality' and 'justice', and to the question on the original poster, 'why should any profession be closed to women?' she added 'who are obliged to work?'[4] Casgrain wrote much later that Idola St-Jean was openly accused by some 'of presenting our demands with too much bitterness' (1972: 54-5).

Yet the words of Idola St-Jean more closely anticipated the spirit of the second wave of the women's movement, some 35 years later. In a 1936 editorial in *Women's Sphere* St-Jean pronounced: 'The word of order of the feminists should be "A liberated woman in a liberated world". In fact the freedom of women is subordinated to the total freedom of society' (Canadian Alliance for Women's Vote in Quebec 1936: 31). In 1936 those were fighting, but not winning, words.

THE HIGH BIRTH RATE RECONSIDERED

If the declining birth rate threatened nationalists in the 1920s and 1930s, what happened between 1950 and 1970 transformed nightmare into reality. By 1961 the average number of births per 1,000 Quebec women aged 15 to 49 was the second-lowest in Canada, after British Columbia; and it continued to fall. If the nationalist rhetoric had contained the first feminist movement, it had been singularly unable to curb the plummeting birth rate. For the falling birth rate in Quebec was a response to the same imperatives operating elsewhere. When it makes economic sense for people to have large families, many do. Children are easier to support on family farms than in industrialized cities and can contribute sooner to their own support. And in cities, it became more and more difficult for children to contribute to family survival because of compulsory education and laws prohibiting child labour (Bradbury 1979). When women contribute to family income by remaining at home, they tend to have more children. Once they seek waged labour outside the home, child care becomes intensely difficult, and they tend to have fewer children. Birth rates reflect these economic realities, which influence but do not determine the decisions made by women and couples.

Until recently no one asked if all French-Canadian women in Quebec actually did produce more babies than women elsewhere. In a feminist reappraisal of the demographic data, Marie Lavigne (1986) challenged the belief that women in Quebec shared a common fertility experience. While some women (but a declining number) throughout this century had many children, 40 per cent of those in the cohorts of 1887, 1903, and 1913 had two or one—or no children at all.[5] More recently, Danielle Gauvreau (1991) elaborated on Lavigne's thesis. Single women who became pregnant with no possibility of marriage were confronted with economic destitution, social ostracism, and the wrath of the clergy. With no access to abortion, no secular services for adoption, and—eventually—only huge church-run orphanages, these women scarcely fitted the model of heroic and virtuous mothers of the nation; nor were they treated as such. Also on the excluded list of women were married women with few children, married women who raised the children of others; women who died in childbirth, and women who practised birth control with varying degrees of success.

Why then did apparently everyone *believe* that all lay women in Quebec willingly gave birth to many children? That women in Quebec had many children was confirmed by the experience of the majority of children, who did grow up in large families—or whose friends did. Very large families are noticeable, Lavigne points out, and many more people come from large families than small, so many believed them to be the normal, even the only, experience. But although it was the norm to grow up in a large family (of six children or more), until at least the half-century mark, producing many children was the work of a decreasing minority of women (Lavigne 1986: 308). Lavigne provides a satisfying explanation of the gap between what is believed to be true about women and fertility and the actual range of prevailing practices. But the widespread belief in women's inexhaustible and unbemoaned fertility also dovetailed with the hopes of the nationalists and the fears of the English.

Although it seems that when women in Quebec had large numbers of children, it was neither to save the nation nor foil the English (McLaren and McLaren 1986: 124-45);[6] it is also clear that they did not stop having children, as the nationalists claimed, because they had become feminists—at least not in the years before 1970, when feminism in Quebec, as elsewhere, had a limited public presence (Stoddart 1973; 1981). This does not mean that women's lives had not changed during this period. Increasingly, married women with children were juggling waged labour with the bearing and raising of children (Clio Collective 1987). Without maternity leave, day care, or salaries that permitted the hiring of baby sitters or nannies, they did not need books or outside feminist agitators to suggest a solution. With each generation, more women limited the size of their families and more severely (Henripin and Peron 1973).

The assumption that women in Quebec had children in response to entreaties from Church or state-based nationalists has at the least been overstated. An empirical investigation may show that it deserves as much—or as little—credence as the belief that English women heeded the (perhaps apocryphal) admonition of Queen Victoria to 'lie still and think of the Empire' when performing their conjugal duty. But ideas can often have a tenuous link with social practices yet still resonate strongly with what people believe is happening.

The first wave of feminism did coincide with the growing realization in Quebec that the birth rate was falling, and people anxiously cast about for causes. Feminism seemed a logical suspect. Not surprisingly, early twentieth-century feminists responded that they simply wanted to enable women to be better mothers. Not only was this an attempt to mollify their opponents, but also recognition that the potential terrain for women to do anything else was narrow indeed. The professions remained closed to women, and the social service work undertaken by their sisters in English Canada had in Quebec long been the prerogative of nuns (Danylewycz 1987). Waged work for women was scarce, badly paid, and incompatible with child care. Working-class women stretched the family income by working at home—taking in boarders, children, and laundry (Bradbury 1979).

Nonetheless, despite the disclaimers of the early Quebec feminists, their critics argued that feminism was a profound threat to national survival. Before writing off the nationalists' fear as paranoia or sexism, therefore, let us ask rhetorically and with the clarity of hindsight: had the critics of feminism grasped something important? By insisting on equality between the sexes, in however tenuous and guarded a fashion, these first-wave feminists indeed unlocked a Pandora's box. This became evident decades later with the Women's Liberation Movement, when the theoretical logic of feminism found itself on more receptive terrain.

SECULAR NATIONALISM, PRO-NATALISM, AND FEMINISM

By the time second-wave feminism arrived in Quebec in the late 1960s, the economic, social, and family situation of women had changed dramatically. Indeed, Quebec now looked much more like the rest of the country. The Quiet Revolution had dismantled the Church's control of education and social services, replacing it with state bureaucracies and secular services.

Many nuns left their convents and joined other middle-class women as teachers, social workers, nurses, and secretaries in the expanding state bureaucracy. Women, including married women with children, entered the labour force in large numbers, albeit in the same kinds of job ghettos with salaries appropriate to second-class status that characterized women's work elsewhere (Clio Collective 1987). And there were far fewer children as women tried to do waged work without day care, maternity leave, or sufficient income, and as they tried valiantly to manage with the never-ending double work day. The assault on marriage-for-life by those seeking divorce or separation, by those opting for unions (with opposite- or same-sex partners) unsanctified by Church or state, and by those settling into permanent singlehood, with or without children, had made independence—from husbands—a way of life for many, and equality—with men—a pressing political demand (Quebec 1978).

In this environment feminists developed and propagated critiques of the family and marriage and demanded reproductive control—free access to birth control and *avortement, libre et gratuit* (abortion free and on demand). The simple slogan of the Comité de lutte pour l'avortement libre et gratuit—'We will have the children that we want to have'—expressed what most women appeared now to be doing. The nationalist fears articulated with such outrage 50 years earlier had been realized. Young women especially became harsh critics of their male-dominated society, in particular the Church, the institution they now held responsible more than any other for the successful defence of patriarchal relations. They castigated the Church for deeming birth control and abortion to be sins, for exhorting women to have many children, for railing against 'working' mothers, and for keeping women out of its inner sanctum. Secularization in Quebec came with a great rush, and second-wave feminists could hardly wait to dance on the Church's grave.

When the Church fell from power, however, patriarchy shuffled but did not collapse. Perhaps this should not have been surprising. Feminists knew that Quebec legislators had denied women the vote until 1940, 18 years after the last of the other provincial governments had succumbed. But surely that was because the links between the men of the Church and the men of the state had been deep and enduring, involving overlapping interests, beliefs, and kinship networks. Once the state was free of its religious fetters, surely subsequent governments would usher in a new age of sexual equality.

Or would they? The test case was about abortion. During the 1970s the Liberal government of Premier Bourassa was so committed to prosecuting Dr Henry Morgentaler for performing abortions that it appealed three jury acquittals. Over this issue, and many others, the secular state in Quebec was on a collision course with the growing number of feminists.

But the feminists were only a small part of the opposition to Bourassa. Nationalism in Quebec grew stronger, and in 1976 the Parti Québécois, an explicitly pro-independence political party led by René Lévesque, won the election. This victory, on 15 November 1976, occasioned a rejoicing which has never had—and could not have—any counterpart in English Canada, which gained its statehood through a grand business deal that promised even better deals to come (Whitaker 1977). Many feminists took part in the rejoicing, believing with so many others that they had a better chance of realizing their aspirations in an independent Quebec.[7] By the mid-1970s half of the party's members were women, many of whom insisted that the party incorporate feminist demands in its platform. Far from seeing any contradictions between feminism and nationalism, these feminists saw only possibilities for creating an independent and egalitarian nation.

And with good reason. For like bourgeois revolutions, movements of national liberation develop and articulate an ideology of equality. The colonized assert equality with the colonizers, the bourgeoisie with the aristocracy. But the language of national liberation is more inclusive and generous. For it is hard to call for the tearing down of some hierarchies while insisting on the maintenance of others. Moreover, if such movements are to succeed, more general mobilization is necessary. Not just owners and employers, but workers; not just men but women; not just the advantaged but the disadvantaged must be willing to struggle actively for what they believe will be a better society for everyone. In Quebec many important differences divided those who became *indépendantistes*: some were socialists or social democrats, including many working people who believed that their vision of society could be struggled for more effectively once Quebec was a nation; many were frustrated because their careers were blocked in an economy controlled by English capital; some were the successors of a long line of clerical nationalists who feared the loss of the French language, culture, and religion. And some were feminists who believed that their struggle for equality between men and women should be part of the struggle for national justice (Dofny 1977; Hamilton 1980; Milner 1978).

The support of such disparate groups brought the Parti Québécois into office. But how could the PQ *as government* fulfil the expectations of people with such competing and conflicting goals? Deep differences among nationalists, hastily papered over during the election campaigns, soon resurfaced in conflicts over social and economic policy. Not only were most nationalists not feminists, but most were deeply committed to, and privileged by, patriarchal practices.

But in 1975, when everyone was being wooed, anything seemed possible. Indeed the nationalist-feminist love affair reached its zenith in the two or three years after the election of the Parti Québécois. Though that affair went unconsummated, the flirtation had results.[8] Along with the reform of the Civil Code, issues like day care, violence against women, and abortion became mainstream political issues (Hamilton 1980).

Everywhere, the raising of these issues has been the work of feminists. But the ways in which political parties and governments deny, appropriate, or embrace them differ. In Quebec the controversies generated by issues like day care and abortion were shaped by nationalist concern with survival and the birth rate. Will state-subsidized day care mean that women will be more or less likely to have children? Will access to abortion further reduce the birth rate and therefore contribute to the decline of the 'nation'?

Three years into the PQ mandate, these questions and the particular fears they unleashed surfaced in a government-sponsored conference called 'Naître au Quebec' (To Be Born in Quebec). Ambivalence towards feminism and women's participation in the public sphere was masked in a discourse strikingly reminiscent of that of the 1920s nationalists: the nation was in jeopardy because couples had reduced the size of their families in order to pursue pleasure and possessions. The dean of Quebec demographers, Jacques Henripin, put it clearly in an address to the conference: 'The child becomes the object of more and more intense competition: he is threatened by the first or second automobile, by a second residence, by trips to the east or south, by sports equipment, by the taste for freedom, by meals in restaurants, and by a panoply of trinkets offered by the consumer society' (Quebec 1979: 32, my translation).

Henripin supported day care and other 'family' policies because he believed they might encourage women to have more children, who would then ensure the survival of Quebec. His rationale for day care departed radically from that of feminists, who insisted upon the right, need, and desire of women to participate fully in economic and political life. The Minister of Social Affairs at the time, Denis Lazure—one of the strongest supporters of feminist issues in caucus—nonetheless closed the conference on this note: 'The incredible growth from 60,000 Québécois in New France at the moment of conquest, to more than 6,000,000 now, constitutes a sharp example of the passionate will of a people to survive' (p. 130, my translation).

By the end of the PQ's first term, the feminist-nationalist honeymoon had ended. Lévesque's second-term election platform included monetary incentives for having that important third baby—incentives that the subsequent Liberal government enhanced. The highest-ranking feminist in the cabinet, Lise Payette, chose not to run again after a seemingly small blunder on her part led to personal and political disgrace, the disaffection of her colleagues, and, arguably a defeat for the government on its primary policy: sovereignty-association. This blunder, which triggered the so-called 'Yvette' phenomenon, confirmed, if somewhat more indirectly than the subsidy for third-time parents, the continuing resonance in Quebec of the link between women, maternity, and national survival.

THE YVETTE PHENOMENON

The background to these events ranged from the referendum on sovereignty-association to the content of primary school readers. Central to the PQ's 1976 election campaign was a promise to hold a referendum on Quebec's future relationship with Canada. Pre-referendum polls showed that the two groups least likely to vote 'yes' were the English and women. The PQ feared that women, encouraged through the decades by nationalists to maintain their traditional role, would, in fact, behave in a traditional way and support the status quo by voting 'no'. The person responsible for persuading women to change their minds was Lise Payette, minister for the status of women. On 9 March 1980, she addressed a partisan crowd in Montreal. Women, she proclaimed, should stop being afraid of change. She reminded them of Madeleine de Verchères, heroine of New France, and told them that, as always, women held the nation's destiny in their hands. (Notice here Payette's own reference to the 'special destiny' of women.) All women in Quebec, she went on, had been brought up to be 'Yvettes' and it was time they jettisoned this role. (Yvette was the little girl in the primary school readers who dutifully helped her mother in the kitchen while her brother, Guy, played exciting games outside.)

As yet, the feminists, despite considerable effort, had not succeeded in releasing Yvette and Guy from their gender stereotypes, and each year Quebec school children discovered them in their unreconstructed incarnations in their compulsory textbooks. Thus far, Payette was on politically uncontentious ground. But spontaneously she added another comment: Claude Ryan (then leader of the Liberal Party and provincial leader of the No campaign) was the kind of man who wanted women to remain Yvettes; he was, moreover, 'married to an Yvette'.

No one, let alone the minister, who quickly apologized, denied that she had made a faux pas in calling Madeleine Ryan an Yvette. But in this case apologies proved irrelevant. A few days later when, for the first time, the polls showed that a majority of decided Quebeckers would vote Yes in the campaign, the federal No forces cast about for a new strategy. They found it in Payette's *ad feminem* remark. Women in Quebec, rankled by her apparent attack on Madeleine Ryan, began to show more interest in the campaign. Many of them, in the weeks that followed, became the most energetic workers for the No side. Starting with small numbers, Yvette breakfasts and rallies throughout the provinces culminated in a giant gathering of 15,000 women at the Montreal Forum on 7 April. The participants sported buttons proclaiming 'Je suis une Yvette'.

These events were carefully orchestrated by the Quebec Liberal Party, representing the No campaign, and the rally featured well-known women in Quebec—including Thérèse Casgrain, veteran leader of the suffrage campaign—who led lives quite unlike the life for which little Yvette seemed destined. Yet many women responded favourably to the campaign. Not only was the Yvette movement the only excitement that the No forces generated throughout the campaign, but the momentum developing for the Yes vote was halted and reversed.

The big question that remains is why no countervailing support was mobilized by the women on the Yes side? If the PQ represented the best hope for feminists, and if many of them had supported the party, why did they not move to give Yvette and Guy, and what they represented, a decent burial? There are several reasons. First, the media read the Yvette movement as anti-feminist, and as more recent events bear out all over North America, the news media are far more interested in anti-feminist mobilization than feminist action (Faludi 1991).[9] Second, Payette's cabinet colleagues responded to her faux pas with anger or silence. Third, the minister, acknowledging that she had lost her credibility inside and outside the cabinet as a spokesperson for women, dropped out of the campaign (Payette 1982). Fourth, many feminists—now disillusioned with the PQ—were unhappy to see Payette 'using the feminist issue' to further nationalist goals.

Finally, it must be asked why Payette's remark motivated so many women to identify with Yvette and to organize for the No side. Though the women who organized the Yvette rallies were hardly full-time home-makers, this was not true for the majority of participants. These women took exception to Payette's rejection of the Yvette role, while men and women on both sides of the referendum issue thought of their mothers and their grand-mothers, of old history lessons, of the importance of large families, of what would happen if women continued to have so few children. On the No side virtue reigned supreme; here was a motherhood issue in every sense. The Yes side countered with stunned silence, caused by anger, guilt, and anxiety. The image of mother—as defender of the nation, the main force behind national survival—proved inviolable.

Such an interpretation is consistent with the theme of this chapter. The Yes side was defeated. The Parti Québécois ran again and won in 1980. This time feminists did not provide the blueprint for policies on women and the family (Payette 1982). In the aftermath of the Yvette affair, Premier Lévesque staked out a strong defence of the traditional nuclear family, including incentives for producing children—a policy reminiscent of Intendant Talon's (failed) attempt 300 years earlier. This election promise was kept, but it offered no more chance (media reports to the contrary[10]) of increasing the birth rate than such incentives did in Talon's day.

'WOMEN', FEMINISM, AND NATIONALISM

Another reading of the Yvette affair will be offered for those who would be both nationalists and feminists—or indeed for any politician who dares tell women en bloc what to do. During the last US presidential election cam-paign Vice-President Dan Quayle castigated the fictional television charac-ter Murphy Brown for having a child when she was not married. Many women responded angrily, and not just those who intended to have children alone. Like Quayle—in this sense only—Payette's mistake may simply have been to tell women what they should do as women—or more precisely what they SHOULD NOT BE—that is, they should not be 'Yvettes'. If so, these women were not the first group to convert a label intended to denigrate them into a badge of honour. Consider how some gays and lesbians refashioned 'queer' into a symbol of pride and resistance. Such an interpretation sits easily with the evidence that in the early decades of the twentieth century women did not have large families to fulfil the edicts of clerico-nationalist ideology and the need for national survival. Nor were they persuaded by Payette's nationalist argument to reject a traditional label. Temporary though it was, send-up though it might have been, women wore the button 'Je suis une Yvette'—even though none of them, even the most traditional, were eight-year-old girls who wanted to spend their whole life in the kitchen.[11]

In her interesting essay on the category of 'woman' in history, Denise Riley (1988) examines how problematic the term 'woman' has become for feminism. Not only have women 'rarely, if ever . . . step[ped] forward as completely unified candidates for emancipation' (p. 94), but the category of 'woman', while strategically necessary to feminism, has also led to its undoing. In the past decade, for example, many women from different locations have faulted feminism for invoking a universal category— 'woman'. In Quebec, women of colour whose families may have been in Quebec for generations, as well as first- and second-generation immigrants, have called feminists to task for practices, ideas, and policies that are exclusionary and racist (Maroney 1992). If this is a dilemma for feminism, the acknowledgement of diversity also poses a fundamental challenge for nationalist politics.

Women reject injunctions to act, vote, and mother in certain ways *because they are women*. Indeed, at the largest conference of feminists ever held in Quebec, the delegates refused to take a position on the constitutional referendum of 1992 because there was no unanimity among them (Cauchon 1992). Non-white women, in particular, fear a nationalist agenda predicated on racist notions of 'real' Québécois (Bula 1992), such as those captured in the title of the state-sponsored conferences called 'Naître au Québec'. Pronatalism as a symbol of national survival poses a threat to women with its insistence that there is only one way to be a 'good' woman and a good Québécoise, and a double threat to women of colour and non-French ethnic backgrounds by suggesting that only *some* women can be 'good' women and 'good' Québécoises.[12]

If there is to be another meeting of minds between feminists and nationalists in Quebec, as in 1976, it would presumably have to be on different terms. Certainly the apparent contradiction between feminism with its emphasis on autonomy, equality, and diversity—and the nationalist myth that equates women, mothering, high birth rates, and *survival*—will have to be confronted. Like women everywhere in the industrialized world, women in Quebec are having fewer babies than they once did. Their decisions, then and now, have to do with their economic, social, and personal circumstances and inclinations. The historical record shows that they are neither nationalist heroines nor dupes of feminism. Women's identification with feminism and feminists' support for particular nationalist agendas are not there for the asking.

There is much irony in the nationalist discourse on mothers and children. While women who have children are still considered the best servants of the nation, once women have had children they are on their own—government bonuses notwithstanding. If feminists and nationalists together confronted the myths from the past and jointly insisted upon the collective responsibility for child care and the world they create for all children, their next joint encounter with political power might well have quite a different outcome (d'Augerot-Arend 1991; Dumont 1991).

NOTES

I would like to thank Jennifer Stoddart for her helpful suggestions on an earlier draft of this chapter.

1 In *The Vertical Mosaic* John Porter (1965, 95-6) documented the unequal relationship between members of the two 'charter' groups in Quebec. For example, between 1931 and 1961 people of British origin became increasingly over-represented in the professions and in financial institutions while the French became increasingly under-represented. Though Porter attributed the difference to cultural factors, including the emphasis on classical education in Quebec, recent studies suggest that the French-Canadian petite bourgeoisie, the rising middle class, and the large capitalists behaved in ways similar to their English-speaking counterparts. The difference was that historically the ownership, control, and management of capital were all conducted in English. See, for example, Ronald Rudin (1985; 1990) and Paul-André Linteau (1985). While the Quiet Revolution ensured that the growing state bureaucracy offered places to French-speaking people, it was not until Bill 101 made French the official language of work in 1977 that the corporate world in Quebec began to conduct business in French. Until then, French-speaking Quebeckers who wanted to succeed had to do it in English. See also Christopher Beattie 1975.

2 As Hubert Guindon (1977: 28) wrote, 'True to form the victory of the Parti Québécois last November 15th [1976] came as a "shock" to English Canada. Everything that happens in Quebec always comes as a shock; in fact, if political events in Quebec do not come as a shock they are non-events.'

3 This popular view slipped quietly into the English historiography of Quebec. See, for example, Mason Wade (1968: 47): French 'survival was not dependent upon either British magnanimity or the force of circumstances; for French Canada possessed an indomitable will to live, witnessed in the first decade after the Conquest by the attainment of the highest birthrate (65.3 per 1,000) ever recorded for any white people.'

4 For an analysis of Casgrain's politics and for evidence that she tailored her remarks and posters differently for French and English audiences, I am indebted to Maureen Smith (1980).

5 To quote Lavigne (1986: 320): 'it is clear that the history of the mother with a large family is that of only a minority of women born at the turn of the century. The prolific minority did, however, have an immense impact on the statistics. . . . It is the averages provided by this minority that provided the basis for theories as to the fertility of the Québécoise.'

6 But see Henripin and Peron (1972: 229): 'Perhaps nowhere in the world was the Catholic large-family ideal more efficiently put into practice. It was reinforced by outspoken nationalist propaganda in favour of the *revanche des berceaux* and there can be no doubt about the success of these ideas.'

7 Indeed, as in the first wave of the women's movement, but for different reasons, many French feminists in Quebec found it difficult to work in the same women's centres and organizations with English women. Differences of language and culture might have been transcended, but their hierarchical ordering made that impossible. Those who were both feminists and nationalists insisted that the struggles for sexual equality and independence be linked.

8 But for a more critical analysis of the nationalism-feminist encounter see Diane Lamoureux (1987).

9 It should be noted that neither Dandurand and Tardy (1981) nor Jean et al. (1986) found evidence that the Yvette movement was anti-feminist. These authors argue convincingly that this was the media's immediate, but incorrect, interpretation.

10 Since 1988 such incentives have been enhanced greatly by subsequent Liberal governments. A media interpretation of a Statistics Canada report (*Kingston Whig-Standard* 1992) stated categorically, in the words of the headline 'Cash for Babies Plan Sends Quebec Births Up.' The report notes that the fertility rate in Quebec 'increased dramatically'—to 1.7 children per woman aged 15-44 from 1.4 in 1987. There are serious reasons to question this conclusion. The Quebec rate is 'still lower than the national average of 1.82', and the national average (with no incentives) has also gone up in the past few years. The author of the report makes it clear that there is no way of making a causal connection between the bonuses and the higher birth rate and that there are other more likely explanations (personal communication).

11 For a further elaboration of this interpretation see Roberta Hamilton (1993).

12 For a systematic discussion of the creation of a 'demographic crisis' in Quebec and the implications for women and feminism, see Maroney (1992).

BIBLIOGRAPHY

D'Augerot-Arend, Sylvie (1991), 'Concilier nationalisme et féminisme: un défi pour le Québec de l'avenir', *L'Action nationale* 81, no. 1 (Jan.): 56-68.

Beattie, Christopher (1975), *Minority Men in a Majority Setting: Middle-Level Francophones in the Canadian Public Service* (Toronto: McClelland and Stewart).

Bradbury, Bettina (1979), 'The Family Economy and Work in an Industrializing City: Montreal in the 1870s'. *Historical Papers* (Ottawa: Canadian Historical Association), 71-96.

Brunet, Michel (1980), *Les Canadiens après la Conquête* (Montreal: Fides).

Bula, Frances (1992), 'New Coalition Must Adapt to Our Needs—Minority Groups', *Gazette* (Montreal), 1 June.

Canadian Alliance for Women's Vote in Quebec (1936-37), *Women's Sphere* (Montreal).

Casgrain, Thérèse F. (1972), *A Woman in a Man's World*, trans. by Joyce Marshall (Toronto: McClelland and Stewart).

Cauchon, Paul (1992), 'Les mouvements de femmes donnent naissance à "Québec féminin pluriel"', *Le Devoir*, 1 June.

Cleaverdon, Catherine (1970), *The Woman Suffrage Movement in Canada* (Toronto: University of Toronto Press).

Clio Collective (1987), *Quebec Women: A History*, trans. by Roger Gannon and Rosalind Gill (Toronto: Women's Press).

Dandurand, Renée, and Evelyne Tardy (1981), 'Le phénomène des Yvettes à travers quelques quotidiens'. In *Femmes et politique*, ed. Yolande Cohen (Quebec City: Le Jour), 21-56.

Danylewycz, Marta (1987), *Taking the Veil* (Toronto: McClelland and Stewart).

Dofny, Jacques (1977), 'The P.Q. Government: Year One'. In *Nationalism and the National Question*, ed. Nicole Arnaud and Jacques Dofny (Montreal: Black Rose), 114-23.

Dumont, Micheline (1991), 'L'expérience historique des femmes face à l'avenir politique et constitutionnel du Québec', *L'Action nationale* 81, no. 5 (May), 610-22.

Eisenstein, Zillah (1981), *The Radical Future of Liberal Feminism* (Boston: Northeastern University Press).

Faludi, Susan (1991), *Backlash: The Undeclared War Against American Women* (New York: Crown).

Gauvreau, Danielle (1991), 'Destins de femmes, destins de mères: images et réalités historiques de la maternité au Québec', *Recherches Sociographiques* 32, no. 3: 321-46.

Gorham, Deborah (1979), 'Flora MacDonald Denison: Canadian Feminist'. In *A Not Unreasonable Claim*, ed. Linda Kealey (Toronto: Canadian Women's Educational Press), 47-70.

Groulx, Lionel (1960), *Histoire du Canada français depuis la découverte* (Montreal: Fides).

Guindon, Hubert (1977), 'Quebec Notes', in *This Magazine*, Oct.

————— (1988), 'The Modernization of Quebec and the Legitimacy of the Canadian State'. In *Hubert Guindon, Tradition, Modernity, Nation: Essays on Quebec Society*, eds Roberta Hamilton and John L. McMullan (Toronto: University of Toronto Press), 60-93.

Hamilton, Roberta (1980), 'Sexual Politics', *Canadian Forum*, Feb. 27-30.

————— (1988), *Feudalism and Colonization: The Historiography of New France* (Gananoque, Ont.: Langdale).

————— (1993), 'Les Yvettes douze ans après'. In *Thérèse Casgrain: Une femme tenace et engagée* (Sainte-Foy: Presses de l'Universite du Québec), 171-7.

Henripin, Jacques, and Yves Peron (1972), 'The Demographic Transition of the Province of Quebec'. In *Population and Social Change* eds D.V. Glass and Roger Revelle (London: Edward Arnold), 213-32.

————— (1973), 'Evolution démographique récente du Québec'. In *La Population du Québec: études retrospectives*, ed. Hubert Charbonneau (Montreal: Boréal), 45-72.

Jean, Michèle, Jacqueline Lamothe, Marie Lavigne, and Jennifer Stoddart (1986), 'Nationalism and Feminism in Quebec: The Yvette Phenomenon'. In *The Politics of Diversity: Feminism, Marxism and Nationalism*, eds Roberta Hamilton and Michèle Barrett, trans. Joy Holland (London: Verso), 322-38.

Laflèche, L'Abbé (1866), *Quelques considérations sur les rapports de la société civile avec la religion at la famille* (Montreal: Eusèbe Senécal).

Lamoureux, Diane (1987), 'Nationalism and Feminism in Quebec: An Impossible Attraction'. In *Feminism and Political Economy: Women's Work, Women's Struggle*, eds Heather Jon Maroney and Meg Luxton (Toronto: Methuen), 51-68.

Lavigne, Marie (1986), 'Feminist Reflections on the Fertility of Women in Quebec'. In *The Politics of Diversity: Feminism, Marxism and Nationalism*, eds Roberta Hamilton and Michèle Barrett, trans. David Macy (London: Verso).

Lavigne, Marie, and Jennifer Stoddart (1977), 'Women's Work in Montreal at the Beginning of the century'. In *Women in Canada* rev. edn., ed. Marylee Stephenson (Don Mills: General), 129-47.

Lavigne, Marie, Yolande Pinard, and Jennifer Stoddart (1979), 'The Fédération Nationale Saint-Jean-Baptiste and the Women's Movement in Quebec'. In *A Not Unreasonable Claim*, ed. Linda Kealey (Toronto: Canadian Women's Educational Press), 71-88.

Linteau, Paul-André (1985), *The Promoters' City: Building the Industrial Town of Maisonneuve, 1883-1918*, trans. Robert Chodos (Toronto: Lorimer).

Macdonald, Ian L. (1984), *From Bourassa to Bourassa* (Montreal: Harvest House).

Maroney, Heather Jon (1992), '"Who Has the Baby?" Nationalism, Pronatalism and the Construction of a "Demographic Crisis" in Quebec, 1960-1988', *Studies in Political Economy* 39 (Autumn): 7-36.

McLaren, Angus, and Arlene Tigar McLaren (1986), *The Bedroom and the State: The Changing Practices and Politics of Contraception and Abortion in Canada, 1880-1980* (Toronto: McClelland and Stewart).

McRoberts, Kenneth, and Dale Posgate (1980), *Quebec: Social Change and Political Crisis* (Toronto: McClelland and Stewart).

Milner, Henry (1978), *Politics in the New Quebec* (Toronto: McClelland and Stewart).

Payette, Lise (1982), *Le pouvoir? Connais pas!* (Quebec City: L'Amérique).

Porter, John (1965), *The Vertical Mosaic: An Analysis of Social Class and Power in Canada* (Toronto: University of Toronto Press).

Quebec (1978), Conseil du statut de la femme, special issue of the *Bulletin*, 'Québécoises! égalite et indépendence', vol. 5, no. 5 (Oct.).

――― (1979), Conseil des Affaires sociales et de la famille. *Rapport des déliberations du colloque du CASF sur le thème: 'Naître au Québec'* (Quebec City).

Riley, Denise (1988), *'Am I That Name?' Feminism and the Category of 'Women' in History* (Minneapolis: University of Minnesota Press).

Rudin, Ronald (1985), *Banking en français: The French Banks of Quebec, 1835-1925.* (Toronto: University of Toronto Press).

――― (1990), *In Whose Interests? Quebec's Caisses Populaires, 1900-1945* (Montreal and Kingston: McGill-Queen's University Press).

La Semaine Social (1923), *La Famille* (Montreal).

Smith, Maureen (1980), 'French-Canadian Women and the Struggle for Provincial Suffrage', unpublished paper, Concordia University. In possession of author.

Stoddart, Jennifer (1973), 'The Woman Suffrage Bill in Quebec'. In *Women in Canada*, ed. Marylee Stephenson (Toronto: New Press), 90-106.

――― (1981), 'Quebec's Legal Elite Looks at Women's Rights: The Dorion Commission, 1929-31'. In *Essays in the History of Canadian Law*, vol. I, ed. David H. Flaherty (Toronto: University of Toronto Press), 212-48.

Trifiro, Luigi (1978), 'Une intervention à Rome dans la lutte pour le suffrage féminin au Québec (1922)', *Revue d'histoire de l'Amérique française* 32, no. 1 (June): 3-18.

Trofimenkoff, Susan Mann (1977), 'Henri Bourassa and the Woman Question'. In *The Neglected Majority: Essays in Canadian Women's History*, eds Susan Mann Trofimenkoff and Alison Prentice (Toronto: McClelland and Stewart), 106-15.

――― (1983), *The Dream of Nation* (Toronto: Gage).

Wade, Mason (1968), *The French Canadians, 1760-1967* (Toronto: Macmillan).

Whitaker, Reg (1977), 'Images of the State in Canada'. In *The Canadian State*, ed. Leo Panitch (Toronto: University of Toronto Press), 28-68.

CHAPTER 8

Women of Quebec
and the Contemporary
Constitutional Issue

Micheline Dumont

Translated by Carol Cochrane

Since the early 1970s, various authors have noticed the ambiguous ties between the women's movement and revolutionary, national-liberation, and leftist movements in general. A classic on the subject is *Women, Resistance and Revolution* by Sheila Rowbotham (1972), who shows that all revolutions have welcomed women as militants, but have rejected their specific demands. In *Le féminisme libertaire*, Micheline De Sève (1985) analyses the shortcomings of the Marxist theory of women's issues. In *Personal Politics*, Sara Evans (1979) analyses the emergence of radical feminism from the civil rights movement and the New Left in the United States. Alice Echols (1989) explores its manifestations in *Daring to Be Bad: Radical Feminism in America, 1967-1975*.

In Quebec the leaders of the 'patriots' of the nineteenth century presented a basically male image, as indicated by the recent studies of the patriots of Lower Canada or the rebels of Upper Canada (Greer 1991; Morgan 1991). It was the patriots who, in 1834, took away women's right to vote, which had been acquired 'by mistake' in 1791. And in 1838 the short-lived declaration of independence of the Republic of Lower Canada abolished the widow's dower, which ensured financial protection for widows according to the *coutume de Paris*. Women in those days may have endorsed the aspirations of the patriots, but history has not seen fit to record their words or actions. Of course there was no women's movement in those days.

When the nationalist undercurrent became much more conservative at the beginning of the twentieth century, the very concept of feminine protest was seen as a dangerous Anglo-Saxon import. But Quebec women were not passive. Indeed, women of the French-Canadian élite were aware of the actions of feminists around the world. They spoke of the 'féminisme chrétien' in their magazine *Le coin du feu* (1893-6); they joined the Montreal chapter of the National Council of Women in 1893 (Pinard 1983); and finally, in 1907, they formed their own feminist association, La Fédération nationale Saint-Jean-Baptiste (Lavigne et al., 1983), and published their own feminist journal *La Bonne parole*.

We know that the religious and political élite of Quebec associated feminism with Protestantism and, more importantly, assigned women a special responsibility for French-Canadian survival. The Quebec difference fed upon, among other things, the patriarchal constraints of the Civil Code and the concept of Catholic submission, and, in the end, women found themselves imprisoned by the national need for them to be subordinated. They were responsible for the revenge of the cradle. They were considered the foundation of the patriarchal family, which has vaguely been presented as a form of matriarchy. Most of all, society counted on the complete gratuitousness of their work, which involved most of the farm work and domestic chores performed by wives and mothers, and various jobs in the educational system and the social services performed by members of religious communities (Laurin et al. 1992). The national role of women is a constant theme in discussions of nationalism. On three occasions the Montreal Saint-Jean-Baptiste parade, the annual patriotic celebration, chose the theme of the French-Canadian woman (or mother).[1] Almost all aspects of this conservative ideology were endorsed by the feminists of the first feminist association, the Fédération nationale Saint-Jean-Baptiste, as Roberta Hamilton explains elsewhere in this volume.

However the relations between feminism and nationalism no longer correspond to that old model. Since 1960 a new nationalism has been confronted with a new feminism. But feminist issues are not easily viewed as nationalist issues; this is particularly true within the constitutional debate. A new look at the women's movement in Quebec demonstrates that, on the contrary, these two issues are inextricably linked. This chapter will examine the provincial and federal scenes, the recent constitutional crisis, and especially the evolution of the Fédération des Femmes du Québec.[2]

THE QUIET REVOLUTION AND AFTER (1960-1985)

The first manifestation of the 'new' Quebec nationalism, the Quiet Revolution, presented itself as a champion of equality for women. This was not because its leaders were feminists, but because its reformist legislation afforded new tools for women. The first female member of the Quebec legislature, Claire Kirkland-Casgrain, was responsible for the adoption of Bill 16, which changed the status of married women in 1964. In the same year, the Parent report, which concluded the important government commission on the educational system, introduced major changes at all levels of education, including co-education, equality between girls' and boys' education, and free education up to the end of the CÉGEP. This reform made new job opportunities possible for women. Labour leaders adopted a favourable attitude to paid work by women. Quebec's birth rate was declining. The list goes on.

At the beginning of 1965, a number of women realized that, although Quebec women had had the vote for 25 years, the franchise had not been celebrated collectively. Thérèse Casgrain, who initiated the idea, asked representatives from women's associations to organize the celebration. The anniversary of the right to vote was celebrated with a two-day conference in Montreal, called *La femme du Québec: Hier et aujourd'hui*. Committees studied the legal status of women and the participation of women in the Quebec economy and in society. Claire Kirkland-Casgrain, Quebec's first female MLA, gave the keynote address, and Mariana Jodoin, only woman senator from Quebec, was honorary chair.

At the closing session, the conference voted unanimously to found the Fédération des femmes du Québec. The federation was to have representatives from all the women's associations as well as individual members; its first objective would be to co-ordinate all activities aimed at promoting the interests and rights of women. The participants adopted the organizational structure chosen by the National Council of Women in 1893 and in 1907 by the Fédération nationale Saint-Jean-Baptiste. The Fédération des femmes du Québec was soon represented regularly on parliamentary committees, and it lobbied for the creation of the Conseil du statut de la femme in 1973. Its agenda was clearly reformist and feminist: revision of the Civil Code, legalization of divorce, equality in the workplace, protection of part-time workers, minimum work standards, maternity leave, day-care centres, educational opportunities and orientation for girls, information about family planning, and protection of women in the reform of pension plans. One of the federation's main demands in 1975 was made in its 'Mémoire sur l'égalité des hommes et des femmes' (Brief on the equality of men and women) at the time of the creation of the *Charte des droits et libertés de la personne*. Most important, during every election campaign, it published information about each party's policies on women's issues, pointing out that one voter in two is a woman. The FFQ was a leader in offering specialized courses for women in political education, political action, and political process.

But the FFQ was soon joined by new women's groups. From 1969 on, the women who fought for the radical left or for the 'new' nationalist groups posed the fundamental question of what the role of women was in these protest movements. The Front de libération des femmes (FLF) was the first group formed in 1969. Corresponding to the famous *Manifeste du FLQ* of 1970 was the *Manifeste des femmes québécoises* in 1971, and the slogan of *Québécoises deboutte!* the first Quebec radical feminist newspaper, was 'No liberation of Quebec without the liberation of women! No liberation of women without the liberation of Quebec!' The specific character of the radical Quebec feminist movement, in contrast with radical Anglo-Saxon feminism, was evident from its beginnings in Montreal (Lanctôt 1980). 'The first public action of

Toronto Women's Liberation had been, in 1968, an intervention in a winter bikini contest, protesting the marketing of women as sex objects. In contrast, the first public action of the Feminist Front was a protest in 1969 against governmental repression of trade-union and other leftist-nationalist activity in Montreal' (Black 1988: 90). 'American feminists provided the catalyst for the first women's liberation group, but they were soon expelled; their anglophone presence was incompatible with Quebec's Nationalist emphasis on French culture and language' (Black 1992: 96). Though the theorist of the Movement de Libération des Femmes in France played an important part in the theoretical formation of radical feminists in Quebec, the movement cannot be understood without considering its nationalistic leanings (De Sève 1992). For example, on 6 May 1970, the Front de libération des femmes refused to take part in the Abortion Caravan to Ottawa because its members did not want to address the federal government.

After the actions of the FLF (1969-71) and the Centre des femmes (1972-5) (O'Leary and Toupin 1982), various small groups were formed around specific issues: abortion, day-care centres, feminist publishing houses, popular theatre, magazines, women's centres, health centres, and pornography (Brodeur et al. 1982). After *Québécoises deboutte!* ceased publishing in 1974, many magazines were founded: *Plurielles* (1978), *Des rires et des luttes de femmes* (1978-81), *RAIF* since 1973, *Communiqu'elles* (1973-91), *Les Têtes de pioche* (1976-9), *Féminin pluriel* (1981-3), *La vie en rose* (1981-7). Unlike these magazines (and the groups that published them), the FFQ presented a quiet image of feminism.

But in the United States, radical feminists succeeded in pushing liberal feminists to the left (Echols 1989: 4), and the same thing happened in Quebec. By the end of the 1970s, the FFQ itself was dealing with abortion, violence against women, rape, pornography, sexism in the media, health issues, and so on. In 1976 it described abortion as women's right for desired motherhood. The leaders of the FFQ knew this claim would change its public image, but in the minds of the public, the whole idea of feminism was becoming radical.

During that time, women attempted to integrate into traditional political parties. Sylvia Bashevkin (1985: 74), analysing women's presence in party politics in English Canada, shows that feminist consciousness can affect female representation within a party. Very early, the Parti Québécois became known for the important role played by militant women in the party. In 1973 it was the first party to include issues specifically affecting women in its platform. In 1976 it was the first party to elect four women. In 1978 it was the first party to create a ministry for the status of women and to promote an overall policy for all matters concerning the condition of women. The policy was published under the title *Pour les Québécoises: égalité et indépendance* (For the Women of Quebec: Equality and Independence). Its most eminent female members were declared feminists. This is demonstrated by Hamilton elsewhere in this volume. While raising many hopes, the party also disappointed the militants who emphasized the specific nature of women's issues. When René Lévesque vetoed a clause approving abortion, women's committees in several ridings disbanded, and many women tried to establish an autonomous women's organization, Le regroupement des femmes québécoises, which lasted only one season in 1978.

In the Liberal Party, the situation was completely different. Since 1950 women members of the party had been organized into a sizeable federation, completely independent of the male structure. Chantal Maillé (1990: 90, 112) explains how this organization succeeded in promoting proposals concerning women and organizing committees in most local ridings. In 1971 the federation, with its 25,000 members, agreed to integrate into the structure of the official party. But this move was negotiated on the condition that 50 per cent of every riding delegation to party conventions be women. They also succeeded in obtaining two members in every riding association. With this strategy, the women of the Liberal Party chose to work through an action committee called the 'Commission d'action politique féminine'. Their objective was to train women for political activism (Maillé 1990: 90, 113). Although most of these women were not clearly labelled as 'feminists', they endorsed many feminist demands and many of them had been active in various women's associations. In all likelihood, this different strategy enabled many women to make their mark in the Liberal Party, even though their involvement in women's issues was never as evident as that of women in the Parti Québécois. Liberal militant women relied more on a strategy of equality.

By the late 1970s, it appeared that feminists of all leanings were divided equally between the two political parties. However, it seemed impossible to distinguish between the different types of feminist demands, reformist and 'radical', in the two political parties. Political distinctions in no way corresponded to the distinctions in women's demands. One study reveals that one female Member of the National Assembly out of two supports feminist demands, mostly reformist demands. But there is no sharp division between the two main parties (Tremblay 1990). The members of the FFQ came from both parties, and political partisan issues were officially and politely set aside.

In 1980, when all of Quebec was polarized by the referendum, the Yvette incident transformed the public debate. (The story is told elsewhere in this volume by Roberta Hamilton and does not need repeating here.) At the time, the Yvette movement was easily interpreted by some as an expression of women's anger at the radical feminist position of the minister for the status of women, Lise Payette. For it was she who accused the women who supported the 'No' side of conforming to the traditional model of nationalism, comparable to the little stereotypical Yvette of the old school readers. However, this interpretation did not stand up to scrutiny. Today, an anti-feminist emphasis in the debates which brought together the Yvettes is sought in vain (Dumont 1990). It is easier to find old-fashioned nationalist arguments in the comments of the participants. 'In difficult times, the country relies on its women,' some said reassuringly. Furthermore, among their ranks were such well-known feminists as Thérèse Casgrain, who had been the leader of the suffrage campaign; Solange Chaput-Roland, prominent member of the Voice of Women; Monique Bégin, general secretary of the Bird Commission; Sheila Finestone, former president of the FFQ; Yvette Rousseau, former president of the Canadian Advisory Council on the Status of Women, and many more. In fact, the Yvettes developed a magnificent strategy for organizing Liberal militants. With Louise Robic at the head of the Commission d'action politique féminine, they gambled on Lise Payette's political mistake, as well as on the anger of the Liberal militants, to organize the Yvette rallies under the obliging eye of the media. There, a great number of Yvettes found their initial inspiration to get involved in politics. One participant revealed, a few years later, that at the Montreal Forum, she had discovered the incredible solidarity of women.

A few days later on 26 April 15,000 women gathered at Place Desjardins for the fortieth anniversary of women's right to vote in Quebec. Thérèse Casgrain declined to participate. Consequently, the event became a Yes rally attended by Lise Payette, the minister; Madeleine Parent, a union leader from the 1940s; Hélène Pelletier-Baillargeon, who declared that 'all steps taken toward autonomy and liberty resemble one another', comparing women's autonomy with Quebec's autonomy. At the Yvette rally, the women had sung 'O Canada'; at Place Desjardins they sang 'Gens du pays'. Unlike the speeches at the Yvette rally, which barely mentioned women's issues, most of the speeches dealt with women's equality and women's autonomy together with the sovereignist issue. As Dandurand and Tardy (1982: 23) explain, most of 'the so-called "autonomous" groups that usually stand apart from all traditional political parties rallied in favour of the Yes vote.'

On referendum day, 60 per cent of the Quebec population said No to the Parti Québécois, and many analysts believe that there was no gender gap apparent in the results (Blais 1980; Tardy 1980). The one thing that is certain, however, is that many women placed their political option, Yes or No, ahead of women's issues. As Susan Trofimenkoff suggests, 'the Liberals proceeded to specify so many and so intricate changes that the federation was barely recognizable while the Parti Québécois talked so sanguinely of association that its separation could hardly be discerned. While the two smudged their options for political purposes, only the feminists implied that the debate might be irrelevant' (Trofimenkoff 1982: 330).

The anti-feminist backlash predicted by the media as a result of the Yvette incident did not occur; there was no decrease in the demands of women in the 1980s. Not only were there continuous demands concerning the condition of women, but women's groups were transforming Quebec's feminism. In 1985 there were more than 300 groups engaged in political action at many levels (Ouellette 1986).

Women were also becoming more and more prominent in various political spheres. Eighteen women were elected to the National Assembly in 1985
and 23 in 1990. An increase could also be seen in municipal politics and in
the labour unions. Throughout the autumn of 1989, three union leaders
were in the news. Representing the avant-garde, the openly feminist union
leaders were Lorraine Pagé, of the CEQ (Centrale de l'Enseignement du
Québec), Monique Simard, from the CSN (Confédération des Syndicats
nationaux), and Diane Lavallée, from the Nurses Union, a trio that con-
trasted strongly with the trio of union leaders who had directed the 'Front
Commun' in 1972. At that time, Yvon Charbonneau, of the CEQ, Louis
Laberge, of the FTQ (Fédération des Travailleurs du Québec), and Marcel
Pépin, of the CSN, had conducted a strong labour contestation, defying a bill
imposed to stop a general strike. In 1972 the government had imprisoned
the leaders, thus creating martyrs. But in 1989, for the same offence, it
passed the notorious Bill 160, which abolished the seniority of defiant members and was aimed directly at solidarity in the unions with a female majority.

The close relationship between women's movements and party politics
finally became apparent when the reputedly conservative Association féminine d'éducation et d'action sociale (AFEAS)[3] published a brochure called
Comment prendre sa place en politique (How to take one's place in politics) and
gave workshops to help its members become active in the public forum.
Whether the militants' involvement in politics was a springboard for women
or feminist issues will be discussed below. Before answering this important
question, however, we shall look at the federal scene.

The Women's Movement on the Federal Scene (1967-1987)

Since the beginning of the century, feminists across Canada had rallied
around common demands. But this consensus was broken in 1922 when
Quebec women were refused the right to vote in provincial elections. We
know today that it was the renewal of the dialogue between the English- and
French-speaking movements, after 1960, notably in the Voice of Women and
the FFQ, that enabled women to obtain the Royal Commission on the Status
of Women from the federal government in 1967 (Bégin 1992). The strategic
importance of the commission's report (the Bird Report) no longer had to be
demonstrated in the awakening of feminist awareness which occurred across
Quebec after 1971 (Collectif Clio 1992). The FFQ played a central role by
publishing a discussion guide on the recommendations of the report that was
used in hundreds of women's groups.

Thus, in 1971, three women were elected to the House of Commons,
and all of them—Jeanne Sauvé, Monique Bégin, and Albanie Morin—came
from Quebec. In 1973 the federal government established the Canadian

Advisory Council on the Status of Women. Strangely enough, the first federal ministers responsible for the condition of women were men, a strategy suggested by the women of the party themselves (Bégin 1992). The Secretary of State undertook to give generous financing to the major feminist associations in the country united under an umbrella organization, the National Action Committee (NAC). Under this policy, the large Quebec women's associations were inevitably relegated to a status of regional association, and the Quebec militants often found themselves marginalized within the Canadian women's associations. Images of this can be found in the leaflets of the organization. The English version presents a drawing of women in a circle under the heading 'NAC's members'. The French version shows a group of women with their backs to each other. Under the heading 'Funds', the English version is illustrated with figures of ten-dollar bills and the French version shows nickels and dimes! As the 1970s passed, there was less sharing of ideas between the feminists of the two linguistic groups. Radical feminism in Quebec was not on the same wave length as the rest of Canada (Black 1988; Lamoureux 1986). Furthermore, the Quebec feminists almost lost track of French-speaking feminist movements in other provinces. In those circumstances the referendum only crystallized attitudes and latent misunderstandings. At the time of the referendum in 1980, many Canadian women observed the speakers for the Yvettes and thought; 'In Quebec, feminists are federalists!'

The first crisis occurred in 1981 around the question of patriating the Constitution. A national conference on women and the constitution organized by the Liberal Party created a split among the feminists and the members of the Canadian Advisory Council on the Status of Women and was boycotted: this episode was called the Anderson-Axworthy duel (Baines 1988: 174-8). An ad hoc conference attracted hundreds of women from English Canada, but only two small groups came from Quebec: the Réseau d'Action et d'Information pour les Femmes (RAIF) and the Ligue des femmes du Québec. As in the 1980 referendum, the Liberal Party was at the origin of a split between women. The fact that English-Canadian feminists were united behind Doris Anderson's resignation from the presidency of the Advisory Council and that Lucie Pépin accepted the chair did not help to explain what was going on. Was it a nationalist or a feminist issue? As a member of the Fédération des femmes du Québec, was Lucie Pépin speaking in the name of Quebec feminists? She certainly had no mandate to do so. The subsequent events were due more to the gap between the two linguistic communities than to divergences in feminist principles. In March the FFQ delegates left the National Action Committee on the grounds that the Advisory Council should settle its problems alone and should not ask for Axworthy's resignation. They objected also that Quebec had not given approval to the patriated Constitution (Black 1992: 104). In June Claire Bonenfant, president of the Conseil du statut de la femme, took part in the official conference

organized by the Advisory Council. She certainly could not be seen as a fed-
eralist partisan. In Quebec, the RAIF stood alone with the other feminists of
English Canada against the nomination of Lucie Pépin, whose liberal leanings were suspect, as chair of the Advisory Council.

In this matter, everyone claimed to be speaking for women. It can be
suggested, however, that the real question was the whole process of the patri-
ation of the Constitution, since the Parti Québécois had been re-elected in
April 1981.

During the fall, the feminists of English Canada mobilized to have a
clause on the rights of women included in the Canadian Constitution. This
mobilization was called the 'taking of 28' (Kome 1983), and for the feminists
of English Canada it was a memorable struggle—which went nearly unno-
ticed in Quebec. The RAIF, which was the only Quebec group publicly active
in this matter, devoted the fall issue of its magazine (no. 69-70) to the question
with a 66-page report. The FFQ sent one telegram during the negotiations.

The new minister in Ottawa, Judy Erola, was facilitating the lobbying
(Erola 1986: 48), and the new minister for the condition of women in
Quebec, Pauline Marois, explained after Trudeau's gamble that isolated
Quebec: 'Women's solidarity . . . cannot be confused with uniformity, and
Quebec women must ask for a constitutional framework that respects the
specificity of Quebec. . . . It is the nearest government that can ensure the
most the protection of women's rights' (RAIF 1981: 72, my translation). As
Micheline De Sève suggests,

> The truth is that the claim for a specific amendment to the Constitution
> could not be approved by Quebec feminists, since the Constitution itself
> was not recognized as legitimate by our own democratic institutions in
> Quebec, women and men united. This was an English-Canadian issue
> which Quebec-identified feminists could not address without strong reser-
> vations. Furthermore, the issue was complicated by English Canadians'
> silence with respect to the lawfulness of the Quebec Charter of Human
> Rights and Freedoms. Feminists from Quebec had just obtained recognition
> of affirmative action programs in this provincial charter. It was not clear at
> the time if the Canadian equality proposal would be as strong as our own
> charter on this matter. (De Sève 1992: 114-15)

It is interesting to note that this event has disappeared from the collective memory in Quebec. Chronologies on Quebec feminism do not mention
it, nor do books on the same subject (Lamoureux 1986; Brodeur 1982). With
the exception of the RAIF the feminist periodical press of the time did not
mention the 'taking of 28'.[4] Obviously, Quebec women were not mobilized
on the issue. In 1981, it was before the provincial parliamentary commission
that the FFQ presented its important proposal for amending the Quebec
charter of human rights.

It might appear that Quebec women had rejected federal politics, but that was certainly not the case. In the 1984 elections, to the amazement of English Canada, Quebec sent 14 women to the House of Commons. Far from being elected by mistake, 13 were re-elected in 1989. During the more recent debate on abortion, they lobbied intensely in an attempt to defeat the bill that would have recriminalized abortion. All the women in the House of Commons took advantage of a free vote to vote against the bill. Though personally opposed to the voluntary interruption of a pregnancy, Gabrielle Bertrand said: 'Every woman has her own conscience, every woman has her freedom. Who am I to judge this woman as a criminal who for personal and different reasons decides to interrupt her pregnancy?' (Collectif Clio 1992: 546).

At the time of the Meech Lake Accord in 1987, the feminists of Canada assembled once again to examine its consequences for women. The differences then became evident. Barbara Roberts (1988) analysed their respective positions in *Smooth Sailing or Storm Warning*. The feminists of English Canada challenged the concept of the 'distinct society', which, in their eyes, could eventually threaten the rights of women. The feminists of Quebec thought that, on the contrary, they would be able to defend their rights vis-à-vis 'provincial' political institutions. In the words of the FFQ's brief,

> The women's groups outside of the Province of Quebec are usually much more distrustful of the provincial authorities than we are. . . . According to our analysis, the Meech Lake Agreement does not pose an explicit, nor even a potential threat to Quebec women's rights. . . . The concept of a distinct society is a neutral concept within the context of women's rights. . . . In Quebec, the respect of women's rights is more and more becoming part of the political culture. As a matter of fact, the progress we have made with regard to the status of women is linked to the concept of a distinct society. (FFQ Archives 1990)

This document marks a turning point in the history of the FFQ. For the first time, its feminist objectives were linked to a constitutional option. Three years later, the breach was completed. The Federation of the Women of Quebec withdrew again from NAC and the English-Canadian feminists realized that a common stand by all women's groups in Canada was impossible. For many Canadian women, it became obvious that women's issues, far from being marginal, were at the heart of the constitutional debate.

The Constitutional Debate after the Failure of the Meech Lake Accord (1990-1994)

The situation created by the defeat of the Meech Lake Accord in 1990 proved nevertheless that this conviction was not shared by the entire

Canadian political community. The constitutional debate pouring out of the media remained stubbornly androcentric. Women's groups were not invited to choose a representative to sit with the commissioners on the Bélanger-Campeau Commission. In reply to their protests, it was said, as Lorraine Pagé, a member of the Commission, reminds us:

> That they were exaggerating, that the point of view of women would be amply heard, amplified repeatedly at their appearance, and that it would most certainly be taken greatly into account. It was also brought out, said Pagé, that being a woman, a unionist, an educator, and a feminist, I could very well fill that function and assume that role. This should not give me the right to speak four times as often as my co-commissioners but we must believe that the system of double, triple, and quadruple tasks applies to extended parliamentary commissions. (Pagé 1990, translation by Carol Cochrane)

Still too few briefs were presented by women's groups: 16 out of 596. Moreover, they were totally eclipsed by the other briefs. Thus, in Sherbrooke, the media devoted considerable space to a group of 'Townshippers' demanding a land corridor between Ontario and New Brunswick in the event that Quebec seceded but hardly mentioned the two briefs presented by women's groups. The FFQ, on this occasion, made a clear sovereignist stand:

> 1. because we believe that Quebec's sovereignty will give the government the powers necessary to build the kind of society where the equality goals of the women's movement will be endorsed.
> 2. because we believe that women will have more chance to influence the government and to participate in it when the government is nearer. (FFQ Archives, 1990)

But the organization makes it clear that it is a non-partisan option: 'Our choice is related to a political project; it is not related to a political party. Our stand is political, but without allegiance to any party' (FFQ Archives 1990).

The commissioners required expert opinions. At the last minute, they realized that there were no women among the invited experts, and they hurried to find a few to add to the list. One hundred and nine people were approached, 24 of whom were women. From this number, 53, 10 of whom were women, agreed to present briefs. In fact, among all the briefs, only two broached the subject of women's rights.[5] In the end, the Bélanger-Campeau report contained one small paragraph on the question of women's equality.

At the beginning of fall 1991, two Quebec commissions, one appointed by the provincial government, the other by the Parti Québécois, attempted to find a solution to the constitutional impasse. Among the matters discussed, the issue of women simply did not appear. The pre-referendum debate showed clearly that it was difficult to associate the autonomy of women with national autonomy. The questions raised by the specialists were mainly economic. In the autumn of 1990, the two commissioners, Bélanger and Campeau, reminded everyone that the rules of the economic game, as we know them, are untouchable. Commenting on this statement, Lise Bissonnette (1990) wrote in *Le Devoir*: 'Quebec can well change its political status if it eventually decides to do so but it will not change its type of society. It must retain a fair and rational economic programme. Let it be said that there will always be an orthodoxy of money even if there is no longer a constitutional one' (translation by Carol Cochrane).

One must regret the narrowness of the path presented to the people of Quebec by the commission and in the subsequent discussions. In fact, few briefs mentioned the social and cultural problems that are inextricably related to the economy and the Constitution. These questions would, in all likelihood, be more difficult to manage and would require much more imagination and determination than the economic problems that have already been given so much consideration. Are the questions of women and of the political and constitutional future really unrelated? The women of Quebec still think that the two issues are linked.

In fact, in 1990, women had enthusiastically celebrated the fiftieth anniversary of obtaining the right to vote. The special event, 'Femmes en tête', was a great success even though it had been denounced by immigrant groups because it was chaired by Lise Payette, author of a controversial documentary, *Disparaître*, on immigration. If the nation was at stake after the failure of Meech Lake, the women's movement in Quebec was at a turning point too.

Once again the FFQ was at the centre of the debate. But the Quebec umbrella association was now going through important structural changes. First, as we have seen, its agenda had become quite radical. Second, the number of associations soliciting membership was growing: 35 in 1980, 58 in 1987, and 115 in 1992. This was the result of the transformation of feminism, a phenomenon that has been called strategic feminism (Collectif Clio 1992: 480-6). It characterizes the multiplicity of groups that are polarized on a specific issue (health, violence, family, law, immigrant women, women's economic needs, etc.) and dispersed in every cities. Third, the individual members of the FFQ were now busy women struggling with families and professions: they had less time for activism. In contrast, members from the associations were often salaried feminists, employed by organizations that provided services to women, and hence dependent on government funds. These changes explain how the leadership of the FFQ shifted from the individual members to the members from the associations.

This transformation took place in a political and administrative climate that was also changing. As we have seen, the FFQ had taken a sovereignist stand in its brief to the Bélanger-Campeau Commission in November

1990. But this political option was chosen after the board had been having organizational problems for several years.[6]

At the close of its orientation convention in 1991, before the referendum, the FFQ undertook to gather women's ideas on a feminist proposal for Quebec society. Quebec was at a turning point, and its women were eager to propose a new society.

> For years, we, the women of Quebec have questioned, imagined, written about, sung about, composed, demanded, and proposed our vision of the world. Some among us belong to an organization, a group, a political party; others not. Some advocate a constitutional preference, some do not. From the first of us to the last, we work daily on different levels, beyond our political allegiances, to diversify the approaches for attaining equality. United by our gender, strong through our differences, we agree in the plural. It is time for us, with our wide experience and our concerted efforts, to propose a society centred on people. (FFQ Archives 1992, translation by Carol Cochrane)

In the eyes of the women's movement, the future could not be reduced to a choice between two constitutional options. Many women felt it was essential to define the society in which they wanted to live and to choose the constitutional option that would best ensure that they attained it. Militants from various parts of the women's movement of Quebec had to agree on the principles that would serve as guidelines for a feminist proposal for society.

This project was called Un Québec féminin pluriel and was discussed by all women's groups on International Women's Day on 8 March 1992. Following that, a national forum took place in Montreal at the end of May of the same year and attracted more than 1,300 women.

The money to finance the event came from different sources: unions, the provincial council on the status of women, and the federal Secretary of State. All groups were there, from the traditionalist Cercles des fermières to the radical Syndicat des agricultrices; women from every ethnic group, from every union, from every 'regroupement'; and even members of the AFEAS who had never before taken part in a rally of this kind.

But the political path was narrow. On the one hand, individual delegates from the FFQ pleaded for a constitutional stand and a clear sovereignist declaration. On the other, the member organizations and the organizing committee knew this strategy would not be possible because it would break the consensus.

At the close of the meeting, the dream of a new super-coalition of all women's groups in Quebec, united and strong enough to influence the whole political process, was formed. From the workshops came a list of goals and means of action on key issues: economy, feminism, pluralism, state, power, and education.

In short, women were proposing a feminist framework for society: 'To speak of Quebec's political future is to speak of objectives we, as a community, wish to pursue: a fair, egalitarian, democratic, peaceable, and non-violent society, open to pluralism, healthy, and in charge of its own future. These are the values upon which the women's movement wishes to build our future' (FFQ Archives 1992, Québec féminin pluriel).

History moves on: the Charlottetown Agreement and the Canadian referendum of 1992; the federal election of 1993; the Quebec provincial election of 1994. But the outcome of the 'Québec féminin pluriel' project is not yet certain. The 1992 referendum was another example of the 'tension between non-partisan and independent feminism, on the one hand, and the demands of a party-structured parliamentary system on the other' (Bashevkin 1985). On that occasion, NAC's arguments and political stand on the constitutional proposal revealed a new understanding by English feminists of Quebec's demand. But while NAC recommended that its member vote No, the FFQ, which had made the same recommendation, was threatened with the loss of its grants from the Secretary of State. This was another example of manipulation by a political party, and Quebec feminists seemed more threatened than NAC. However, it was clear also that women were not united with respect to a solution. They were divided in English Canada and they were divided in Quebec.

In Quebec, a superficial analysis of the arguments, pro and con, formulated by various women, suggests that many No partisans were speaking mainly of women's issues and made their political decision on that basis. There was a Regroupement des Québécoises pour le Non (Association of Quebec Women for a No Vote). In contrast, women partisans of the Yes were mostly silent on women's issues. For them, those questions did not seem to fit easily into the constitutional jargon. Needless to say, the old traditional masculine discourse did not change at all. As a women's group said, 'On n'aurait rien dit que ça aurait été pareil' (What we said didn't make any difference). Do men listen to what women have to say?

In the political vacuum that emerged from the results of the 1992 referendum, is it possible to re-examine the links between Quebec feminism and Quebec nationalism? Is Diane Lamoureux right in claiming that 'nationalism provided women with a political vocabulary with which they could analyse their oppression' but in practice constitutes an 'impossible attraction' between the two political movements? (Lamoureux 1987: 51).

On the provincial scene, feminist politicians have been openly disappointed by the Parti Québécois (Payette 1982; Boily 1984). But women in the provincial Liberal Party are more critical of the women's movement than of their own political party (Maillé 1990: 151-78).

As we have seen, many activists, like those in the FFQ, take a soveignist stand because of their feminist involvement. They refer to a new collective image of Quebec that is more 'autonomist' than 'nationalist'.

This is the position of Claire Bonenfant, who explains the stand of the FFQ:

In concentrating our action on the provincial level, we have made real progress on the women question, progress that is not out of keeping with the distinct character of Quebec. From a feminist standpoint, we understand the importance of autonomy and identity. Those aims were and still are at the heart of women's struggle. We know the price of autonomy, but we also know its value. (FFQ Archives 1991)

On the federal scene, the 'taking of 28' in 1981 has led many analysts to ask whether it was a real gain for women (Buist 1988; Brodsky and Day 1989; Gotell 1990; Black 1992). And the critics come mainly from women's groups. Women active in federal politics find women's groups too critical. They seem reluctant to criticize their own party (Erola 1986; Bégin 1992).

Since 1984 Quebec women active in the main Canadian parties have not made many statements about women's issues, and it is regrettable that this question has never really been examined. Obviously, there are not many links between them and Quebec women's groups. The only exception has been the abortion bill.

If the 1980s saw the institutionalization of feminist demands both in Canada and Quebec (Findlay 1988; Lamoureux 1988), it can also be observed that 'the site of struggle has shifted or has been shifted from the parliamentary sphere to the bureaucracy and the criminal justice system' (Findlay 1988: 8).

In this new conjuncture, the recent episode of Québec féminin pluriel illustrates the contradictions in the Quebec women's movement. Can women from 'institutionalized feminism' or 'services for women' maintain the leadership of a pressure group? Can a super-coalition of women's groups be a real political tool? And most important: is a sovereigntist option the basis for political action for women's issues? In November 1993, the shift of power within the FFQ was clearly formalized by a new constitution and a new orientation that gave more importance to demands by groups representing disadvantaged women, by giving them more votes (Boileau 1994: 29). With this change, individual members lost their leadership. Three out of five 'regional councils' consisting of individual members were disbanded, notably the Montreal Council, which was largely responsible for the constitutional policy. During the provincial electoral campaign, in August 1994, the FFQ initiated the 'Women Coalition 94', which questioned the two leaders 'on the policy they intend to put in place in order to construct Quebec for the year 2000, considering women's values and realities' (FFQ Archives 1994). But the FFQ no longer mentioned the question of sovereignty. This question will remained unanswered as long as the whole political class does not understand what has really happened in Quebec since 1960. All the economic and cultural changes occurred concurrently with the transformations in the status and condition of women. We must ask whether the former would have been possible without the latter.

Now, thirty years later, it may be the time for the male decision makers of the Quebec nation to invite women decision makers to take part in their deliberations. Among all the transformations that have taken place, one of the most important is that the aspirations and the values of the female half of the population have changed. Women are marching towards autonomy. This fact is clearly demonstrated by all the statistics on education, economy, family, and demography. How can it not be recognized that henceforth the autonomy of women is an integral part of the new Quebec identity and that it can no longer be ignored. The participation of women in politics, the integration of issues affecting women into the political agenda, and most of all, the new conception and organization of power will be a sign of a real revolution. At the present time, it requires great faith and hope to believe that could happen.

APPENDIX

Briefs submitted to various government bodies by the Fédération des Femmes du Québec since 1979

L'avortement (1990)
Mémoire de la FFQ présenté au Comité parlementaire sur le projet de loi C-43.

La réforme électorale et le financement des partis (1990)
Mémoire de la FFQ à la Commission royale sur la réforme électorale et le financement des partis.

Front de défense des non syndiqué-e-s (1990)
Présenté à la Commission des affaires sociales dans le cadre de l'étude de l'avant-projet de loi.

Regroupement pour des congés de maternité et parentaux (1990)
Mémoire présenté à la Commission des affaires sociales concernant l'avant-projet de loi modifiant la Loi sur les normes du travail et d'autres dispositions législatives.

Sages-femmes (1989)
Présentation de la FFQ devant la Commission des affaires sociales de l'Assemblée nationale dans le·cadre du projet de loi 4 'Loi sur la pratique des sages-femmes dans le cadre des projets-pilotes'.

Pour un meilleur équilibre (Services de garde) (1989)
Mémoire préparé pour la consultation générale afin d'étudier ce document.

Pour une politique de sécurité du revenu (1988)
Mémoire préparé pour la consultation générale afin d'étudier ce document.

Les droits économiques des conjoints (1988)
Mémoire préparé pour la consultation générale sur le document et présenté à la Commission des institutions et à l'Assemblée nationale.

Loi sur le cinéma et le vidéo (1988)
Mémoire présenté par le Front commun contre la pornographie à la Commission permanente des affaires culturelles sur le projet de loi 109.

Les femmes et la fiscalité (1987)
Présentation lors de la rencontre organisée par la Ministre déléguée à la condition féminine du Québec.

Accord constitutionnel de 1987 (lac Meech) (1987)
Présentation de la FFQ devant le Comité mixte du Sénat et de la Chambre des communes.

L'emploi et la formation (1987)
Mémoire présenté au sous-comité du Sénat.

Propositions sur le logement et les sans-abri à Montréal (1987)
Document présenté au Comité exécutif de la ville de Montréal par le Comité conjoint de la FFQ.

Secrétariat d'État (1987)
Présentation de la F.F.Q. devant le Comité permanent sur le Secrétariat d'État.

Les municipalités (1986)
Mémoire présenté à la Commission d'études sur les municipalités.

Santé et services sociaux (1986)
Mémoire aux audiences de la Commission d'enquête sur la santé et les services sociaux.

Assurance chômage (1986)
Mémoire à la Commission d'enquête sur le régime d'assurance chômage.

L'équité en matière d'emploi (1985)
Mémoire conjoint de la FFQ et de PANFD sur le projet de loi C-62 concernant l'équité en matière d'emploi.

Allocations familiales (1985)
Mémoire présenté au Comité législatif sur le projet C-70 modifiant la loi de 1973 sur les allocations familiales.

Accès à l'égalité (1985)
Mémoire à la Commission parlementaire des institutions sur le projet de règlement concernant les programmes d'accès à l'égalité.

Politique familiale (1985)
Mémoire présenté par le Comité famille de la FFQ aux audiences de consultation sur la politique familiale.

Travail (1984)
Mémoire présenté à la Commission consultative sur le travail (Commission Beaudry).

Étude de la pornographie et de la prostitution (1984)
Mémoire présenté devant le Comité Fraser.

Les femmes et le collège (1984)
Mémoire présenté au Conseil des collèges.

L'union économique et les perspectives d'emploi au Canada (1983)
Mémoire à la Commission royale.

Mode de scrutin (1983)
Mémoire à la Commission de la représentation électorale du Québec.

Émissions à tendances sexuelles abusives (1983)
Mémoire au sous-comité sur les émissions à tendances sexuelles abusives du Comité permanent des communications et de la culture.

Les femmes et la réforme des régimes de retraite (1983)
Mémoire au Comité de la Réforme des régimes de retrait.

Garderies (1982)
Rappel des prises de positions sur les garderies suivi de commentaires sur le document de consultation soumis par l'Office des services de garde à l'enfance.

Travail à temps partiel (1982)
Mémoire à la Commission d'enquête sur le travail à temps partiel.

Microtechnologie et emploi (1982)
Mémoire au groupe d'étude sur la microtechnologie et l'emploi.

Modification de la Charte des droits de la personne du Québec (1981)
Mémoire à la Commission parlementaire.

Cinéma et audiovisuel (1981)
Mémoire à la Commission d'étude sur le Cinéma et l'audio-visuel.

Formation des adultes (1981)
Mémoire à la Commission d'étude sur l'éducation des adultes (Commission Jean).

Réforme du droit de la famille (projet de loi 89) (1980)
Mémoire au Ministre de la Justice du Québec sur la loi instituant un nouveau Code civil.

Divorce (1980)
Propositions relatives à la loi sur le divorce.

Infractions sexuelles (1979)
Commentaires sur le rapport de la Commission sur la réforme du droit au Canada.

Réforme du droit de la famille (1979)
Mémoire au comité chargé de la révision du Code Civil pour le droit de la famille.

NOTES

A first version of this chapter was published, in French, in *Zeitschrift für Kanada-Studien*, the journal of the Gesellschaft für Kanada-Studien, in 1992. The present version has been extended considerably.

1 In 1931, *Vive la Canadienne*; in 1943, *Hommage à la mère canadienne*; and in 1961, *Hommage à la femme canadienne-française*.

2 I have used mainly the various publications of the federation: *Bulletin de la Fédération des femmes du Québec* (1969-80); FFQ *Petite Presse* (1981-87); *Le féminisme en revue* (1987-92); *Le féminisme en bref* (from 1990); and briefs presented to various commissions and committees; and papers from the project Québec féminin pluriel. (See note 7.)

3 AFEAS was created in 1966 from the amalgamation of two traditional groups : the *Union catholique des femmes rurales* (UCFR) and the *Cercles d'économie domestique* (CED), founded, respectively, in 1945 and 1952.

4 In the television series *Democracy*, Patrick Watson gave a good illustration of this situation. All six programs were translated except the one on feminism. It was shown in two different versions. The English version was about 'the taking of 28' and the French version concentrated on the ideas and actions of Lise Payette.

5 Diane Lamoureux, a political scientist at Laval University presented 'Mémoire sur l'avenir politique et constitutionnel du Québec', and Micheline Dumont, a historian at Sherbrooke University presented 'L'expérience historique des femmes'.

6 There were two short presidencies in the year 1989-90. The following year, the organization was run by a 'collective' chair. During those years, the FFQ had serious financial and administrative difficulties.

7 Québec féminin pluriel has published many documents, including the following:

Un Québec féminin* pluriel. Pour un projet féministe de société *Le féminin comprend le masculin. (1991).
Texte d'appel. Synthèse des travaux du Forum (Mai 1992).
Éléments de réflexion en vue d'un regroupement national du mouvement des femmes au Québec (Nov. 1992).
Pour changer le monde. Le Forum pour un Québec feminin pluriel (Montreal: Les Éditions Écosociété, Dec. 1994).

BIBLIOGRAPHY

Baines, Beverley (1988), 'Women and the Law'. In *Changing Patterns: Women in Canada*, eds S. Burt, L. Code, and L. Dorney (Toronto: McClelland and Stewart), 157-83.

Backhouse, Constance, and David H. Flaherty (1992), *Challenging Times: The Women's Movement in Canada and in the United States* (Montreal and Kingston: McGill-Queen's University Press).

Bashevskin, Sylvia (1985), *Toeing the Lines: Women and Party Politics in English Canada* (Toronto: University of Toronto Press).

Bégin, Monique (1992), 'The Royal Commission on the Status of Women in Canada: Twenty Years Later'. In Backhouse and Flaherty (1992), 21-38.

Bissonnette, Lise (1990), 'Le minimum de courant commun', *Le Devoir*, 7 Nov.

Black, Naomi (1988), 'The Canadian Women's Movement: The Second Wave'. In Baines (1988), 80-102.

—— (1992), 'Ripples in the Second Wave: Comparing the Contemporary Women's Movement in Canada and the United States'. In Backhouse and Flaherty (1992), 94-109.

Blais, André (1980), 'Le vote: ce qu'on en sait, ce qu'on n'en sait pas'. In *Québec: un pays incertain: Réflexions sur le Québec post-référendaire* (Montreal: Québec/Amérique), 157-82.

Boileau, Josée (1994), 'Un vent de renouveau souffle sur la FFQ', *Gazette des Femmes* 15, no. 6: 29.

Boily, Nicole (1984), 'Les femmes en politique, encore une exception', *Politiques* 5: 7-25.

Brodsky, Gwen, and Shelagh Day (1989): *Canadian Charter Equality Rights for Women: One Step Forward or Two Steps Back* (Ottawa: Canadian Advisory Council on the Status of Women).

Brodeur, Violette, et al. (1982), *Le Mouvement des femmes au Québec* (Montréal: Centre de formation populaire).

Buist, Margaret (1988), 'Elusive Equality: Women and the Charter of Rights and Freedoms', *Feminist Perspectives on the Canadian State/Perspectives féministes sur l'État canadien* (Resources for Feminist Research/Documentation sur la recherche féministe), 17, no. 3: 103-5.

Collectif Clio (1992), *Histoire des femmes au Québec depuis quatre siècles* (Montreal: Jour).

De Sève, Micheline (1985), *Le féminisme libertaire* (Montreal: Boréal).

—— (1992), 'The Perspectives of Quebec Feminists'. In Backhouse and Flaherty (1992): 110-16.

Dandurand, Renée, and Evelyn Tardy (1982), 'Le Phénomène des Yvettes à travers quelques quotidiens'. In *Femmes et politique*, ed. Y. Cohen (Montreal: Jour).

Dumont, Micheline (1990), 'Les Yvettes ont permis aux femmes d'entrer dans l'histoire politique', *L'Action nationale* 71, no. 8: 1041-5.

Echols, Alice (1989), *Daring to be Bad: Radical Feminism in America, 1967-1975* (Minneapolis: University of Minnesota Press).

Erola, Judy (1986), 'Women in the eighties'. In *The Forty-Ninth and other Parallels* (Boston: University of Massachusetts Press), 41-53.

Evans, Sara (1979): *Personal Politics: The Roots of Women's Liberation in the Civil Rights Movement and the New Left* (New York: Knopf).

Findlay, Sue (1988), 'Feminist Struggles with the Canadian State, 1966-1988', *Feminist Perspectives on the Canadian State* (RFR/DRF), 17, no. 3: 103-5.

Gotell, Lise (1990): *The Canadian Women's Movement, Equality Rights and the Charter* (Ottawa: Canadian Research Institute for the Advancement of Women/Institut Canadien de Recherche sur les Femmes).

Greer, Allan (1991), 'La république des hommes: les Patriotes de 1837 face aux femmes', *Revue d'histoire de l'Amérique française* 44, no. 4: 507-28.

Kome, Penney (1983), *The Taking of Twenty-Eight: Women Challenge the Constitution* (Toronto: Women's Educational Press).

Lamoureux, Diane (1986), *Fragments et Collages: Essai sur le féminisme québécois des années 70* (Montreal: Remue-Ménage).

―――― (1987), 'Nationalism and Feminism in Quebec: An Impossible Attraction'. In *Feminism and Political Economy: Women's Work, Women's Struggle*, eds H.J. Maroney and M. Luxton (Toronto: Methuen) 51-68.

―――― (1988), 'De la quête de l'argent de poche au renforcement de l'État-providence', in *Feminist Perpectives on the Canadian State* (RFR/DRF), 17, no. 3: 72-5.

Lanctôt, Martine (1980), *Genèse et évolution du mouvement féministe à Montréal*, MA thesis, Université du Québec à Montréal.

Laurin, Nicole, et al. (1992), *À la recherche d'un monde oublié: Les communautés religieuses de femmes au Québec, de 1900 à 1970* (Montreal: Jour).

Lavigne, Marie, et Yolande Pinard (1983), *Travailleuses et féministes: Les femmes dans la société québécoise* (Montréal: Boréal Express).

Lavigne, Marie, et al. (1983), 'La Fédération nationale Saint-Jean-Baptiste et les revendications féministes au début du 20e siècle', in Lavigne and Pinard (1983), 199-216.

Maillé, Chantal (1990), *Les Québécoises et la conquête du pouvoir politique* (Montreal: Saint-Martin).

Morgan, Cecilia (1991), 'When Bad Men Conspire, Good Men Must Unite: Gender, Reform and Rebellion in Upper Canada', paper presented to the Canadian Historical Association, Kingston.

O'Leary, V., and L. Toupin (1982): *Québécoises deboutte!* (Montreal: remue-ménage), 2 vols.

Ouellette, Françoise-Romaine (1980), *Les groupes de femmes du Québec en 1985: champs d'intervention, structures et moyens d'action* (Quebec City: Conseil du statut de la femme).

Pagé, Lorraine (1990), 'Les femmes dans le Québec de demain', *Le Devoir*, 7 Mar.

Payette, Lise (1982), *Le pouvoir, connais pas!* (Montreal: Québec/Amérique).

Pinard, Yolande (1983), 'Les débuts du mouvement des femmes à Montréal, 1893-1902', in Lavigne and Pinard (1983), 177-98.

Quebec (1991), Commission sur l'avenir politique et constitutionnel du Québec [Commission Bélanger-Campeau], *Rapport* (Quebec City).

RAIF, *Bulletin du Réseau d'Action et d'Information pour les Femmes*, no. 69-70 (1981): 'La Marche de l'égalité et ses aventures', 17-83.

Roberts, Barbara (1988), *Smooth Sailing or Storm Warning: Canadian and Quebec Women's Groups and the Meech Lake Accord*, CRIAW Feminist Perspectives, no. 12 (Ottawa: CRIAW).

Rowbotham, Sheila (1972), *Women, Resistance and Revolution* (London, Penguin).

Tardy, Evelyn (1980), 'Les femmes et la campagne référendaire'. In Blais (1980), 185-203.

Tremblay, Manon (1990), 'Les élues du 31e Parlement du Québec et les mouvements féministes: de quelques affinités idéologiques', *Politiques*, no. 16: 87-109.

Trofimenkoff, Susan Mann (1982), *The Dream of Nation: A Social and Intellectual History of Quebec* (Toronto: Macmillan).

PART III

Portraying Gender

CHAPTER 9

The Portrayal of Women Politicians in the Media

Political Implications

Gertrude Robinson and Armande Saint-Jean

Most studies of the media's coverage of women politicians give an ahistorical description of particular individuals in a specific campaign. Usually these studies concentrate on the 'biases' that sneak into these reports. But the term 'bias', as is well known, is difficult to define. Usually it refers either to an absolute standard against which the media are supposed to be measurable, or, more critically, it is viewed as a process of creating meaning which is, itself, embedded within certain social power structures. Since all news reports are written from a 'point of view' the term 'bias' fails to illuminate the assumption on which a report is based. And finally, studies of media coverage of women politicians are often methodically flawed in that they are based on content categories that are imposed on, rather than emerge from, the material itself.

The purpose of this study is to move from the descriptive level to a contextualized analysis that permits us to explain how Canadian women politicians have been publicly portrayed and discussed. It therefore seeks to answer the following three more general questions:

- Has there been a *change* over a 30-year period in the way in which the activities of Canadian women politicians have been reported?
- What are the narrative characteristics that differentiate the descriptions of female politicians from those of male politicians?
- What are the implications of these different narrative styles for a female incumbent's ability to legitimate herself politically?

THEORETICAL SETTING

In Canadian political life, three generations of women politicians can be distinguished. The first, our interviews show, were born in the 1920s, the second in the 1940s, and the third in the 1960s. Each of these generations was thus born into a unique historical time with its own attitudes towards women's role in public life. The relationship between each of those three cohorts of women politicians and the media descriptions of them is determined by the women's movement's own understanding of its goals, which have undergone a three-stage development (Descarries and Roy 1988). In the 'egalitarian reformist' stage of the 1960s, well-educated, older professional women, as well as younger activists, spontaneously joined together to analyse the malaise that had 'no name' (Friedan 1963). Action and consciousness-raising groups studied the meaning of 'equality' in the legal realm and the workplace. Because the movement was so young, there were few avowed feminists among the first generation of Canadian women politicians. They assumed that they were being treated equally and therefore concentrated on the implications of their own minority status and the relation of women to the state. In Canada, this decade was important because it led to the appointment in 1967 of the Royal Commission on the Status of Women, which drew attention to women's changing position in society and, in 1970, presented 166 recommendations for making women more equal to men in Canadian life (Brown 1989: 143-4).

After its early focus on gender equality, the women's movement in its second period (the 1970s) became radicalized and, spurred on by student demonstrations in the United States and Europe, and the anti-war sentiments engendered by the Vietnam War, it turned to issues of systematic discrimination. For second-cohort women politicians, it became clear that their minority status was not an accident, but the result of inadequate access to federal party structures and party support. Consequently, they called for women's networks in the major Canadian parties and for an active search for women to take part in party caucuses and election campaigns.

By the beginning of the 1980s, the neo-conservative backlash that coincided with the Reagan and Thatcher regimes once again changed the emphasis of the North America women's movement. Women's groups now focused directly on social and political issues and split up into various interest groups. Third-generation women politicians reflected this diversity in their own party ranks, with the Liberals and Progressive Conservatives less open than the New Democrats to the recruitment of women. The 'pluralistic feminism' of the 1980s also penetrated media descriptions, which were sensitized by organizations like Media Watch, meetings of feminist activists with editors, and demands from other women's groups for fairer reporting (Schneider 1988: 9).

In the 1980s the proportion of women among political candidates reached about 20 per cent, and party restructuring haltingly began. Our interviews suggest that, for the first time, a new breed of third-generation, self-declared feminist politicians was being elected. Unlike the other two generations, many of these women viewed politics as a career for which specific qualifications were necessary. Such qualifications did not have to be acquired through long years of party work, as before, but could be gained through scholarly, legal, or business training. In the process, the militant feminists, the original trail-blazers, vanished from the public scene.

In addition to the generational analysis, this study also makes use of the 'minority' approach to explain the different status in their parties that the three groups of women politicians enjoyed. This approach, which maps power structures, draws attention to the fact that internal party structures and the 'culture' of politics were created by men for men. They are thus neither easy to penetrate nor comfortable to work in for women aspiring to hold office (Brodie 1985; Bashevkin 1985). The kinds of barriers that political parties place in the way of women candidates become an important index of women politicians' inequality in the political realm.

To sketch the connections between women's changing social position in Canada and the symbolic legitimation of women's participation in public life, our pilot project also undertook a narrative analysis. In this analysis we probed both the context of the media's descriptions and the patterns these descriptions formed. Such an analysis permits us to link the changing media portrayals of women politicians to the three historical periods in which they occurred. This analysis shows that the media used different kinds of narrative for female politicians at different times in the 30-year period. Three different kinds of narrative styles can be distinguished: the traditional 'first-woman' approach, the current special-interest 'transitional' narrative, and a new 'egalitarian' discourse, which began to emerge in the late 1980s, that invokes not gender but competence as the main characteristic by which both male and female incumbents will be judged. The narrative patterns were derived from 250 newspaper and magazine articles published over the 30-year period. Each of these reports was analysed for choice of adjectives, nouns, and personal characteristics associated with women politicians; gender focus—type of headline used; and topics associated with women politicians. Together these characteristics form the basis for describing the generational stereotypes of women politicians.

The generational, minority, and narrative analyses demonstrate that the media institutions and the journalists associated with them are not merely passive mirrors of the Canadian scene but active participants in the continuing process of social change.

WOMEN POLITICIANS AND THEIR COVERAGE BY THE MEDIA

Political Barriers: Scanty Coverage of Women Politicians

Much has been written about the minority status of women politicians in Canada. It is sufficient to remember, here, that at both the provincial and federal levels, the number of women elected was insignificant until 1970.

During the last two decades, however, women have made substantial gains, so that in 1988, they made up 19.5 per cent of all federal candidates and 13.2 per cent of all federal MPs. At the provincial level, the representation of women politicians varied from an insignificant 2 per cent in Newfoundland, to 19 per cent in Quebec, to a maximum of 22 per cent in Ontario. Even though these figures constitute progress for women politicians, they show that Canada has only about half the female political representation of Scandinavian countries, such as Sweden, where 38 per cent of members of parliament are women. Sociologists have suggested that it takes a threshold of between 20 and 30 per cent for a minority to succeed in improving its access to a gendered profession like politics.

The implications, for media coverage, of politicians' minority status are twofold: women politicians have virtually no visibility in three of the country's 10 provinces; and even the women politicians who are elected constitute a very small subgroup of candidates available for media attention. Because women are rarely selected for strategic and visible party positions, they also receive less media exposure *before* they become candidates. This disproportion is the outcome of two sets of gender-related party practices: women candidates have unequal access to the parties' available seats, and they are assigned in disproportionately high numbers to run in 'lost-cause' ridings (Brodie 1985: 113-17). Furthermore, female candidates are usually unable to contest all open seats. In the 1988 federal election, women were able to contest only 133 out of a total of 263 seats (Burt 1988: 154; Brodie and Vickers 1982: 19-22). Data collected by François-Pierre Gingras show that the picture improved somewhat in the 1993 federal election in that 22 per cent of all candidates were women; nevertheless, 56 of the 295 ridings had no women candidate.

Both of these gender-related constraints have serious consequences for the media coverage of female contenders. The electronic media, with scarce personnel and a 'games' approach to election coverage, associate 'winning' with male politicians, while women politicians, whose campaigns are often for 'lost-cause' ridings, are associated with the 'Flora syndrome'. Sheila Copps had to contend with this phenomenon in her 1982 campaign against David Peterson for the leadership of the Ontario Liberal Party. Although she obtained many votes, she was never credited with having done well in the campaign nor with having leadership potential. The scarcity of female contenders also helps to keep women from becoming visible in electoral campaigns unless their party achieves a surprise upset. Together, these gender-linked party barriers translate into additional biases against women politicians in the media.

A third set of gender filters that affect female, but not male, politicians arises from the unique narrative styles that the largely male reporters use in relation to women politicians. Just as politics, until recently, was a largely male activity, so, too, has broadcast journalism been a male profession with traditional notions about women's place in society (Jeffrey 1989; MacBeth-Williams et al. 1986). A historical comparison, based on generational analysis, permits us to make a connection between changes in ways of thinking and professional reporting and, thus, to identify changes in reportorial styles concerning women politicians (Lee 1989).

The Traditional Narrative (before 1970): Focus on Biology

In the period up to 1970, society generally assumed that women's 'natural' place was in the home, while the public sphere of politics, business, and work was inhabited by men. Although the Second World War had drawn more women into the paid labour force, the ideology of the 1950s reverted to the conservative outlook (Friedan 1963). Not until the late 1960s did larger numbers of women, both with and without children, enter the labour force to help cover the rising costs of a middle-class standard of living. At that time, as we have seen, the North American women's movement was in its infancy, and the contradictions between women's public work and private family roles were not yet well understood. The lack of women MPs indicates the formidable barrier which the traditional role assignment represented for women's recruitment (before 1970) into the male domain of Canadian politics. Only 17 women were elected to Parliament in the 50 years between 1920 and 1970. Clearly, these social attitudes also affected the ways in which the first generation of women politicians, among them Pauline Jewett, Judy LaMarsh, and Flora MacDonald, were written about.

The traditional narrative style concentrates on women's 'biological difference' and describes women politicians as 'first woman' and 'token' in the non-traditional domain of politics (Robinson 1978). The traditional topic assignment associated with the first-woman approach also leads male reporters to query female politicians on a small number of 'women's' issues. These include social welfare, education, and health rather than the 'hard' issues of economics and foreign affairs. Flora MacDonald was distressed by this restricted reportorial topic assignment after the Iranian hostage crisis in which she played a crucial but unacknowledged role as Canada's Minister for External Affairs.

In addition to restricting the topic assignment, which marginalizes women politicians and their interests, the traditional narrative style undervalues women politicians' professional backgrounds and wide-ranging capacities. 'First-woman' reporting highlights primarily the *biological* characteristics and *family relationship* of the female politician and ignores her training and professional qualifications. Judy LaMarsh (1968: 303) reports, in her memoirs *A Bird in a Gilded Cage*, that 'columnists asked me about anything and everything except about my job. . . . My home, my cooking, my hobbies, my friends, my tastes, my likes and dislikes, all became public property to a degree suffered by none of my colleagues, including the Prime Minister [Trudeau].' When women politicians are constructed as gender 'tokens', they are also assumed to be undergoing a great deal of strain caused by the supposed conflict between their political and family responsibilities. Both Flora MacDonald and Judy LaMarsh report that they were frequently asked by reporters, 'Are you a politician or a woman?' as though the two were mutually exclusive.

Through the first-woman lens, women politicians become identified as the 'other', as those who are different, though their biographies show that they have more in common with male politicians than with other professionals. Women politicians are equal to their male counterparts in their level of education; they have professional backgrounds in law, political science, and management, and have usually worked more years in their parties and ridings (Brodie 1985: 60) than the male contenders. Yet, in spite of this, their *visible biological difference* becomes the primary point of reference. Judy LaMarsh (1968: 305) sums it up this way: 'Where there are twenty-five men, the public's interest is split; when there is one woman, she becomes a focus for criticism and for curiosity.'

Communications theorists have pointed out that reporters, who are short of time and are given too little space for their stories, condense social complexity into a series of colourful typifications. These stereotypes, which crystallize socially accepted values and expectations, change over time. Because the public role of the first generation of women politicians was considered to be in conflict with their private lives, the descriptions of them in the 1960s were designed to 'normalize' these presumed social contradictions between their biology and their public role. Two kinds of stereotypes were used for this normalization. The first, which describes the woman politician in terms of her family relationships, obliterates her political contributions. Women MPs like Martha Black (1935-40) and Cora Casselman (1941-45), who were *elected* to Parliament, were represented as the wife or widow, and thus as appendages of powerful husbands whose seats, it is implied, they inherited. This suggested that they held power, not in their own right, but in someone else's name.

The second set of stereotypes—*spinster, women of easy virtue,* and *club women*—achieved the same obliteration of qualifications by focusing on a female politician's sexual characteristics, instead of her political capacities. In politics, the label 'spinster' serves to describe someone who is single, has liberal ideas, and is free of the obligations usually expected of a wife (Gray 1989: 19). Women politicians viewed through this lens are portrayed as serious, preachy, competent, and hard-working because they lack household responsibilities. The label was applied regularly to Flora MacDonald, Pat Carney, Pauline Jewett, among others. Carole-Marie Allard (1987: 106) catches the negativism implied in this label: 'Comments can label the woman MP. If she is a widow, she is suspected of having killed her husband. If she is divorced, she is unstable. If married, she neglects her husband, and if single, she is abnormal' (our translation). Not only were these female politicians' governmental activities implicitly belittled by this label, but three of them acknowledged that reporters had had the audacity to ask them *explicitly* about their sex lives. A male contender would have been shocked to be asked such an improper question. Linda Goyette (1986), quoting Susan Crean, puts it well: '"The reigning notion is that if you're a man, sex comes with the territory. If you're a woman, you're expected to be celibate."'

The 'woman of easy virtue' label is attached to, and stigmatizes, women politicians who do not play by the traditional social rules. This label, like all others, highlights a woman's gender and looks rather than her competence. The coverage of Claire Kirkland-Casgrain, who in 1964 introduced the revolutionary Bill 16, giving full legal status to married women in Quebec, is an excellent example of this kind of reporting. Under the headline 'A Striking Political Heroine Plans to Save Quebec Women from Their Medieval Bondage', the *Financial Post* commented: 'This charming champion of women's rights, herself the first woman ever elected to the Quebec legislature, has brought two years of campaigning to a climax with a bill she describes as the first step towards first-class citizenship for Quebec women. . . . The lady from Jacques Cartier . . . is a lot easier on the eyes than any of the current inhabitants of [Quebec's] Red Chamber' (Booth 1964).

One final label, that of the 'club woman', is applied to women politicians who espouse opinions that are in opposition to those of the male establishment in Parliament and elsewhere. Although this label is not as negative as the other two, it is by far the most tenacious put-down. It suggests that women politicians are amateurs in the public realm and that their opinions should therefore be disregarded. An extreme example of this type of reporting can be found in the Trois-Rivières newspaper, *Le bien public*, which suggested Thérèse Casgrain should tend to her knitting and return to her hearth. 'Let her cook, sew, embroider, card wool, play bridge—anything rather than persist in her dangerous role of issuer of directives' (quoted in Casgrain 1972: 107).

Biology also provides the basis for the gender stereotyping of certain departments and portfolios that were considered suitable for women incumbents. Women from the first generation were initially entrusted with the departments of Health (LaMarsh), Social Services (Fairclough), Citizenship and Immigration (Fairclough), and Communications (Sauvé). Lester Pearson made a biological classification when he found nothing wrong with ignoring the external affairs qualifications of Pauline Jewett on gender grounds. 'When in 1965 Jewett expressed her dissatisfaction at not receiving a cabinet appointment, Pearson told her: "You know we already have a woman in the Cabinet." "Prime Minister," Pauline urged, "let's have two . . . or three . . . or whatever!" But it was not to be' (Anderson 1987: 44). It took until the late 1970s to open up the 'hard' and powerful ministries to female incumbents. Monique Bégin became Minister of National Revenue in 1977; Flora MacDonald, Minister for External Affairs in 1979; Ursula Appolloni,

Parliamentary Secretary to the Minister of Defence in 1980; and Jeanne Sauvé, first female Speaker of the House of Commons in 1980.

Until the late 1960s, there were so few women politicians that they were generally considered the exception to the norm, as tokens in the male world of politics. Their aberrant position was reinforced in the media representations of women politicians who confused 'gender' with 'competence'. Media descriptions that are based on the fixed characteristics of biology erase the fact that gender is a *socially constructed* and therefore changeable set of characteristics that are anchored in the male gaze. The emphasis on gender creates special expectations with respect to the looks, figure, hair colour, and clothing of a woman politician. It also leads to confusion between gender and political substance. One article, entitled 'Un ministre bien chapeauté,' notes, 'Our immigration minister Mrs Ellen Fairclough travels, meets people and wears a hat much more often than do the majority of Canadians. Since becoming a federal cabinet minister in 1957, Mrs Fairclough has travelled some 240,000 miles, mostly in Canada, and has worn more than three dozen hats' (*La Presse*, 18 January 1962 [our translation]). Such a narrative construction systematically erases women's contributions to political life, and also implies that these contributions are less important solely because they have been made by women.

The 'Transitional' Narrative (1970-90): Focus on Power

In the 20 years between 1970 and 1990, political scientists point out, the public's view of women's place in society has changed dramatically. Three events, as we have seen, contributed to this change: the report of the Royal Commission on the Status of Woman (1970); the changing market requirements of the post-industrial society; and the growth and radicalization of the women's movement since the 1980s. The Status of Women report explicitly called on the parties to recruit more women into politics (Kieran 1968: 42). The post-industrial economy, with its multiplication of service jobs, propelled 68 per cent of married women and 54 per cent of mothers into the labour market and created the concept of the 'working mother' (Bashevkin 1983: 147-8). Women's experiences outside the home led to calls for pay equity in the 1970s and government initiatives for full legal equality in the 1980s (Burt et al. 1988: 140-1). The 1982 Charter debate furthermore made women's groups realize the need for political input by women. Only concerted action by female legislators and grassroots lobbying by women's groups together made women's opinions important enough to solicit (Hosek 1989: 507).

The support for women's legal equality led to qualified public acceptance of women in the political sphere. Although there is as yet little active support for women candidates in the Liberal and Conservative parties, the NDP adopted gender criteria for various party positions in the 1970s (Brown 1989: 144). Consequently the number of women politicians has grown to about 20 per cent in at least three provincial legislatures and to an average of 20 to 30 per cent in the municipal governments of Canada's major cities (Vancouver, Toronto, Montreal, and Halifax) (Lavigne 1990: 5; Maillé 1990: 14). These figures show that since the 1980s, women legislators, at least at the municipal level, are coming close to the 'take-off' point where a minority can begin to effect institutional change.

Two additional social factors have profoundly influenced women's political power in both the United States and Canada. The first was an increase in the percentage of women who vote, the second, an emergent difference in the way women and men vote. Together these became known as the 'gender gap'. In the United States, the differential voter turnout, which amounted to 10 per cent in favour of men in 1950, has been reversed. By 1984 women had a 7 per cent lead over men in voter participation (Mueller 1988b: 22). In Canada, Janine Brodie (1985: 126) noted a similar numerical shift in favour of women and, in addition, discovered that by 1983 women preferred the Liberal Party by a margin of 10 per cent. Flora MacDonald confirmed that all parties in the 1984 election campaign took this gender gap extremely seriously, because it seemed to suggest that women were voting as an interest group.

The 'transitional' narrative approach takes account of these socio-political shifts and frames female politicians in a 'power' network which is superficially more complimentary than the earlier narrative. Three new stereotypes emerge: the *superwoman*, the *champion*, and the *gang member*. Yet the potential positive connotation of these stereotypes is undercut by another journalistic device, which labels some women politicians as 'feminist'. Our analysis will show that journalists use this discourse in two very different ways: either as a simple *classifying* device or as an *interest group* argument. As a classifying device, the label 'feminist' is attached to an individual female politician and used as though it describes a type of party membership. When it denotes an interest group, it implies that women *as a group* have gained political power and influence that is somehow illegitimate. In both uses, the 'feminist' designation is shunned by women politicians, who dislike the negative connotations of the 'new F-word,' as Charlotte Gray calls it (1989: 19).

The most spectacular and most visible of the new stereotypes is that of the *superwoman*. It is applied to a young, intelligent, active, and ambitious woman who succeeds on 'all levels' and 'has it all'. She combines a family with her career, and she is as well groomed as she is competent in her ministerial responsibilities. The superwoman is a hybrid: she embodies both the traditional characteristics of the wife and mother with the modern traits of the businesswoman (superior IQ, enormous capacity for work, and an iron constitution, as well as charm and generosity). Some Canadian politicians described in this manner are Liza Frulla-Hébert, Sharon Carstairs, Chaviva Hosek, Iona Campagnolo, and Janice Johnson. Hubert Bauch (1982) applied this narrative style to Campagnolo when he wrote: 'Campagnolo has been an instinctive climber all her life . . . from the time she blew into Ottawa eight years ago [she] has been tagged as a contender for the whole bag of marbles. . . . As if to prove them right, she made it into the Cabinet in less than two years. . . . She was Iona 'la Camp' who had clawed her way from Cannery Row to Parliament Hill (*Gazette*, 13 Nov. 1982).

The second stereotype for describing women politicians in the 1970s and early 1980s is the *champion*. This narrative approach is close to that of the *superwoman* but tends to be applied to middle-aged women politicians who have led a more traditional life. Often a woman described in this way has come to politics after proving herself in another domain, perhaps business, sports, or various charitable organizations. Her children are usually grown, and her family obligations more compatible with her duties as a representative of the public. She, too, pays attention to her grooming, is open to the media, and aware of her previous accomplishments. Among the politicians who have earned this classification are Pat Carney, Monique Landry, Monique Vézina, Margaret Thatcher, and Lucie Pépin. An example of the 'feminist' *champion* narration is provided by the *Toronto Star*: 'On being a feminist in 1984, Lucie Pépin has a cool-down approach. She's been called a male-oriented feminist, and says that women have to be ready to work with men to help the advancement of women' (quoted in Truman 1984).

The third label we encountered in our analyses is what we have called 'being *one of the boys*'. This narrative scheme is applied to women politicians who have been accepted into the ranks by the male political establishment, which counts them as part of the 'gang'. This type of female politician adopts a 'masculine' stance in politics, which means either that she does not resort to what are called feminine wiles (charm, coquetry, or wheedling) to achieve her goals or that she plays by the conventional rules of the game. A woman politician who is one of the boys benefits from this kind of acceptance but at the same time is continually reminded that she is an anomaly and may be placed in the unenviable position of being used as an alibi *against* women's interests. Examples are legion, such as the woman minister who had to salvage the reputation of a male colleague who had made a sexist remark in a constituency speech. Or the first female justice minister, who was appointed just as anti-abortion legislation (Bill C-43) was being reintroduced. This narrative approach has been applied to, among others, Barbara McDougall, Mary Collins, Kim Campbell, Lorna Marsden, and Sheila Copps, who is outspokenly cheerful about being described as a feminist and as one of the gang. In her autobiography *Nobody's Baby*, she says: 'I take pride in being a feminist. Look at the word itself; it comes from the Latin *femina*, woman; and being a woman is cause enough for being proud. I take pride, too, in representing my constituency—not only the riding which sent me to Parliament, but my larger constituency, the women of Canada' (Copps 1986: 89).

Unlike the first set of stereotypes—*spinster, woman of easy virtue, club woman,* and *wife of*—which have to do with the *traditional social roles* of women, the new stereotypes, applied to the second generation of women politicians during the 1970s and early 1980s, are a little more positive because they are constructed around the realization that women as an interest group can make an electoral difference. The political *superwoman* is described as a success in both the private and the public spheres. The *champion* is an accomplished woman in business, a profession, or charitable organizations. The members of the *gang* have learned the rules of the political game and use them like men.

Yet in spite of 1980s attempts to redress women's inequality in the male worlds of politics, business, and the media, only slow progress has been made. Women are now found in provincial and local politics but are still very under-represented at the top, in the federal domain. A 'glass ceiling' is also in place in the media professions (Robinson 1975; Crean 1987), where women have gained access to middle management but not the top. In the 1990s, women make up only 9 per cent of editors-in-chief and 6 per cent of managing editors in the Canadian Daily Newspaper Publishers Association. Furthermore all 33 people promoted to senior management jobs in 1989 were men (Cornacchia 1990). The situation is no better in television and film production, where, according to an American study by the National Commission on Working Women, 'women made up 15 per cent of producers, 25 per cent of writers and 9 per cent of directors of shows aired in 1990. In prime-time shows women held 43 per cent of the roles but were rarely depicted at all after age 40' (*Gazette* 1990).

CONCLUSION

Though there have been changes, and older stereotypes have been replaced by new ones, for the second and third generations this does not constitute progress in itself. In the late 1980s and early 1990s there has been a backlash and much greater resistance to, and worry about, feminist demands for women's social equality. No wonder then that powerful élites, among them journalists, try to eradicate women from the public domain by proclaiming the 'post-feminist era' or the 'death of the women's movement' (though there is no sociological evidence to corroborate these pronouncements).

So the media coverage of politicians continues to be different for women and men. Both the narrative angles and the evaluative criteria continue to belittle the political qualifications of women politicians. The typical narrative approaches

- tend to ignore the substance of a female incumbent's speeches in favour of her looks, clothing, and hair;
- fail to give recognition for prior political activities, with the result that no one knows the stages in a woman's political career, which together signify her competence;

- make women politicians responsible for women *as a class* when gender is known to be only one of many factors in interest-group formation; and
- use 'feminism' as a negative personal characteristic, and thus erase the group dimensions of this diversified social movement.

The evaluative criteria are also different for women and men:

- Women have to meet a considerably higher standard of excellence than men do.
- The political performance of women is judged only by the extremes of the scale (good and bad), while men are evaluated across the whole scale, including the mediocre middle range.
- Women politicians have to adhere to a moral code of sexual abstinence not imposed on men.
- Women politicians can be branded 'feminist' and thus have their political contributions denigrated.

Such different treatment of women and men raises a series of questions. To what extent do the media adequately perceive the difference in attitudes, goals, and understandings that motivate female and male politicians? Why are women drawn in greater numbers to local, municipal, and regional than to provincial and national politics? How adequate is the picture that the media draw of the political arenas in which women prefer to operate? And even more fundamentally, is there any difference in the reasons why women and men go into political life? Since the media provide society with the words and concepts for naming and constructing social and political reality, how adequately are they performing this task for women and women's concerns? The veracity and accuracy with which the media represent women politicians and their views are inextricably linked to the effectiveness with which political women can shape their society. Conversely, inaccurate and elliptical media descriptions deprive both female representatives and citizens of their voice and their contribution to the public domain.

There is evidence today that women readers and viewers are deeply troubled by the restrictive media reporting of modern women's social concerns and by the irrelevance of many media reports to their common life experience. Recent analyses confirm that newspapers, which supply their readers with an overwhelmingly white, male, middle-class view of the world, have lost 25 per cent of their female readers in the past decade (Cornacchia 1990; Walker 1990). This kind of evidence suggests that women have different notions about the nature of political activity and that they are becoming alienated from Canada's governing bodies such as Parliament and the Senate. Our own interviews show that women politicians feel uncomfortable in the 'boys' school' atmosphere of these institutions and come to politics with different expectations. Women politicians also complain that journalists and politicians alike do not acknowledge, or mistrust, the female networks and female solidarity which women's groups of all kinds have generated around women's issues.

A third characteristic that distinguishes female from male politicians is their attitude toward power. This difference was noted by Denise Falardeau during the Royal Commission symposium in Montreal (Canada 1990). Here Falardeau noted that women politicians she knew looked for power, but not at any price and not in general. Women tended to look for power to do something concrete. For many women politicians power is an instrument rather than an object in itself. Thérèse Lavoie-Roux echoes this sentiment in an interview with Marie-Jeanne Robin (1983: 177-8). However, personal power alone is no match for hierarchical team-based power, through which high-ranking bureaucrats or ministerial advisers can, and do, affect legislative decisions. In these bureaucratic behind-the-scene realms, women continue to be under-represented (Brown 1989: 232).

The question for the future is how to translate these differing outlooks into effective programs for institutional change and more women-friendly legislation. Political scientist Carol Mueller (1988a: 291), exploring the historical development of women's political agendas, points out that two different strategies have been proposed. One argues that equal rights are the best foundation for meeting women's needs; the other contends that women have special needs with respect to their reproductive capacities and that 'human difference' must therefore inform social legislation. This leads us to conclude that women in government do make a difference. The women ministers we talked to or whose biographies we consulted all have provided stepping-stones for improving women's condition: Claire Kirkland-Casgrain established married women's legal rights in Quebec; Monique Bégin introduced universal health insurance; Pat Carney provided for greater job equality in the federal bureaucracy; and Flora MacDonald inserted a women's equality clause into the latest Broadcasting Act. Second- and third-generation politicians like Audrey McLaughlin, Léa Cousineau, Chaviva Hosek, and Sheila Copps, among others, are continuing this agenda. Extra commitment will be needed in the 1990s as North American economic restructuring submerges women's political agendas. It is at these times that the growing number of feminist politicians among third-generation incumbents in municipal and provincial councils will make the greatest difference, for they will have the fresh ideas and thus will set the course for the future.

NOTE

This paper is based on a more extensive study entitled 'Women Politicians and Their Media Coverage: A General Analysis' in Kathy Megyery, ed., *Women in Canadian Politics: Toward Equity in Representation*, vol. 6, Research Studies of the Royal Commission on Electoral Reform and Party Financing (Ottawa and Toronto: RCERPF/Dundurn Press, 1992).

BIBLIOGRAPHY

Allard, Carole-Marie (1987), 'Ottawa: les femmes emménagent', *Commerce*, Oct.: 102-6.

Anderson, Doris (1987), *To Change the World: A Biography of Pauline Jewett* (Richmond Hill: Irwin).

Bashevkin, Sylvia (1983), 'Social Change and Political Partisanship: The Development of Women's Attitudes in Quebec, 1965-79'. *Comparative Political Studies* 16 (July): 147-72.

———— (1985), *Toeing the Lines: Women and Party Politics in English Canada* (Toronto: University of Toronto Press).

Bauch, Hubert (1982), 'Campagnolo: Can She Climb to PM's Job?' *Gazette* (Montreal), 13 Nov.

Booth, Amy (1964), 'A Striking Political Heroine Plans to Save Quebec Women from Their Medieval Bondage', *Financial Post*, 23 May.

Brodie, M. Janine (1985), *Women and Politics in Canada* (Toronto: McGraw-Hill Ryerson).

Brodie, M. Janine, and Jill McCalla Vickers (1982), *Canadian Women in Politics: An Overview*. CRIAW Papers no. 2 (Ottawa: Canadian Research Institute for the Advancement of Women).

Brown, Rosemary (1989), *Being Brown: A Very Public Life* (Toronto: Random House).

Burt, Sandra, Lorraine Code, and Lindsay Dorney, eds (1988), *Changing Patterns: Women in Canada* (Toronto: McClelland and Stewart).

Canada (1990), Royal Commission on Electoral Reform and Party Financing, *Proceedings of Symposium on Women's Participation in Political Parties*, Montreal, 31 Oct.-2 Nov.

Casgrain, Thérèse (1972), *A Woman in a Man's World*, trans. Joyce Marshall (Toronto: McClelland and Stewart). Originally published as *Une femme chez les hommes* (Montreal: Jour, 1971).

Copps, Sheila (1986), *Nobody's Baby* (Toronto: Deneau).

Cornacchia, Cheryl (1990), 'Pressing On: Women's Perspective Important to the News', *Gazette* (Montreal), 19 Nov.

Crean, Susan (1987), 'Piecing the Picture Together: Women and the Media in Canada', *Canadian Woman Studies* 8 (Spring): 15-21.

Descarries, Francine, and Shirley Roy (1988), *Le mouvement des femmes et ses courants de pensée: essai de typologie*, CRIAW Papers No. 19 (Ottawa: Canadian Research Institute for the Advancement of Women).

Friedan, Betty (1963), *The Feminine Mystique* (New York: Dell).

Fruman, Leslie (1984), 'Lucie Pépin Is a Proven Feminist' *Toronto Star*, 7 Dec.

Gazette (Montreal) (1990), 'TV Downplays Women on, off Screen: Study'. 21 Nov.

Goyette, Linda (1986), 'Big Federal Win a Modest Step into Power Circle'. *Edmonton Journal*, 20 Apr.

Gray, Charlotte (1989), 'The New F-Word', *Saturday Night*, April: 17-20.

Hosek, Chaviva (1989), 'How Women Fought for Equality'. In *Women and Men: Interdisciplinary Readings on Gender*, ed. Greta Hoffmann Nemiroff (Toronto: Fitzhenry and Whiteside).

Jeffrey, Liss (1989), 'Waiting for the Results'. *Scan*, March/April: 7-10.

Kieran, Sheila H. (1968), 'Who's Downgrading Women? Women', *Maclean's*, Aug.

LaMarsh, Judy, (1968), *Memoirs of a Bird in a Gilded Cage* (Toronto: McClelland and Stewart).

La Presse (1962), 'Un ministre bien chapeauté: Madame Ellen Fairclough'. (Montreal) 18 Jan.

Lavigne, Marie (1990), 'Femmes et pouvoir politique: une intégration à réussir'. In *Women and Power: Canadian and German Experiences*, eds Gertrude J. Robinson and Dieta Sixt (Montreal: McGill Studies in Communications and Goethe-Institut Montreal).

Lee, Robert Mason (1989a), *One Hundred Monkeys: The Triumph of Popular Wisdom in Canadian Politics* (Toronto: Macfarlane Walter and Ross).

MacBeth-Williams, Tannis, D. Baron, S. Philips, L. Travis, and D. Jackson (1986), 'The Portrayal of Sex Roles on Canadian and U.S. Television'. Paper presented at a conference of the International Association for Mass Communication Research, New Delhi. In *Psychology* (Vancouver: University of British Columbia Press), 1-25.

Maillé, Chantal (1990), *Primed for Power: Women in Canadian Politics* (Ottawa: Canadian Advisory Council on the Status of Women).

Mueller, Carol M. (1988a), 'Continuity and Change in Women's Political Agenda'. In *The Politics of the Gender Gap*, ed. Carol Mueller (Beverly Hills: Sage).

———— 1988b. 'The Empowerment of Women: Polling and the Women's Voting Bloc'. In *The Politics of the Gender Gap*, ed. Carol Mueller (Beverly Hills: Sage).

Robin, Marie-Jeanne (1983), *La politique au féminin*, interview with Thérèse Lavoie-Roux (Montreal: Inédi).

Robinson, Gertrude Joch (1975). 'Women Journalists in Canadian Dailies: A Social and Professional Profile'. In *McGill Working Papers in Communications* (Montreal: McGill University).

———— (1978), 'Women, Media Access and Social Control.' In *Women and the News*, ed. Laurily Keir Epstein (New York: Hastings).

Schneider, Beth E. (1988), 'Political Generations and the Contemporary Women's Movement', *Sociological Inquiry* 58, no. 1: 4-21.

Walker, Robert (1990), 'In Byline Game Men Win 67-30: National Study Suggests *Gazette* Ratio Is Typical', *Gazette* (Montreal), 24 Sept.

CHAPTER 10

Daily Male Delivery

Women and Politics in the Daily Newspapers

François-Pierre Gingras

LAMENT FOR AN IDENTITY

A generation ago, the late Thérèse Casgrain (1972) lamented that even the most respectable newspapers presented a superficial image of women and were thus shirking their responsibility to educate the public. She certainly had first-hand experience of how the media had been treating women in general and militant women in particular for most of this century: her involvement in politics extended from the early 1920s, as a suffragette, to the 1970s, as a senator.

The chapter by Robinson and Saint-Jean in this volume and numerous other studies conducted since Casgrain's autobiography have demonstrated the persistence of sex-role stereotyping in the Canadian media, particularly the broadcast media.[1] Head counts of men and women on the air, published by the Canadian Radio-Television and Telecommunications Commission (Canada 1986), have illustrated the relative absence of women among experts interviewed, especially in the fields of politics and economics. International studies have also concluded that the media tend to ignore or misrepresent women's achievements and needs (Beauchamp 1987; Creedon 1989; Gallagher 1981; Mattelart 1986; UNESCO 1987). Female politicians have deplored the biased attitude of the media towards them (cf. Robinson and Saint-Jean in this volume; LaMarsh 1968; Marois in Robin 1983; Robinson, Saint-Jean, and Rioux 1991). American studies have also reported that in election campaigns, women candidates receive less attention and more negative coverage than their male counterparts (Kahn and Goldenberg 1991).

Nevertheless, with a few exceptions (such as the excellent analysis by Robinson and Saint-Jean), there is an apparent lack of systematic analyses of the media coverage of Canadian women involved in politics. It is indeed appropriate to examine the relevance today of Thérèse Casgrain's criticism in the light of four general hypotheses:

- The media pay more attention to men than to women, whatever field of activity is considered.
- The media pay more attention to men than to women, whatever indicator is considered.
- Politics is a subject found less often in media items referring to women than in items referring to men.
- The media refer to women more often in negative than in positive terms, specially in fields traditionally associated with men.

To gather sufficient information to submit all these hypotheses to rigorous testing would require considerable resources. It would be necessary to consider a wide variety of media across the country: radio, television, newspapers, and magazines; large and small audiences or readerships; local, regional, Canada-wide, ethnic, specialized, and professional media (such as those devoted to sport or the medical profession). The media should also be surveyed during a long period, to avoid biases introduced by special occasions (such as Mother's Day) or events (such as political scandals). Before undertaking such an ambitious project, it was decided to conduct an exploratory case study to determine whether the general hypotheses had any basis at all.

THE OTTAWA DAILIES

For practical reasons, it was decided to concentrate on the three daily newspapers in the very politically aware National Capital Region (the *Citizen*, *Le Droit*, and the *Ottawa Sun*) and to examine about 50 consecutive issues of each.[2] The sample consisted of all issues during nine consecutive weeks, from 14 May (two days after Mother's Day)[3] to 10 July 1991. There is no claim that the data collected are representative of any other media or period. Because the sample is not a systematic random sample but rather the total universe of cases for a given period, no statistical test was performed.

Altogether, 3,662 salient items were collected: 1,703 articles and 1,268 titles referring explicitly to men or women,[4] plus 691 photographs of men or women. But notices of births, weddings and deaths; cartoons; travel and automobile sections; and advertisements of all kinds were excluded. Articles, titles, and photographs are hereafter referred to as the 'indicators'.[5] The items were sorted into five mutually exclusive categories, or 'fields':

- Politics, public policy, and public administration;
- Entertainment, arts, and culture;
- Economy, business, and finance;
- Sport, fitness, and outdoor life;
- Social life, a residual category including general news, natural disasters and most other catastrophes, crime-related and other legal items, organized and volunteer activities (church, cadets, scouts, etc.), fashion, cooking, and life style.

Each category was given a precise definition. When an item seemed to pertain to more than one field, judgement was exercised to determine the dominant one, using as cues the title, the content of the article, the position in the newspaper, as appropriate.

Given the scope of this book, it is useful to quote in full the operational (and unfortunately not very elegant) definition of the Politics category:

> Any item referring to a person currently associated (or having been or aspiring to be associated) with any government or public administration, at any level, through support or challenge or the exercise of authority, power or influence, including (but not limited to) elections, lobbying, demonstrations, public activities or public speeches or other commentaries. Items related to Education, Justice, the Armed Forces, Environment, etc. are classified under Politics or Social or Economy, depending on the context; when an item refers to a person occupying a public office or identified with a political party or a pressure group trying to influence public policy, there is a presumption of political relevance of the item; for instance, hearings on the environmental impact of a proposed regional dump are likely to be politicized, while the intervention of the army on the site of a natural disaster rarely is. Items concerning the Royal family are classified under Social unless they have a direct bearing on public policy.

This definition may not satisfy feminists who believe that what is political for women differs from the traditional political science definition of the field and that this diverseness is essential to understanding women in politics (Vickers 1989; Evans 1986; O'Brien 1989). Elsewhere in this book, Jacobs, Ralston, Tremblay, Robinson, and Saint-Jean discuss one aspect or another of the private-public dichotomy. The argument has considerable merit, and the classical distinction between what is private and what is public is no longer authoritative (Irigaray 1989). But in practice, it would be a methodological nightmare to try to devise two different and parallel sets of definitions[6] in a content analysis that seeks to compare the treatment of men and women. Many items collected refer explicitly to men as well as women. Such occurrences were not counted twice: men and women were assigned fractions corresponding to their proportion of space in number of lines for the articles and in square centimetres for the photographs.

Simultaneously, items related to women were also evaluated as being 'favourable' (or 'positive'), 'neutral', or 'unfavourable' (or 'negative'), following Carney's (1972) guidelines for content analysis. Although there is always some subjectivity in any evaluative exercise, as much consistency as humanly possible was maintained by using the following qualifying definitions of 'image':

- Favourable, positive: any item that lauds, supports or looks with favour upon its female subject(s), whether or not it appears founded or unfounded; also includes any focus on a female's good luck or any other nice thing that happened to her. Examples: adulation of female movie stars, approval of a female minister's 'rapping the knuckles of CSCE member ministers'.[7]

- Unfavourable, negative: any item that criticizes, degrades or looks with disfavour upon its female subject(s), whether or not it appears founded or unfounded; this also includes association with scandals and criminality, as well as reports of failure, dependence, fragility, violence and willful misadventures visited upon a female. Examples: article on female circumcision, report that 'mother of molested boy says justice failed her'.

- Neutral: any article not evaluated as favourable or unfavourable. Examples: 'A female tennis player will compete in such and such tournaments this coming season', 'A female minister spoke on such and such an issue' (without positive or negative leaning). When an item includes both positive and negative references to women, classification followed what appeared to be the dominant image (often evidenced by the title or the accompanying photograph); complete ambivalence of an item prompted a 'neutral' classification.

The coding and analysis of the presence and images of women in the newspapers were done with consistency and relevance in mind, but no reliability test was performed, as no panel or jury was used to classify items in the different fields or to assign a positive, neutral, or negative trait to items referring to women. Therefore other researchers using the same raw data might come up with slightly different results.

Presence

Women and Men in Ottawa Newspapers

Three Canadians out of four feel that daily newspapers and other media have special responsibilities towards the public (Kubas 1981; Canada 1981). Daily newspapers are also considered to play a vital role in agenda setting for the general population and for all levels of government (Fletcher 1981; Canada 1981). To what extent do Ottawa daily newspapers acknowledge or ignore the presence of women in society? Are women on their agenda?

A first look at the data reveals how little space women occupy in the three Ottawa dailies: the share of women consists of anything from a low of 8 per cent (*Ottawa Sun*) to a high of 23 per cent (*Le Droit*) of gender-related articles (Figure 1).[8] On average, women are present in 16 per cent of all gender-related titles and in 21 per cent of photographs showing humans. Women are rarely found in the headlines. If media coverage is an indicator of relevance, then women are relatively unimportant social actors in the National Capital Region, for, on the whole, the three daily newspapers give five units of contents to men for each unit they give to women.[9]

Although it is clear that, generally speaking, women do not get as much newspaper coverage as men do, are there any categories where they get 'equal' treatment? To paraphrase Cohen (1981: 199), are there any fields from which women are not almost excluded?

Unfortunately, no. At least, not quite. In all five fields (Politics, Culture, Economy, Sport, and Social), the men's share of articles is overwhelming, ranging from 65 per cent of *Le Droit*'s Social articles to 99 per cent of the *Ottawa Sun*'s economic and financial pages (Figure 2). The average male share for five categories in three newspapers is 86 per cent.

Generally speaking, the Social category is where women get the largest number of gender-related *articles*: an average of 25 per cent. But this is not necessarily a recognition of great accomplishments. For instance, in the *Ottawa Sun*, more than half of these articles are related to crime, with women portrayed as victims accounting for 43 per cent of all Social articles about women in this daily. In two fields, Sport and Economy, the three Ottawa newspapers print very few articles about women, with averages of 8 per cent and 9 per cent, respectively.

FIGURE 1   WOMEN AND MEN IN OTTAWA NEWSPAPERS

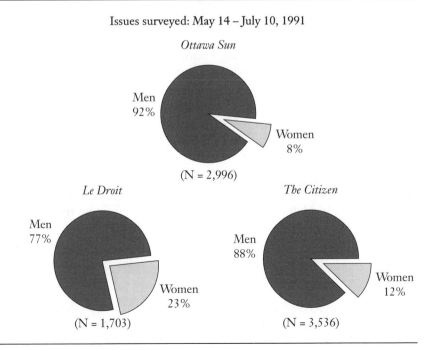

Issues surveyed: May 14 – July 10, 1991

Ottawa Sun

Men 92%

Women 8%

(N = 2,996)

Le Droit

Men 77%

Women 23%

(N = 1,703)

The Citizen

Men 88%

Women 12%

(N = 3,536)

Figure 2 Men and Women in Ottawa Newspapers

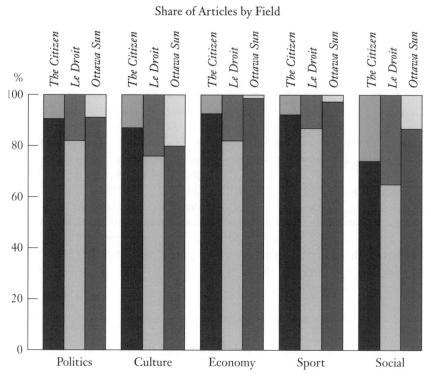

Share of Articles by Field

Note: The bottom of each bar refers to men, the top to women.

Women's share of *titles* is also highest in the Social category, with a maximum of 36 per cent in the *Citizen*. The Culture category comes next, in the 23 to 31 per cent range. Women rank again lowest in both Economy and Sport, plunging to a low of 5 per cent in the *Citizen*'s gender-related titles about the economy.

Women are not better off when photographs are considered. They account for up to 32 per cent of the *Citizen*'s Social pictures and an average of 25 per cent in the Culture category. They are virtually absent from *Le Droit*'s Economy section, with a pitiful 2 per cent of the photos. In the *Ottawa Sun*, the most obvious women pictured are the scantily dressed 'Sunshine Girls'.

Whatever the field, whatever the indicator (articles, titles, or photographs), whatever the newspaper, women consistently get much less coverage than men.

The data presented so far would lead to the expectation that women are much less present than men in the political coverage done by Ottawa newspapers. The first set of bars in Figure 3 shows that the women's portion of

FIGURE 3 POLITICS AND NEWSPAPERS IN OTTAWA — SPRING 1991

Coverage of women and men compared to their proportions of elected politicians

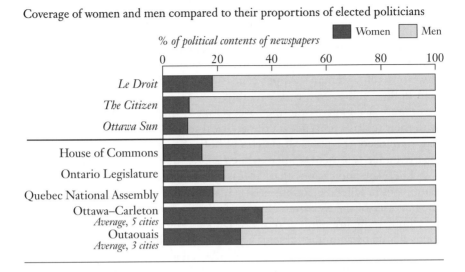

% of political contents of newspapers

political articles ranges from a high of 18 per cent in *Le Droit* to a low of 9 per cent in the *Citizen* and the *Ottawa Sun*.

Women's share of political titles and photographs is of the same magnitude, from 11 to 15 per cent and from 16 to 19 per cent, respectively. Furthermore, the photographs are often of women who have little political power, such as the wives of the Prime Minister and other male politicians.

It may be argued that the newspaper coverage of political women merely reflects their relative absence from the political scene (as Robinson, Saint-Jean, and Rioux 1991, suggest); their confinement to peripheral roles (Black and McGlen 1979; Payette 1982; Robin 1983; Tardy et al. 1982); or the long-standing male disregard of the historical influence of women (Dumont-Johnson 1981; Brossard 1981). This research has not investigated whether newspapers systematically discriminate against women when decisions are made to cover public events, but journalists quoted by Beauchamp (1987) seem to be of the opinion that they do. Such claims, related to the broader systemic sexism in Canadian society, cannot be substantiated, but some may be explored.

One of the easiest ways of investigating the triangular relationship between women, media, and politics is to compare the presence of women in newspapers to the proportion of women in the governments situated nearest to the readership.[10]

The readers of the three Ottawa dailies are drawn from a territory bridging the Ottawa River and including several communities in the Regional

Municipality of Ottawa-Carleton and the Communauté urbaine de l'Outaouais. In the spring of 1991, in five city councils on the Ontario side, women held on average 36 per cent of the elected seats, ranging from 17 per cent in Nepean to 50 per cent in Kanata; on the Quebec side, the three-city average was 28 per cent (from 20 per cent in Aylmer to 38 per cent in Gatineau). At the same time, the women's share of seats was 14 per cent in the House of Commons, 22 per cent in the Ontario Legislature and 18 per cent in the Québec National Assembly.

Figure 3 compares the media coverage of men and women in politics with their relative presence on the political scene. Even when such low standards are used, the political articles of both the *Citizen* and the *Ottawa Sun* clearly under-represent women, while *Le Droit* does so to a lesser degree.

There are indications that, at least as far back as 1974, the sex of local candidates in federal elections is largely irrelevant to the voting behaviour of the majority of the electorate, but very relevant for party notables, who may discriminate in any number of ways (Deller 1980; Brodie 1985). This opinion is shared by a number of female politicians (Robin 1983) and discussed in this volume by Tremblay. Survey data collected locally by the author indicate no significant differences in the attitude of the electorate towards male and female politicians, although interviews with local politicians reveal persistent sexist attitudes.

NEWSWORTHINESS

When women do make the news, what is it about? Is what's newsworthy about women different from what's newsworthy about men? Figure 4 answers that question. Articles about men deal mainly with Sport (in the 28-30 per cent range), Politics (24-29 per cent), and Social events (19-29 per cent), in that order, whereas articles about women are overwhelmingly Social (in the 35-52 per cent range), with Politics running as a distant second (17-25 per cent). Economy comes last both for men (in the 6-16 per cent range) and for women (in the 2-9 per cent range). In all three newspapers, only the field of Culture offers a larger slice of articles about women[11] than of articles about men.

The pattern is roughly the same when one examines titles and, to some extent, photographs. Although the ranking of categories varies when men and women are compared with these two indicators, the slice of Politics is consistently smaller for women.

It must therefore be concluded that the 'feminine' contents of the Ottawa daily newspapers is systematically less politicized than the 'masculine' contents.

For social scientists who believe that politics is about power and influence and who have heard Caroline Andrew's (1984) call for an articulation of the relations between gender and politics (see also Lamoureux 1989), there is only one slightly encouraging way to look at the data presented so far:

FIGURE 4 ARTICLES ABOUT MEN AND WOMEN IN OTTAWA NEWSPAPERS

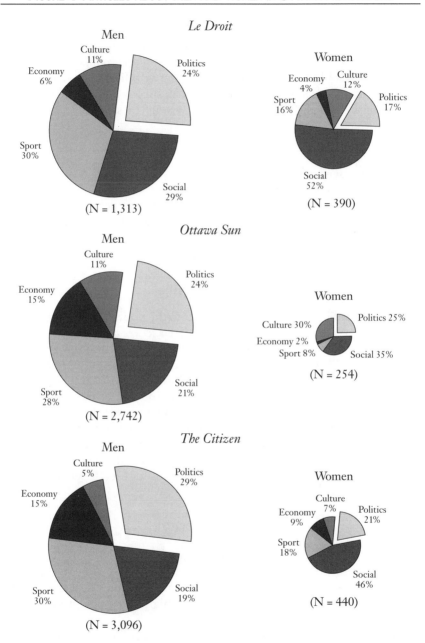

For each daily, the size of the 'women' pie is proportional to women's share of articles in that daily.

Politics ranks in second position in the 'feminine' contents of Ottawa news-papers[12] as it does for men.

Even this parallel has its limitations, however. It must be remembered that, for women, there is a much greater distance between the first and sec-ond ranks than there is for men. Surely Ralston (in this volume) would com-ment that this is like saying that the chief executive officer of a multinational corporation and a homeless woman in Halifax spend similar proportions of their income on food. Should the homeless woman be satisfied?

IMAGE

There is a consensus in previous research that advertising and the broadcast media reinforce sex-role stereotyping. The chapter by Robinson and Saint-Jean is quite eloquent in that respect. This paper does not attempt to repli-cate well-documented studies but simply asks: Do the Ottawa daily newspapers look upon women with favour or disfavour? The relevant data appear in Figure 5.

Overall Image

The Ottawa dailies vary widely with respect to the positive or negative image they present of women in their articles: *Le Droit* scores high with 67 per cent of images being favourable; the *Ottawa Sun* has the worst record with only 26 per cent, in addition to having the lowest proportion of articles about women. The *Citizen* stands half-way with 46 per cent positive articles.

It is difficult to get a clearer picture by looking at individual fields because different patterns are found in the various papers. For instance, Figure 6 shows that only 10 per cent of articles about women in *Le Droit*'s sport section are negative, while 31 per cent are negative in the *Ottawa Sun*'s sport section. The *Citizen* tops the other dailies for the negative image of women in the Social category (42 per cent) but is lowest (10 per cent) in the Culture category.

Political Image

Only in the field of Politics is there some apparent similarity in the profiles conveyed by the three newspapers, with 34-40 per cent and an average of 38 per cent of images about women being negative. Ironically, as Figure 6 shows, Politics is also the category with the highest average proportion of unfavourable articles about women.[13]

Any similarity among newspapers vanishes when one looks at the posi-tive instead of the negative image of women presented in their coverage of Politics: the range of 'positiveness' extends from a mere 14 per cent of the articles in the *Ottawa Sun* to a substantial[14] 60 per cent in *Le Droit*.

FIGURE 5 IMAGES OF WOMEN IN OTTAWA NEWSPAPERS

Size of pie is proportional to women's share of articles in each daily*

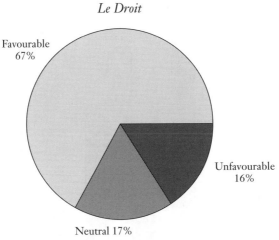

Le Droit

Most positive

Favourable
67%

Unfavourable
16%

Neutral 17%

*women's share = 23%

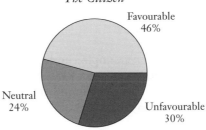

The Citizen

Favourable
46%

Neutral
24%

Unfavourable
30%

*women's share = 12%

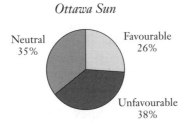

Ottawa Sun

Least positive

Neutral
35%

Favourable
26%

Unfavourable
38%

*women's share = 8%

FIGURE 6 WOMEN IN OTTAWA NEWSPAPERS

Scope of Negative Images, by Field

Percentage of unfavourable articles in each field
(remainder of articles are neutral or favourable)

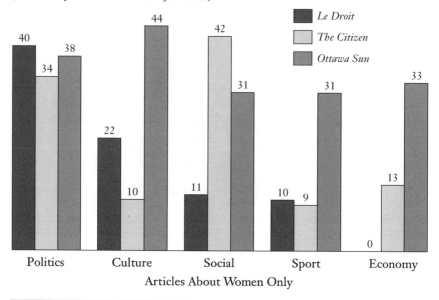

Articles About Women Only

It is difficult to discover a simple, homogeneous political image of women through the quantitative content analysis of the three Ottawa newspapers.[15] When one considers articles about women in the Politics category, one fact stands out: about two stories out of five present a negative image of women.

UNIMPORTANT PERSONALITIES

This chapter is primarily a quantitative description of the place of women in the three Ottawa daily newspapers during nine consecutive weeks of 1991. Some regularities are observable and they tend to support the general hypotheses derived from Casgrain's lament about the media treatment of women. These regularities are worth recapitulating:

- If media coverage is an indicator of social relevance, then women are relatively unimportant in the National Capital Region, for on the whole, the three daily newspapers publish five units of contents about men for each unit of contents about women.

- Whatever the field, whatever the indicator (articles, titles, or photographs), and whatever the newspaper, women consistently get much less coverage than men.
- Political articles in all three Ottawa daily newspapers under-represent women, in view of their actual representation on the political scene.
- Despite the fact that Politics actually ranks in second position in the 'feminine' contents of Ottawa newspapers, the 'feminine' contents are systematically less politicized than the 'masculine' contents.
- For every two positive articles about women in the field of Politics, about five are negative.

Aside from these findings, there are considerable variations from one newspaper to another. There are also numerous questions still to be answered: Is the period studied representative or at least typical?[16] Is the situation in other parts of Canada similar to what it seems to be in Ottawa?[17] Do the print media and electronic media have similar patterns, specially in the treatment of Politics?[18]

Despite the obvious need for more research, the findings reported here show that 'the problematic relationship between women and the mass media' is more than a question of mere visibility (Gallagher 1981). This case study may be easily replicated, and the results would be of use to individuals, groups, and institutions concerned with the needs and interests of women.

As Beauchamp (1987) has shown, the sexism of the media is not always unconscious or systemic, that is, the result of institutionalized and largely unquestioned practices. For instance, some dailies (such as the *Ottawa Sun*) exhibit overt sexism in regularly publishing photos of pinup girls, despite repeated protests from readers and community groups. This is not the kind of coverage women are looking for.

Should women accept de Tocqueville's logic that the more men and women compete for limited goods (in this case media coverage), the less they will be 'inclined to treat one another in an altruistic manner' (Morton 1984)? Or should they believe, as political journalist Lysiane Gagnon (1983) does, that the changing of attitudes is a slow but effective process? The alternatives are clear: the easiest is individual passivity, usually interpreted as passive acceptance of the status quo; the most difficult path is collective mobilization to overcome the unconscious, systemic, and overt forms of sexism in newspapers and to improve the presence and the image of women in the media, from a stereotypical as well as from a 'numbers' perspective.

Of course, this does not preclude efforts to improve the influence of women in politics, which is the subject of other chapters in this book.

NOTES

The title 'Daily Male Delivery' is borrowed from a series of gender-conscious advertisements for TSN, The Sports Network, in *Marketing* (a weekly publication of the Maclean-Hunter group). This chapter is a revised version of Gingras 1992.

1 Content analyses of sex-role portrayal in the Canadian broadcast media has been done for the Canadian Radio-Television and Telecommunication Commission, the Canadian Broadcasting Corporation, the National Watch on Images of Women in the Media (Mediawatch), and even the Alliance of Canadian Cinema, Television and Radio Artists (ACTRA); see bibliographies in Canada 1986. General references are much too numerous to list here. Most of those relevant to Canada may be found in the bibliographies of works cited in this chapter. See also Canada 1982; Bettinotti and Gagnon 1983; Robinson, Saint-Jean, and Rioux 1991.

2 But not necessarily politically correct, as this chapter demonstrates.

3 It was decided to start after Mother's Day to avoid over representation of a certain type of media coverage of women as mothers.

4 Men and women are taken here in the generic sense of male and female human beings, regardless of their age.

5 Other indicators were used too, such as the proportion, size, and position of articles, titles and photographs, but the data are not reported here, because of the complexity (and sometimes highly subjective nature) of any comparison of these indicators across newpapers of different formats. For instance, in the tabloid *Le Droit*, the most important sport feature is usually found on the third-last page, whereas the *Citizen* prints it on the first page of its sport section.

6 The use of distinct, parallel (gender-based) definitions of Politics would require distinct, parallel definitions of all the other fields.

7 The CSCE is the Conference on Security and Cooperation in Europe.

8 To avoid overburdening readers with figures, only part of the data are reported here. Detailed tables are available from the author.

9 According to our calculations, women get 17 per cent of all 'units of contents', a measure averaging the proportions of articles, titles, and photographs.

10 Of course, this quantitative comparison neglects the influence of women and men engaged in politics. For a review of the literature on the participation of women in politics, see Tremblay 1990; and Paré et al. 1991. The topic is discussed in this volume by Arscott, Tremblay, and Whitehorn and Archer.

11 With as much as 30 per cent in *Ottawa Sun*, but even with a low 7 per cent in the *Citizen*. The unusually high proportion of the Culture category in the *Ottawa Sun*'s articles about women should not obscure the fact that only about a third are actually positive; see below.

12 In the Ottawa dailies, the field of Politics occupies an overall average rank only slightly higher in the coverage of men (2.14, behind Sport) than in the coverage of

women (2.42, behind Social). The overall average rank is obtained by averaging the ranks of the Politics category for the three indicators in the three newspapers. The smaller the number, the higher the rank.

13 But because of the considerable differences from one newspaper to another, averages are not very meaningful measures of central tendency in the other four categories.

14 The author might have used a less (or more) emphatic qualifier if he had codified comparable data for men.

15 For instance, *Le Droit*, the newspaper least negative about women generally, publishes more negative comments in the Politics category than in any other; however, most of *Le Droit*'s political articles about women are actually favourable. Similarly Sport comes second in *Le Droit* in the proportion of articles presenting a negative image of women. However, three-quaters of all articles about women in the Sport category are positive. Methodology-minded readers may take note that the *Ottawa Sun*, seemingly the most misogynous newspaper in Ottawa from a general point of view, with 39 per cent of articles unfavourable to women, might appear less negative than *Le Droit* in the Politics category, which contains 25 per cent of all unfavourable *Sun* articles, compared to *Le Droit*'s 36 per cent. However, this would be a misleading interpretation; for the *Ottawa Sun* is actually much less positive than *Le Droit* in the realm of Politics, with only 14 per cent of the articles being favourable, against 60 per cent in *Le Droit*. Another interesting case arises with the Economy category, for which the research has found no negative mention of women in *Le Droit*, but 13 per cent in the *Citizen*; in absolute numbers, however, the *Citizen* published many more positive economic items about women than *Le Droit* did, largely because, in the period studied, the *Citizen* published 39 articles about women in this field, and *Le Droit* only 17. (The figures correspond to the respective proportion of 9 per cent and 4 per cent shown in Figure 4.) The abundant data presented in this paper must be analysed carefully to avoid other possible misinterpretations.

16 A small-scale replication conducted by the author in the fall of 1992 shows essentially similar results.

17 The author's own unpublished research suggests so, however: a content analysis of the Toronto *Globe and Mail* for the same period shows patterns similar to those reported here, and a previous analysis of three Montreal papers—*Le Devoir*, *La Presse* and *Le Journal de Montréal*—also document the relative absence of women. This is consistent with data gathered in 1990, 1991, and 1992 by Évaluation-Médias, the Quebec branch of Mediawatch.

18 Cf note 1 above.

BIBLIOGRAPHY

Andrew, Caroline (1984), 'Women and the Welfare State' [Presidential address to the Canadian Political Science Association], *Canadian Journal of Political Science* 17, no. 4 (Dec.): 667-83.

Beauchamp, Colette (1987), *Le silence des médias* (Montreal: Remue-ménage).

Bettinotti, Julia, and Jocelyn Gagnon (1983), *Que c'est bête, ma belle! Études sur la presse féminine au Québec* (Montreal: Soudeyns-Donzé).

Black, Jerome H., and Nancy E. McGlen (1979), 'Male-Female Political Involvement Differentials in Canada, 1965-1974', *Canadian Journal of Political Science* 12, no. 3 (Sept.): 471-97.

Brodie, Marion Janine (1985), *Women and Politics in Canada* (Toronto: McGraw-Hill).

Brossard, Nicole (1981), 'Notes et fragments d'urgence', pp. 15-19 in *Femmes et politique*, ed. Yolande Cohen (Montreal: Jour).

Canada (1981), Royal Commission on Newspapers, Report. (Ottawa: Minister of Supply and Services).

—— (1982), Task Force on Sex-Role Stereotyping in the Broadcast Media, *Images of Women* (Ottawa: Canadian Radio-Television and Telecommunications Commission).

—— (1986), Canadian Radio-Television and Telecommunications Commission, *Report on Self-regulation by the Broadcasting and Advertising Industries for the Elimination of Sex-Role Stereotyping in the Broadcast Media* (Ottawa: Minister of Supply and Services).

Carney, Thomas F. (1972), *Content Analysis: A Technique for Systematic Inference from Communications* (Winnipeg: University of Manitoba Press).

Casgrain, Thérèse (1972), *A Woman in a Man's World* (Toronto: McClelland and Stewart).

Cohen, Yolande, ed. (1981), *Femmes et politique* (Montreal: Jour).

Creedon, Pamela J. (1993), *Women in Mass Communication*, 2nd edn (Newbury Park, CA: Sage).

Deller, Joanne (1980): 'The Effect of Female Candidatures on Voting Behaviour'. Paper presented at the Canadian Political Science Association annual meetings, Montreal.

Dumont-Johnson, Micheline (1981): 'Découvrir la mémoire des femmes', *Cahiers de recherche éthique* 8: 51-65.

Evans, Judith (1986): 'Feminism within the Discipline of Political Science'. In *Feminism and Political Theory*, eds Judith Evans, Jill Hills, Karen Hunt, Elizabeth Meehan, Tessa ten Tusscher, Ursula Vogel, and Georgina Waylen (London: Sage).

Fletcher, Frederick (1981), *The Newspaper and Public Affairs* (Ottawa: Royal Commission on Newspapers).

Gagnon, Lysiane (1983), *Vivre avec les hommes* (Montreal: Québec/Amérique).

Gallagher, Margaret (1981), *Unequal Opportunities: The Case of Women and the Media* (UNESCO: Paris).

Gingras, François-Pierre (1992), 'Women in Politics and Canadian Media: A Case Study of Ottawa Newspapers'. Paper presented at the Canadian Political Science Association annual meetings, Charlottetown.

Irigaray, Luce (1989), *Le temps de la différence* (Paris: Livre de Poche).

Kahn, Kim Fridkin, and Edie N. Goldenberg (1991), 'Women Candidates in the News: An Examination of Gender Differences in U.S. Senate Campaign Coverage', *Public Opinion Quarterly* 55, no. 2 (Summer): 180-99.

Kubas, Leonard, and Communications Research Center (1981), *Newspapers and Their Readers* (Ottawa: Royal Commission on Newspapers).

LaMarsh, Judy (1968), *Memoirs of a Bird in a Gilded Cage* (Toronto: McClelland and Stewart).

Lamoureux, Diane (1989), *Citoyennes? Femmes, droit de vote et démocratie* (Montreal: Remue-ménage).

Mattelart, Michèle (1986), *Women, Media and Crisis: Feminity and Disorder* (London: Comedia).

Morton, F.L. (1984), 'Sexual Equality and the Family in Tocqueville's Democracy in America', *Canadian Journal of Political Science* 17, no. 2 (June): 309-24.

O'Brien, Mary (1989), *Reproducing the World: Essays in Feminist Theory* (Boulder, CO: Westview).

Paré, Bernadette, Réjean Pelletier, and Manon Tremblay (1991), 'La différence de sexe en politique: les députées et députés du Québec à Ottawa'. Paper presented at the Canadian Political Science Association annual meetings, Kingston.

Payette, Lise (1982), *Le pouvoir? Connais pas!* (Montreal: Québec/Amérique).

Robin, Marie-Jeanne (1983), *La politique au féminin.* (N.p.: Inédi).

Robinson, Gertrude J., Armande Saint-Jean, and Christine Rioux (1991), 'Women Politicians and their Media Coverage: A Generational Analysis'. In *Women in Canadian Politics: Toward Equity in Representation*, ed. Kathy Megyery, vol. 6 of the research studies of the Royal Commission on Electoral Reform and Party Financing (Ottawa and Toronto: RCEPPF/Dundurn).

Tardy, Évelyne, Anne-Marie Gingras, Ginette Legault, and Lyne Marcoux (1982): *La politique: un monde d'hommes? Une étude sur les mairesses au Québec* (Montreal: Hurtubise).

Tremblay, Manon (1990), *La participation des femmes aux structures politiques électorales: une bibliographie* (Sainte Foy, P.Q.: Université Laval, Groupe de recherche multi-disciplinaire féministe).

UNESCO (1987), *Women and Media Decision-Making: The Invisible Barriers* (Paris: UNESCO).

Vickers, Jill McCalla (1989), 'Feminist Approaches to Women in Politics'. In *Beyond the Vote: Canadian Women and Politics*, eds Linda Kealy and Joan Sangster, (Toronto: University of Toronto Press).

CHAPTER 11

Gender and The Canadian Military

Attitudes Toward Peace and Symbolic Politics

François-Pierre Gingras

INTRODUCTION

In Canada, as in other countries, national defence is regarded as a predominantly masculine community, with a strong sense of duty, a conservative
ethos, and *macho* values. Although women have traditionally been considered
to be more conservative than men,[1] the peace movement and the women's
movement have questioned the typically bellicose, male way of settling disagreements. It seems that many women have been more inclined than men to
profess, with the archetypal figure of Antigone, guardian of the 'unwritten
unalterable laws', 'My way is to share my love' (Sophocles [440 BC] 1947). This
chapter examines the differences between the attitudes of male and female
members of the Canadian military to some ethical questions related to peace.[2]

Although it is perhaps considered proper for the Canadian public in
general and even members of the defence community to be in favour of
world peace and of a peacekeeping role for the Canadian Armed Forces,
there are indications from the military of some concern about the so-called
excesses of a love of peace. Survey data and personal interviews are used in
this chapter to determine the extent to which male and female Roman
Catholics in the Canadian Armed Forces differ in their support of peace and
peacekeeping.[3]

This examination is timely. Outside Canada, the topic of gender and the
military has been studied in different contexts (Alt and Stone 1990, 1991;
Enloe 1983; Hough 1979; Larwood, Glasser and McDonald 1980; Reynaud
1988; Savell et al. 1979; Stevens and Gardner 1987; Woelfel et al. 1976).
However, in our country, over half a century after the creation of the
Canadian Women's Army Corps and the Women's Division of the Royal
Canadian Air Force, there are still very few works discussing Canadian
women and the military. A short article by Shannon (1992) was an overdue

account of the early experiences of women in the Armed Forces, and two recent books have at last documented the often painful situation of military wives (Collier 1994; Harrison 1994). Even a modest contribution such as this chapter should be a welcome addition to the literature. The topic of gender and the military also appears particularly relevant now that we have had for the first time a female associate minister of national defence—Mary Collins—and a female defence minister—Kim Campbell—a 'high-profile' (*Maclean's* 1993; *Financial Post Magazine* 1993) politician with a 'pretty face [. . .] and promoting a radical feminist agenda' (Byfield 1993),[4] and with (allegedly) progressive ideas (Frum 1993).[5] Indeed, the initial hostility of part of Canada's male-dominated establishment towards Kim Campbell undoubtedly mirrored 'hidebound traditions and prejudice' against women (Shannon 1992) and expressed the views of a significant number of opinion leaders, both in the business and the military communities.[6] However, one might have expected female editors, like Diane Francis or Maryanne McNellis, of the *Financial Post* and the *Financial Post Magazine* respectively, to say a few words about the unprecedented opportunity for another woman to influence the values of the Canadian military.[7] But nobody saw in her a modern Antigone. On the contrary, the political right did not expect the new minister to make any significant contribution to national defence.[8] Even the media that quoted Campbell's comment that 'for the first time in my lifetime, we have the capacity to make some real changes' in defence and foreign-policy priorities, did not suggest what kinds of changes she might propose.[9]

General Hypotheses

This chapter is first premised on the author's impression that, perhaps more than ever before, the defence community is likely to be nurturing some ambivalent ethical attitudes. On the one hand, it seems obvious that the conservative military ethos[10] is very much alive in the Armed Forces. On the other hand, there is no reason to believe that the defence community is immune to the dominant (and changing) values of Canadian society, including the considerable popular support for Canada's international peacekeeping role[11] and the symbolic appropriateness of promoting peace rather than preparing for war. That is why we should expect to find ambiguous attitudes in the defence community towards a wide set of ethical issues, including matters related to peace, especially if we analyse them by more than one method.

The second premise is that the Canadian defence community has a more or less homogeneous culture and that one should not expect many or deep variations from one category of individuals to another, even between women and men. Roman Catholic members of the defence community may or may not be representative of the entire defence community in Canada. However, if religious beliefs are relevant to ethical attitudes, then it is methodologically safe to control for religious faith before exploring a set of such attitudes and determining whether men and women show similar patterns.[12] Canadian women are becoming more socially autonomous, and Canadian society in general is making fewer and fewer distinctions between men and women. It should then be expected that the attitudes of women, still a minority in the defence community,[13] would reflect numerous contradictory pressures: the traditionalism and support for the existing social order long seen as a characteristic of femininity; the pacifism that is often associated with women's movements; the pressure felt by any minority to over-conform to a community's ethos in order to gain the acceptance of the majority; and the exasperation and other feelings caused by the chauvinism (and harassment) of which numerous women seem to be victim in the male-dominated Armed Forces.[14]

The general hypothesis of this chapter is, therefore, that, within the national defence community, women and men will exhibit apparently similar, equally ambiguous views on many ethical questions. We will call it a null hypothesis because it suggests the absence of any relationship between the variables.

METHODOLOGY

Evidence of the Attitudes of the Military

There are many sources touching on the values and attitudes of the Canadian military, but few are systematic, objective studies, and most tend to ignore the presence of women.[15] General works (such as Stanley 1974; Newman 1983; and Coulon 1991) and even recent studies of Canadian peacekeepers (Beaudet 1993 and Coulon 1994) supply useful information on the Canadian Armed Forces, but their very broad perspective offers little insight into the attitudes of servicemen and -women towards most of the ethical issues of concern here. Other works take a highly subjective approach to picturing the value system of members of the Canadian Forces. This is characteristic of essays by critics of the military (such as Tremblay 1988) and of some documentaries on historically sensitive subjects.[16] Histories written or prefaced by military authorities (for instance, Castonguay 1989 and Preston 1991) are often of a very high intellectual calibre, but some people may fear that they emphasize the glories of military history and neglect the rest (but see Loomis 1984). The same can of course be said of many other works. Some retired members of the Armed Forces have written memoirs filled with anecdotes from which the interested scholar may extract pertinent information about the military ethos at different times and places.[17] Recollections of military chaplains are also especially informative because at times they are critical of the value system and of some established practices of the Canadian Forces.[18] Studies of attitudes about sex roles in the Armed Forces are not uninteresting, but they tend to be concerned more with attitudes *towards* women in the Forces than with differences *between* men and women.[19]

A good but somewhat biased[20] way of acquainting oneself with the system of values in the military is to attend their professional meetings, such as the annual seminar of the Conference of Defence Associations Institute (CDAI) or activities sponsored by the Canadian Institute for Strategic Studies (CISS), and to read defence publications, such as *Sentinel, Canadian Defence Quarterly, Esprit de Corps/Canadian Military Then and Now*, the CDAI *Forum*, and CISS publications. References to the military ethos are omnipresent in all of the above. Participating in the activities of the War Amputees' Association, of the Army, Navy, and Air Force veterans' associations or the Canadian Legion also provides interesting insights.

If qualitative evidence is relatively easy to gather, quantitative evidence is not, with the result that it is difficult to know how widespread specific attitudes are in the military community and especially how they cut across gender lines. Department of National Defence's (DND) Directorate of Personnel Psychosocial Profiles and the Personnel Applied Research Unit conduct and sponsor research on a wide range of questions related to personnel management but apparently not on ethical issues such as peace and disarmament: in recent years, homosexuality and sexual harassment have been the popular topics for investigation. Occasionally results of studies of morale and motivation have been published in scientific publications (see for instance Cotton 1979; 1981).

The 'Challenge 2000' Research

In 1989-90, the Military Ordinary of Canada (the Roman Catholic Bishop of the Canadian Forces) commissioned an extensive survey of Roman Catholics in the Armed Forces. The project was called 'Challenge 2000'. The research used a stratified sample of members of the Armed Forces, their spouses, and civilian employees on all 32 bases in Canada and 2 bases abroad. The 11-page questionnaire investigated a total of 100 variables, mostly, but not exclusively, of pastoral interest. Over 600 people were surveyed.

The purpose of the 'Challenge 2000' survey was 'to draw a more accurate picture of the People of God within the Canadian Forces and better plan the pastoral action to be undertaken'.[21] Some questions, however, dealt with broad ethical issues, such as world peace, disarmament, aid to the Third World, economic justice in Canada, and so on. The data are of exceptional interest because no comparable information is available.

The sample was stratified according to data provided to the author by the Military Ordinariate (MO) and DND headquarters.[22] As already mentioned, the sample consisted of Roman Catholic members of the national defence community. Because the military chaplains serve not only members of the Forces but their families as well, the sample was designed to comprise about two-thirds service members and one third civilians. To provide sub-samples large enough to allow analysis by sex, 42 per cent of the sample were women, 10 per cent were in the service, and 32 per cent were civilians (wives of servicemen and employees). Appendix 1 gives more information on the sample design and the actual responses. Appendix 2 shows selected characteristics of three sub-samples of interest in this chapter: male members of the Forces, female members of the Forces, and civilian women.

This chapter draws heavily upon the quantitative information found in the responses to 20 closed questions and 11 open-ended questions in the Challenge 2000 survey.[23] Great care has been taken to extract relevant information from the voluminous, qualitative responses to the open-ended questions in the self-administered questionnaire. In addition, privately published defence publications, informal discussions, and formal interviews conducted by the author in 1992 and 1993 with members of the Canadian Forces, in all ranks, are used to fine-tune the interpretations proposed here.[24]

ATTITUDES TOWARD WORLD PEACE AND RELATED ISSUES

The military system of values is often characterized as basically conservative and cohesive. Anyone who has had much to do with Armed Forces personnel would agree with the Roman Catholic bishop for the French Army who once said that the qualities emphasized in military training—obedience, authority, solidarity, and personal responsibility—are very much in keeping with the teachings of the Gospel (Fihey 1987: 32). These characteristics are also often attributed to conservative personalities (Viereck 1956).

Defence publications and the conversation of members of the service are filled with colourful phrases that catch the essence of the military ethos such as 'getting the work done', 'ready, aye ready', 'tough and proud', and 'esprit de corps'. Contemporary Canada is sometimes described as a 'free-wheeling and self-indulgent' society, whereas the essential traits of the service member are 'loyalty and courage, . . . intelligence, compassion, equal parts of team member and individual thinker and, of course, self-respect' (Belzile 1992: 9). The regiment (and its equivalent in Navy and Air Force) is 'tradition, . . . a large, closely integrated, extended family, . . . a spiritual relationship' (Sutherland 1991: 31).

Attitudes towards peace

In the Challenge 2000 survey, there are five variables directly related to the issue of peace. Respondents were first asked to what extent they supported world peace and nuclear disarmament and then what their feelings were about the way in which the Roman Catholic Church promoted world peace and nuclear disarmament. A summary of the relevant data appears in Appendix 3.

Respondents were later asked to give their impression of the commitment of people around them in favour of world peace and other ideals.

Not unexpectedly, an overwhelming majority (over 95 per cent) of all respondents, male and female, military and civilian, expressed a clear support for world peace. Very few (3 per cent or fewer) thought that the Roman Catholic Church went 'too far' in promoting world peace. About 28 per cent of the respondents believed that the Church did 'not go far enough' in this direction; the proportion was as high as 35 per cent in the sub-sample of female service members, but the difference is not statistically significant.

For the military, being in favour of world peace is consistent with the conception that the task of Armed Forces includes 'anything which involves the elimination of the causes of conflict' (Belzile 1992: 11). International peacekeeping is cited as one of the primary responsibilities of the Canadian Armed Forces in numerous discussions and interviews with officers, including the Commander of the Mobile Command (Gervais 1992: 12-14). The general feeling of the military is that deterrence is more important than waging war.

Commitment to Peace

Although some variations do occur, a majority of respondents to the Challenge 2000 survey believe that people around them show a definite commitment to world peace. There are no significant differences among the three sub-samples: male and females members of the military and female civilians (see Appendix 3, line k).

Defence publications consider that 'Canadians are proud of the reputation which our Armed Forces have earned for themselves as international peacekeepers' (Taylor 1991: 1), 'as they go off to serve the country and humanity' (Marteinson 1992: 4). Indeed, when surveyed for DND during the Gulf War, Canadians attributed considerable importance to Canada's role as a member of the United Nations (MacDermid 1992).

The journal of the CDAI has as the theme of its winter 1993 issue 'Canada as Peacekeeper'. Though acknowledging the support for peacekeeping among the general public and 'the foreign policy élite', CDAI's director for public affairs contends that 'Canadians have made an icon of peacekeeping without really understanding what it is, or what returns it pays out [and, as a consequence, they] often over rate its importance'. He concludes, 'Too much peacekeeping may not be good' for Canada, as it should remain 'a peripheral activity' of a leading nation (Henry 1993).[25] Another magazine laments that 'with so many new commitments and so many cutbacks, the soldiers are understandably worried about the future'—this is the price of peace (Taylor 1992b).

As one officer pointed out in private, 'We are peace-loving but our job is war'. Members of the military as well as defence writers refer to peacekeeping operations in ex-Yugoslavia as 'going to war', and they like to quote Major General Lewis Mackenzie: 'There's no sense in risking the lives of

[Canadian] soldiers in a country where they don't give a damn about peace' (quoted in Taylor 1992c).[26] Our interviews show that men and women of the national defence community share this point of view almost unanimously.

The Symbolic Appropriateness of Peace

Professional defence writers echo the feelings evident in many discussions and interviews with members of the Canadian military: peacekeeping is 'politically correct', and 'peace' may sometimes be nothing more than a 'code word' for transforming 'any word into a magic ethical talisman' (Scott 1993). There is considerable evidence to support this view. A shipbuilder labels Canadian patrol frigates 'Canada's new diplomats, guardians of the sea, protectors and peace keepers' (Saint John Shipbuilding 1992), whereas the same frigates are called 'warships' by an expert in the field (Shadwick 1993: 23). Under the aegis of CISS, an arms trade show has become a 'peacekeeping exhibition and seminar'.[27] Under the very appropriate title *The Changing Face of Peacekeeping* (Morrison 1993), the CISS published the proceedings of the seminar along with a list of the arms and service companies present at the exhibition. While expressing no sympathy for 'otherwise moribund Coalition of Church Groups and Disarmament Weenies', even hard-line defence publications are not fooled by the 'ruse' of 'altruistic saints . . . out to sell arms [and make] buckets of money' under the guise of peacemaking (Scott 1993).[28]

The publisher of a magazine covering extensively the peacekeeping missions in which the Canadian Forces take part notes with concern that 'the Canadian public are silently supportive' of cutbacks in the defence budget (Taylor 1992b). Defence publications chastise the Canadian government for placing 'Canadian service members once again in the dangerous role of international peacekeepers' (Taylor 1991). The lukewarm attitude towards peacekeeping may be attributed largely to the view that it is becoming more difficult for the Forces to 'do more with less': 'When the resources for defence are insufficient given the tasks at hand, and those "insufficiencies" are imposed upon the forces, a heavy burden of decision-making becomes the senior military planner's lot' ('Viewpoint' 1991: 12). Interviews with (mostly male) officers working at the National Defence Headquarters in Ottawa confirm that the military feel the need for 'essential new equipment' (Marteinson 1992) to 'fight for peace'.

Support for Disarmament

Officially, Canada 'adjusts its military structure in response to the new geostrategic realities, [that is] non-specific threats in a troubled and uncertain world' (Green 1992). And officially the military agrees that 'arms control has an important and necessary part to play in future international security and stability; . . . viable arms control arrangements may well be the key to peace and the foundation of a new world order' (Goetze 1992).

However, it is quite obvious that the defence community strongly resents the 'continuing lowering of defence as a government priority' (Yost 1992). The wife of a serviceman has her own explanation: 'Do you really think that any army would support disarmament?'

In fact, however, the Challenge 2000 survey of Catholics in the defence community reveals only a little less support for nuclear disarmament than for world peace, although over 75 per cent of all respondents endorse nuclear disarmament (see Appendix 3, line [c]). In fact, when asked about the actions of the Roman Catholic Church in favour of nuclear disarmament, few consider that the Church goes 'too far', and from 25 per cent to 32 per cent (depending on the sub-sample) feel that it does 'not go far enough'. But here again there is no statistically significant difference among the sub-samples— military men, military women, and civilian women (see Appendix 3, line [d]).

Among those who are lukewarm towards nuclear disarmament, some feel that 'if hostile countries would heed the call of Christ and the Church for disarmament, then the Church would be on more firm ground asking for nuclear disarmament [of NATO countries]'.

Survey data, interviews, and defence literature point to a relatively homogeneous organizational culture in the defence community with respect to peace-related matters. Beyond a generalized support for world peace, there is a serious concern that Canada's Armed Forces may not be adequately equipped (and staffed)[29] to fulfil their peace missions abroad. Neither data from the Challenge 2000 survey of Catholics nor discussions with members of the defence community show any significant differences between the views of men and women. That finding supports the hypothesis of this chapter.

Attitudes toward Other Ethical Issues

In the Challenge 2000 survey, there are three other variables more or less related to the issue of peace, variables that may also be used to test the chapter's hypothesis on the absence of gender variations. Respondents were asked to what extent they supported help to the Third World, anti-poverty measures, and 'justice in the economic system of our country'. The relevant data appear in Appendix 3, lines (e), (g), and (i). The respondents were also asked to describe their feelings about the way in which the Roman Catholic Church promoted these things (see Appendix 3, lines [f], [h], and [g]). They were finally asked to give their view of the commitment of people around them—in the workplace, in the business world, and in the political world—to youth, to older people, to the poor, to refugees and immigrants, and to the service of the country.

Aid to the Third World
It is often said that aid to development is the key to world peace. This theme has been voiced repeatedly by the Roman Catholic Church, among others. Among the three sub-samples, the support for help to the Third World is

almost as high (91 per cent) as for world peace. Only a small minority (7 per cent or less) feels that the Roman Catholic Church does not do enough in that direction, and from 19 per cent to 26 per cent would like it to do more. Responses from the three sub-samples do not vary significantly.

Anti-Poverty Measures and Economic Justice in Canada

In all three sub-samples, a large majority of respondents (86 per cent and over) are in favour of a 'priority option for the poor', but somewhat fewer are in favour of 'justice in the economic system of our country' (58 per cent to 68 per cent). In all three sub-samples, similar proportions of respondents feel that the Roman Catholic Church 'does not go far enough' in promoting a priority option for the poor (25 per cent to 35 per cent), and hardly anyone thinks that the Church is going 'too far' in that direction. The picture is not as clear with respect to the Church's initiatives concerning economic justice: there seems to be a statistical difference[30] between the attitudes of female civilians and female members of the military, but no statistical relationship[31] between this attitudinal variable and the independent variables (sex and membership in the Forces). Here again, the null hypothesis is supported and this tends to confirm that the organizational culture of the national defence community (at least among practising and non-practising Catholics) across gender lines is relative homogeneous.

Perceptions of Commitment

Respondents were asked to give their impression of the commitment of people around them in the workplace, in the business world, and in the political world to youth, to older people, to the poor, to refugees and immigrants, and to the service of the country. For none of these variables were significant statistical differences found among the three sub-samples of interest here (military males, military females, civilian females), giving further strength to the null hypothesis proposed at the beginning of this chapter.[32]

Private Ethical Issues

The interview and survey data discussed so far have not shown any meaningful variations among the three sub-samples of Roman Catholic respondents drawn from the defence community. Some may consider the set of attitudes investigated to belong to the 'public', as opposed to the 'private', sphere. If the hypothesis is true that the organizational culture of the national defence community is *relatively homogeneous across gender lines*, at least among Roman Catholics, then there should also be no meaningful differences in supposedly more private attitudes, even though women would be more intimately concerned with some of the issues (such as abortion and birth control). The Challenge 2000 survey contained questions about the attitudes towards the positions of the Roman Catholic Church on abortion, family planning, divorce, common law relationships, and 'genetical manipulations (genetic engineering)'. To allow comparison, Appendix 4 summarizes the frequencies of characteristic answers for each of the three sub-samples.

Statistically speaking, there are differences of attitude between male and female members of the military with respect to the Church's position on birth control, divorce, and genetic engineering. There are also differences of attitude between female members of the military and female civilians with respect to the Church's position on abortion and genetic engineering. However, when lambda *b* is used as a proportional-reduction-of-error statistic, the relationship is extremely weak—in fact, so weak as to be meaningless. Given the criteria set out at the beginning of this chapter, it must be concluded that there are no substantial variations among the three sub-samples of respondents from the defence community with respect to the Challenge 2000 set of ethical questions of a private nature.[33]

Methodological Comments

It is always fairly easy to misinterpret quantitative data. A few words of caution are therefore in order. Some might suggest that the absence of variation among the three sub-samples may result from the strong influence of the Catholic Church itself or the ethical values it aims to transmit. This contention does not hold because the data do not always indicate blind support for Church positions. For instance, up to 35 per cent of some sub-samples are of the opinion that the Church does not go far enough on some ethical questions (for example, military men and poverty), and up to 75 per cent of some sub-samples disagree with the Church's condemnation of some more private practices (for example, military women and birth control). Other serious disagreements with the official position of the Church have been substantiated elsewhere (Gingras 1992a).

Nor should the results presented here be used to suggest that the members of the defence community share a *totally* homogeneous set of values. Indeed, Appendices 3 and 4 show how Catholics disagree among themselves on some ethical questions. For instance, 11 per cent of military men think that the Catholic Church 'goes too far' in promoting economic justice in Canada, and 24 per cent think it 'does not go far enough'; 29 per cent of civilian women think the Church 'goes too far' in condemning common law unions, and 15 per cent think it 'does not go far enough'. What the data show is that the differences are not related to sex.

In fact, the author has shown elsewhere that observable differences in attitudes of the military may be related to variables other than sex, for instance language and province of residence (Gingras 1992c). Unpublished data also show that there are some significant differences between members of the air force, the army, and the navy. Other differences can be noted between practising and non-practising Catholics; in the latter case, interestingly enough, the over-representation of practising Catholics in the civilian women sub-sample is not sufficient to produce a biased relationship even between sex and ethical attitudes (see Appendix 3).

CONCLUSIONS

Despite some claims that women may be more in favour of peace and less authoritarian than men, the interview data and data from 25 variables included in the Challenge 2000 survey fail to reveal substantial differences in attitudes in three sub-samples drawn from Roman Catholics in the defence community: male members of the military, female members of the military and female civilian employees of DND and/or wives of servicemen. The author has found no evidence that, among Roman Catholics in the defence community, women are more (or less) in favour of peace or less (or more) conservative than men, with respect to a selection of ethical issues. Though attitudes toward peace may be influenced by the symbolic appropriateness of being in favour of peacekeeping, both among the general public and in the military, the other issues, which belong to the public as well as the private spheres, are not likely influenced by this bias. That is not to say that there are no meaningful differences between the attitudes of men and women in the military community, but only that none has been revealed by the available evidence. Unfortunately, this conclusion may reinforce the view that sociologists and military historians have failed to grasp or convey the importance of women's service to Canada. For instance, there is still no definitive work on the part played by women in Canada's wars. One observer has written that women, considered 'a bit of a pest in peacetime, . . . were reluctantly recruited then casually dismissed and officially forgotten' (Shannon 1992). By all accounts, women's contributions and gender differences in the Canadian Forces have definitely not been sufficiently studied. Ignorance can only lead to echoes of Creon's remark to Antigone: 'We'll have no woman's law here.'

Appendix 1

Sampling Design and Responses

Variable	Population Parameters[a] %	Original Sample[b] %	Responses[c] %
Religious practice			
Practising	15-33	50	63
Non-practising	67-85	50	37
Principal language			
French	51	50	56
English	49	50	42
Other/both/undeclared	—	—	2
Status			
Members of the Forces[d]	—	68	65
Civilians[e]			
DND employees	—	—	13
Spouses of members	—	—	24
Total civilians	—	32	35[f]
Sex and status			
Women in Forces	10	10 (15)[g]	10 (16)
Men in Forces	90	58 (85)	55 (84)
Civilian women	—	32	32
Civilian men	—	0	2
Sex			
All women	—	42	42
All men	—	58	58

Notes for Appendix 1

[a]Military personnel only, declaring Roman Catholic faith, as of 15 June 1989. Information or estimations were supplied by the Roman Catholic Military Ordinariate (MO) and/or the Department of National Defence (DND). No information is available for civilian DND employees. Religious practice refers to MO's estimation of those attending mass at least once a week.

[b]Military personnel and civilians. The figures in parentheses are for the military subsample only, to allow comparison with figures in population parameters column. Percentages are given only for variables used to stratify the sample. For pastoral reasons, it was decided to aim at a total sample comprising 50% of practising Catholics. With an expected rate of return of 60%, the research budget allowed for a maximum of about 1,000 questionnaires to be sent.

^cMilitary personnel and civilians. The figures in parentheses are for the military sub-sample only, to allow comparison with figures in population parameters column. Some percentages may not add up exactly to 100% due to rounding.

^dIncludes persons married to another member of the Forces. The desired minimum number of responses from the military was 400 (to allow statistical analysis without too large a margin of error), and the expected response rate was 60%; therefore the size of the original military sub-sample had to be at least 667 (two-thirds of the total sample).

^eConsidering that DND statistics indicate that 57% of all Roman Catholic members of the Forces were married, that in many instances their spouses were also members of the Forces or civilian employees, and that most DND civilian employees were women, it was decided to sample civilian women to allow comparisons between men and women, as well as between military and non-military female members of the larger defence community. The desired minimum number of responses from civilians was 200 (to allow some statistical analysis), and the expected response rate was 60%; therefore the original civilian sub-sample size had to be about 333 (one-third of the total sample).

^fIncludes 2% that are both spouses and DND employees. We know that some civilian women responded to questionnaires addressed to their husbands who were members of the Forces.

^gIt was decided to slightly over-sample women in the Forces to allow for some statistical analysis of the responses from this sub-sample.

APPENDIX 2

Selected Characteristics of Sub-samples in the Challenge 2000 Survey

Variable	Male Military Sub-sample (N ≈ 331) %	Female Military Sub-sample (N ≈ 64) %	Female Civilian Sub-sample (N ≈ 199) %
Service			
Navy	8	14	—
Army	41	39	—
Air Force	51	49	—
Rank			
Private or Jr NCO	32	51	—
Senior Non-commissioned officer	37	12	—
Junior officer	21	35	—
Senior officer	10	2	—
Principal language[a]			
English	39	46	50
French	61	54	50
Age			
25 and under	15	19	8
26-35	36	58	38
36-45	38	18	32
46 and over	12	5	22
Marital Status			
Single	14	32	4
Married	77	51	86
Other	10	18	10
Religious practice[a]			
Practising (weekly)	58	49	75
Non-practising	42	51	25
Education			
High school not completed	17	4	11
High school completed	36	37	36
Some post-secondary studies	29	32	30
University degree	19	28	23

[a]These variables were used to stratify the sample. See Appendix 1 for sampling information.

Appendix 3

Selected Ethical Attitudes in the Challenge 2000 Survey

	Subsample[a]		
Dependent Variable[b]	Male Military Sub-sample (N ≈ 331) %	Female Military Sub-sample (N ≈ 64) %	Female Civilian Sub-sample (N ≈ 199) %
Peace			
(a) Totally favourable	95	100	96
(b) Church goes			
too far	3	0	1
not far enough	26	35	22
Nuclear disarmament			
(c) Totally favourable	81	75	78
(d) Church goes			
too far	10	9	3
not far enough	28	32	25
Help to the Third World			
(e) Totally favourable	91	91	91
(f) Church goes			
too far	5	7	4
not far enough	26	20	19
Anti-poverty measures			
(g) Totally favourable	88	86	87
(h) Church goes			
too far	1	0	1
not far enough	35	25	31
Economic justice in Canada			
(i) Totally favourable	68	58	68
(j) Church goes*			
too far	11	13	4
not far enough	24	24	26
Perception of the commitment of the people around you to world peace[c]			
(k) They are			
very committed	23	20	19
sufficiently committed	39	52	42
barely committed	27	18	24
not at all committed	4	4	3

Notes for Appendix 3

[a]N is the number of respondents surveyed in each sub-sample. The actual number of substantive answers (excluding those who 'did not know' or did not answer) varies slightly from question to question.

[b]There is no statistically significant difference, as measured by chi-square ($p < .05$), between male and female members of the Forces. The only statistically significant difference between female members of the Forces and female civilians is indicated by * When lambda b is used as a proportional-reduction-in-error statistic, no relationship is identifiable, since the value of lambda b in all sections of Appendix 3 is .0000. In other words, knowledge of what sub-sample a given individual belongs to does not improve at all the prediction of any of his or her attitudes on ethical matters.

[c]There is no statistically significant difference, as measured by chi-square ($p < .05$), between male and female members of the Forces or between female members of the Forces and female civilians for any of the impressions of commitment surveyed: in favour of world peace in the workplace, in the business world, in the political world, to youth, to older people, to the poor, to refugees and immigrants, and to the service of the country. This table gives answers only to the first question (world peace), because it is more closely related to the theme of the chapter.

APPENDIX 4

Attitudes in the Challenge 2000 Survey toward the Condemnation
of Selected Practices by the Roman Catholic Church

Dependent variables[b]	Subsample[a]		
	Male Military Sub-sample (N ≈ 331) %	Female Military Sub-sample (N ≈ 64) %	Female Civilian Sub-sample (N ≈ 199) %
Birth control[#]			
Church goes:			
too far	57	75	59
not far enough	8	6	6
Abortion[*]			
Church goes:			
too far	24	33	17
not far enough	21	10	14
Divorce[#]			
Church goes:			
too far	28	47	31
not far enough	13	6	11
Genetical Manipulation[*#]			
Church goes:			
too far	16	32	10
not far enough	24	27	20
Common law marriage			
Church goes:			
too far	34	48	29
not far enough	16	13	15

Notes for Appendix 4

[a]*N* is the number of respondents surveyed in each sub-sample. The actual number of substantive answers (excluding those who 'did not know' or did not answer) varies slightly from question to question.

[b]Symbols indicate statistically significant differences, as measured by chi-square ($p <$ .05), between male and female members of the Forces (#) or between female members of the Forces and female civilians (*). However, when lambda is used as a proportional-reduction-of-error statistic, no relationship is identifiable, the highest value of lambda in Appendix 4 being .03. In other words, knowledge of what sub-sample a person belongs to virtually does not improve (at the most by 3%) the prediction of any of his or her attitudes on ethical matters.

NOTES

This is a revised version of 'Gender Differences in the Attitudes of the Military towards World Peace, Nuclear Disarmament and Related Issues', a paper given at the 65th Annual Meeting of the Canadian Political Science Association, Learned Societies Conference, Ottawa, 1993. The author thanks Sandra Burt, Jean Pariseau, and Alan Whitehorn, for their comments.

1 Of course, this is a broad generalization, but although exceptions may be observed more and more often, traditionally, in almost all countries for which data are available, women have tended to support the conservative parties and to display conservative attitudes more than men. The conventional explanation attributes the difference to the 'different social role of women' (Lipset 1963: 231), and the way in which this leads them to accept values identified with tradition, law, and order.

2 Although Canada is moving toward an integration of the regular forces and reserve units, this chapter is concerned only with the attitudes of professional service people in the regular forces, unless otherwise specified.

3 In the Armed Forces, as in the population at large, there is a majority of Catholics. It is not assumed here that the values and attitudes of Catholics are identical to those of non-Catholics, as that is not the point. What is investigated is the differences (or lack of differences) between men and women in the same community. For reasons explained below, individual data were available only for Catholics.

4 Discussing the feminist agenda, the author dwells on the 'current extravagances of the feminist movement—featuring everything from government-subsidized lessons in lesbian masturbation at a conference in Banff, to similar technology celebrated in a Vancouver women's festival' and expresses the opinion that Campbell's 'two divorces will not enhance her image in the eyes of people trying to make marriages work and raise children.' *Maclean's* (1993) also describes Campbell as a 'self-avowed feminist', but makes no spiteful remarks about that fact.

5 Frum also condemns Campbell for having 'radicalized Canadian law' and warns the Progressive Conservatives that her popularity was 'bad news'.

6 When Kim Campbell was appointed Minister of Defence by Prime Minister Brian Mulroney, the *Financial Post Magazine* ran a short article under the headline 'Arms and the Woman'. It assessed rather simplistically the move of Campbell from Justice ('where she made decisions about guns and gay rights') to Defence ('where she will make decisions about guns and gay rights'): the difference would be 'superior photo ops' and more 'budget power' but 'lousy patronage ops' and increased 'scandal potential'. However, the magazine's coverage of the appointment of Campbell made only two comments specifically related to gender: 'There are only so many things you can do with judicial robes, but as Defence minister, Campbell gets to wear Tilley hats and pose with peacekeepers. . . . Two previous Defence ministers have been laid low by German strippers and prostitutes. Coincidence?' (*Financial Post Magazine* 1993). The reference to 'photo ops' is an allusion to a controversial front-page photo of Kim Campbell published by the *Ottawa Citizen* on 31 October 1992. For background, see Conn (1993).

7 Little has been written about the contribution of Mary Collins during her term as Associate Minister of National Defence.

8 The *Financial Post* is avowedly 'right-wing' (Byfield 1993).

9 See, for instance, *Maclean's* 1993.

10 The essential element of a '*conservative ethos*' is a favourable view of law, order, and military intervention.

11 The research was conducted before the deplorable actions by members of the Canadian Armed Forces (including peacekeepers) that were widely publicized by the media in 1994 and early 1995.

12 For reasons specified below, individual data were available only for Catholics.

13 About 10 per cent of the Armed Forces are women.

14 'Male chauvinism' is the term used by Preston (1991: chap. 12) to describe the attitude of the military towards women in the 1970s; cf. also General de Chastelain's prefatory remarks, p. viii.

15 Interesting exceptions, largely based on anecdotal evidence, are Collier 1994 and Harrison 1994. See also Mackenzie 1993.

16 See, for instance, the television series 'The Valour and the Horror', produced jointly by the CBC and the National Film Board (and broadcast in January 1992), which created much controversy and resulted in hundreds of letters of protest to a Senate sub-committee.

17 Many references may be found in Cooke 1984. Recent reminiscences include Allard 1985, Larouche 1991, and Mackenzie 1993.

18 References will be found in Gingras (forthcoming).

19 See, for instance, Woelfel et al. 1976; Larwood et al. 1980; Savell et al. 1979; Stevens and Gardner 1987.

20 This approach may be somewhat biased because it tends to overemphasize the views of the officers (mostly men) who are the keenest to maintain traditions and ensure a high profile for the Armed Forces.

21 From the cover letter of the questionnaire. A summary of the results may be found in Gingras 1992a. Preliminary (but not totally accurate) results also appear in Gingras, 1992b. See also Gingras 1992c.

22 The Catholic population of each base was stratified to yield representative sub-samples by rank and military status (commissioned officer, non-commissioned officer, private, civilian employee, spouse), sex (female, male), and language (English, French). Base chaplains provided information that allowed the sample to be stratified further on the basis of religious practice (practising or non-practising). To allow for statistical testing, practising Catholics and women were deliberately over-sampled (see Appendix 1 for details). On each base samples were chosen to reflect both its own profile with respect to the stratifying variables and its weight in relation to the entire defence population. English and French versions of the questionnaire were used as appropriate.

23 The quantitative data from the Challenge 2000 survey has been processed with SPSS-PC statistical software. Statistics used in this chapter are chi-square and lambda b. Here, by comparing the attitudes observed in two sub-samples at a time, chi-square gives the probability (p) of finding significant differences; when the probability is less than 5 per cent ($p < .05$), the difference is considered to be statistically significant. Because 'a difference may be statistically significant without being significant in any other sense [and] significance can be obtained . . . with a very weak relationship and large samples', (Blalock 1972: 293-4), this chapter uses lambda b as a measure of strength of relationship. Lambda b gives the proportional reduction in errors (PRE) when one predicts the attitudes of persons whose category or sub-sample is known. A reduction in errors by less than 30 per cent is generally considered negligible, and therefore only a PRE of .3 or more is considered to show any strength of relationship. This chapter considers a relationship to be meaningful only if it satisfies the criteria of both the chi-square ($p < .05$) and lambda b (PRE > 0.3) statistics.

24 All unattributed quotations are from discussions, interviews, and open-ended survey questions. Quotations from francophone respondents have been translated into English by the author.

25 Even before the infamous videotapes of the Airborne Regiment released in 1995, many professional defence writers had for some time been voicing the opinion that the Canadian public is not well informed about the Armed Forces and that cynicism is widespread precisely because of the lack of information: see Thomson 1992. But even well-researched accounts of the Canadian military experience fail to cover some significant peacekeeping activities of the Armed Forces; a good example is the purportedly exhaustive Bercuson-Granatstein-Morton trilogy, which neglects the role of the Canadian Forces during the Cold War as well as many peacekeeping deployments (Morton and Granatstein 1989; Granatstein and Morton 1989; Granatstein and Bercuson 1991). But see also Granatstein and Lavender 1992 and Gardam 1992.

26 Mackenzie was in command of the United Nations operations in Sarajevo in 1992 (see Mackenzie 1993). Some veterans of Cyprus peacekeeping missions express similar opinions.

27 'ARMX' trade shows took place in Ottawa in 1987 and 1989. 'Peacekeeping '93' was sponsored by Baxter Publications in co-operation with CISS. Baxter Publications publishes the annual *Canada's Aerospace and Defence Industry: A Capability Guide*, *Aviation and Aerospace*, and *Canadian Defence Quarterly*. A CISS flyer advertising 'Peacekeeping '93' stated, 'The exhibition portion of Peacekeeping '93 will bring together representatives of business, industry, non-governmental organizations, governments and other interested parties to exchange ideas and information about the broad subject of peacekeeping. Business and industry representatives will have an opportunity to demonstrate how their companies are responding to the shifting demands for new types of equipment.'

28 The author also refers to those who demonstrated against the Peacekeeping '93 exhibition as the 'Coalition to Impose Their Narrow Viewpoint', the 'Coalition to Oppose Reality', the 'Coalition to Turn the Other Cheek', and the 'Coalition to Make Sure No-One gets Away with Anything'.

29 Reduction of personnel and the concept of 'total force' are matters often mentioned in discussions and interviews with the military, but they are peripheral to the theme of this chapter.

30 $P < .05$, as measured by chi-square.

31 Lambda b = .0000.

32 For an examination of some statistical differences between perceptions of commitment and other variables, see Gingras 1992c.

33 A statistically significant difference (measured by chi-square) simply tells us that the distribution of responses is unlikely to be due to chance alone; a proportional-reduction-of-error statistic (such as lambda b) tells us whether or not the independent variables (here, sex and—for women—membership in the military) can be used to predict the attitudes of individuals. The absence of a relationship between gender and private ethical attitudes (despite statistically significant differences) may be due to the fact that respondents had a choice of four possible answers, not only the two reported in the appendix. In other words, the differences within each sub-sample would be much more important than the differences from one sub-sample to another.

BIBLIOGRAPHY

Allard, Gén. J.V. (1985), *Mémoires* (Boucherville, PQ: de Montagne).

Alt, Betty, and Bonnie Stone (1990), *Uncle Sam's Brides: The World of Military Wives* (New York: Walker).

———— (1991) *Campfollowing: A History of the Military Wife*. (New York: Praeger).

Beaudet, Normand (1993), *Le mythe de la défense canadienne* (Montreal: Écosociété).

Belzile, Lt-Gen. (Ret.) C.H. (1992), 'Loyalty and Courage Still Badge of Infantryman', *Forum*, Journal of the CDAI 7, 2 (Spring).

Blalock, Hubert M., Jr (1972), *Social Statistics*, 2nd edn (New York: McGraw-Hill).

Byfield, Ted (1993), 'Reform Party Will Gain If Campbell Is Tory Leader', *The Financial Post*, 13 Mar., p. S2.

Castonguay, Jacques (1989), *Le Collège militaire royal de Saint-Jean*, with a preface by Brig.-Gen. C. Archambault (Montreal: Méridien).

Collier, Dianne (1994), *Hurry Up and Wait: An Inside Look at Life as a Canadian Military Wife* (Kingston: Armchair General Bookstore).

Conn, Chris (1993), 'The Media's Moulding of Kim Campbell', *Ottawa Citizen*, 20 Mar., p. B1.

Cooke, Owen A. (1984), *The Canadian Military Experience 1867-1983: A Bibliography*, 2nd edn (Ottawa: Directorate of History, Dept. of National Defence).

Cotton, Charles A. (1979), *Military Attitudes and the Values of the Army in Canada*, Research Report 79-5 (Toronto: Canadian Forces Personnel Applied Research Unit).

——— (1981), 'Institutional and Occupational Values in Canada's Army', *Armed Forces and Society* 8, 1: 99-110.

Coulon, Jocelyn (1991), *En première ligne: grandeurs et misères du système militaire canadien* (Montreal: Jour).

——— (1994), *Les casques bleus* (Montreal: Fides).

Enloe, Cynthia H. (1983), *Does Khaki Become You? The Militarization of Women's Lives* (Boston: South End Press).

Fihey, Mgr Jacques (1987), Interview in *Fêtes et saisons* 414 (April).

Financial Post Magazine (1993), 'Arms and the Woman: Kimmie Does Defence', Feb., p. 5.

Frum, David (1993), 'Campbell Odd Choice of "Conservative" Party', *Financial Post*, 13 March, p. S2.

Gardam, Col. John (1992), *The Canadian Peacekeeper / Le gardien de la paix canadien* (Burnstown, Ont.: General Store).

Gervais, Lt-Gen. J.C. (1992), 'Moving SLOWLY toward Total Force', *Forum* 7, 2 (Spring): 12-14.

Gingras, François-Pierre (1992a), 'L'ordinaire militaire en consultation: Les catholiques des Forces armées prennent la parole', *L'Église canadienne* 19 Nov., pp. 435-40.

——— (1992b), 'Attitudes of the Military towards Peace, Nuclear Disarmament and Related Issues', paper given at the 64th Annual Meeting of the Canadian Political Science Association, Charlottetown.

——— (1992c), 'Les militaires québécois sont-ils différents?', *Revue québécoise de science politique* 22 (Fall): 55-74.

——— (1993), 'Gender Differences in the Attitudes of the Military towards World Peace, Nuclear Disarmament and Related Issues', paper given at the 65th Annual Meeting of the Canadian Political Science Association, Learned Societies Conference, Ottawa.

——— (forthcoming), *De mémoire d'aumônier militaire: une bibliographie annotée*.

Goetze, Gen. B.A, Director General, International Policy Operation, National Defence Headquarters (1992), Address to the annual meeting of the Conference of Defence Associations Institute Seminar, January.

Granatstein, J.L., and David Jay Bercuson (1991), *War and Peacekeeping: From South Africa to the Gulf—Canada's Limited Wars* (Toronto: Key Porter).

Granatstein, J.L., and Douglas Lavender (1992), *Shadows of War, Faces of Peace: Canada's Peacekeepers* (based on a film by John Muller; photographs by Boris Spremo) (Toronto: Key Porter).

Granatstein, J.L., and Desmond Morton (1989), *A Nation Forged in Fire: Canadians and the Second World War, 1939-1945* (Toronto: Lester and Orpen).

Green, Lt-Col. D.E. (1992), 'Future NATO Force Structure and Canada's Role', *Forum* 7, 2 (Spring): 17-18.

Harrison, Deborah, and Lucie Laliberté (1994), *No Life Like It: Canada's Military Wives* (Toronto: Lorimer).

Henry, Col. (Ret.) A. Sean (1993), 'The Peacekeeping Legacy: Canada and the New World Order', *Forum* 7, 4 (Winter): 6-10.

Hough, Patricia Lynn (1979), *The Socio-cultural Integration of German Women Married to American Military Personnel*, Ph.D. diss., Freie Universität Berlin.

Larouche, Maryo (1991), *Si l'aventure vous intéresse . . .* (Varennes, PQ: Éd. de Varennes).

Larwood, L.E. Glasser, and R. McDonald (1980), 'Attitudes of Male and Female Cadets toward Military Sex Integration', *Sex Roles* 6, 3: 381-90.

Lipset, Seymour Martin (1963), *Political Man: The Social Bases of Politics* (Garden City, NJ: Doubleday).

Loomis, Dan G. (1984), *Not Much Glory: Quelling the FLQ* (Toronto: Deneau).

MacDermid, R.H. (1992), 'Public Opinion Polling and Canadian Involvement in the Gulf War', paper given at the 64th Annual Meeting of the Canadian Political Science Association, Charlottetown.

Mackenzie, Maj.-Gen. Lewis (1993), *Peacekeeper: The Road to Sarajevo* (Vancouver and Toronto: Douglas and McIntyre).

Maclean's (1993), 'The Rising Star', 18 Jan., pp. 12-14.

Marteinson, John (1992), 'From the Editor', *Canadian Defence Quarterly* 22, 3 (Dec.): 4.

Morrison, Alex, ed. (1993), *The Changing Face of Peacekeeping* (Toronto: Canadian Institute for Strategic Studies).

Morton, Desmond, and J.L. Granatstein (1989), *Marching to Armageddon: Canadians and the Great War, 1914-1919* (Toronto: Lester and Orpen).

Newman, Peter C. (1983), *True North Not Strong and Free* (Toronto: McClelland and Stewart).

Preston, Richard A. (1991), *To Serve Canada: A History of the Royal Military College since the Second World War*, with a Foreword by Gen. A.J.G.D. de Chastelain (Ottawa: University of Ottawa Press).

Reynaud, Emmanuel (1988), *Les femmes, la violence et l'armée* (Paris: Fondation pour les études de défense nationale).

Saint John Shipbuilding Limited (1992), Advertisement in *Esprit de corps/Canadian Military Then and Now* 2, 5 (Oct.): 13.

Savell, J.M., J.C. Woelfel, B.E. Collins, and P.M. Bentler (1979), 'A Study of Male and Female Soldiers' Beliefs about the "Appropriateness" of Various Jobs for Women in the Army', *Sex Roles* 5, 1: 41-50.

Scott, James G. (1993), 'Letter from the Editor', *Esprit de corps/Canadian Military Then and Now* 2, 10 (Mar.): 2.

Shadwick, Martin (1993), 'Current Canadian Defence Industry Projects and Capabilities', *Canada's Aerospace and Defence Industry: A Capability Guide* (Toronto: Baxter).

Shannon, Norman (1992), '50 Years Ago . . . Tommy Atkins in Skirts', *Esprit de corps/Canadian Military Then and Now* 2, 5 (Oct.): 56.

Sophocles ([440 BC] 1947), *Antigone*, in *Three Theban Plays*, trans. E.F. Watling (Harmondsworth, U.K.: Penguin).

Stanley, George F.G. (1974), *Canada's Soldiers* (Toronto: Macmillan).

Stevens, G., and S. Gardner (1987), 'But Can She Command a Ship? Acceptance of Women by Peers at the Coast Guard Academy', *Sex Roles* 16, 3-4: 181-8.

Sutherland, Col. (Ret.) W.B.S. (1991), 'Reflections from an Old Soldier', *Esprit de corps/Canadian Military Then and Now* 1, 3 (July).

Taylor, Scott R. (1991), 'Letter from the publisher', *Esprit de corps/Canadian Military Then and Now* 1, 3 (July): 1.

―――― (1992a), 'Letter from the Publisher', *Esprit de corps/Canadian Military Then and Now* 2, 10 (Mar.): 1.

―――― (1992b), 'As the Understrength Military Struggles to Pay the Peace Dividend the Numbers Don't Add Up', *Esprit de corps/Canadian Military Then and Now*, 2, 5 (Oct.): 8.

―――― (1992c), 'Letter from the Publisher', *Esprit de corps/Canadian Military Then and Now* 2, 3 (Aug.): 1.

Thomson, Roger (1992), 'Total Force Army or Total Farce: A Critical View of Canada's New Military Structure', *Forum* 7, 2 (Spring): 15-16.

Tremblay, Jeanne-d'Arc (1988), *La défense du Québec et la famille Tremblay* (Montreal: Fides).

Viereck, Peter (1956), *Conservatism* (New York: Van Nostrand Reinhold).

Viewpoint (1991), *Esprit de Corps/Canadian Military Than and Now* 1, no. 3 (July): 12-13.

Woelfel, J.C., J.M. Savell, B.E. Collins, and P.M. Bentler (1976), *A preliminary Version of a Scale to Measure Sex-Role Attitudes in the Army*, Research Memorandum 76-3 (Arlington, VA: Army Research Institute for the Behavioral and Social Sciences.

Yost, Brig.-Gen. (Ret.) W.J. (1992), 'Canada: The Noblest of All the Self Governing Nations', *Forum* 7, 2 (Spring): 27.

CHAPTER 12

Gender-of-Interviewer Effects and Level of Public Support for Affirmative Action

David A. Northrup

INTRODUCTION

Over the last two decades there has been an increase in the use of surveys to explore the similarities and differences in the attitudes, values, beliefs, and behaviour of women and men. Studies of the 'gender gap' in voting patterns, attitudes towards violence, and support for social programs—such as medical care, help for the poor, the elimination of discrimination against women, and so on—find, not surprisingly, that the sex of the survey respondent can predict the response to gender-related issues as well as general social-welfare issues (Brodie and Chandler 1991: 19-25; Kopinak 1987; Shapiro and Mahajan 1986; Wirls 1986; Smith 1984). But much less attention has been given to the extent to which the interviewers' sex affects the respondents' answers in surveys.

INTERVIEWER EFFECTS

Critics of survey research have asked to what extent survey answers depend on who is asking the question. The first attempts to examine systematically what has become known as 'interviewer effects' suggested that variations in the behaviour and the characteristics (age, class, race, sex, and so on) of the interviewer and the interaction between interviewer and respondent had an effect on the results of sample surveys (Hyman, Feldman, and Stember 1954). However, three decades later Bradburn (1983) concluded there is little support, 'popular notions notwithstanding', for concluding that the interviewer's characteristics '[have a] consistent effect' on survey results. Bradburn suggested that improved training and the use of professional interviewers has ensured that interviewer effects are minimized. The exception,

Bradburn notes, are those characteristics of the interviewer that are 'visible' to the respondent.

The two characteristics of the interviewer most visible in a face-to-face survey, and easiest for the respondent to determine in a telephone survey, are the race and sex of the interviewer.[1] The affect of race on survey results is well documented (Hatchett and Schuman 1975-6; Cotter, Cohen, and Coulter 1982; Anderson, Silver, and Abramson 1988; Finkel, Guterbock, and Borg 1991). While most researchers report that white respondents defer to black interviewers on questions of racial tolerance, others find evidence that both white and black respondents defer to interviewers of the opposite race. This effect may be seen as an example of what Schuman and Converse (1971) have called the 'desire not to offend a polite stranger'. Race-of-interviewer effects have also been found in surveys of adolescents (Campbell 1981). Ethnicity-of-interviewer effects have been confirmed for ethnically sensitive questions (Reese et al. 1981), but in a survey of Cubans, Chicanos, Native Americans, and Chinese, there were no effects for surveys that dealt with non-ethnic issues (Weeks and Moore 1981).

The effect of the interviewer's sex has received much less scrutiny by survey researchers, and the results of what work there is are much less consistent than those on race-of-interviewer effects. Hyman, Feldman, and Stember (1954) report a survey where the results 'reveal consistencies which are suggestive' of what they term the 'respondent reaction to the interview situation'. Johnson and DeLamater (1976) report that both men and women found their interview more interesting and important when they were interviewed by women rather than by men and that women also reported more willingness to be honest when interviewed by female interviewers. However, after reviewing 144 survey items about sexual behaviour, they conclude that 'interviewer gender is not associated with substantial differences in reported sexual behaviour among youth.' Schofield (1965) finds more honest reporting by both men and women when the age and sex of the interviewer are close to those of the respondent. But Reiss (1967), in his study on premarital sex, found reporting was not influenced by the interviewer's sex.

More recently Fowler and Mangione (1990) have found, by re-interviewing respondents in a face-to-face survey, that both men and women rated female interviewers higher on friendliness, professionalism, and overall performance than they rated male interviewers. Fowler and Mangione speculate about the reasons why female interviewers seem able to establish rapport quickly with survey respondents. They caution, however, against drawing firm conclusions about gender-of-interviewer effects until more data are available, and they suggest that these types of differences may be reduced in telephone interviews. In perhaps the most substantial examination of gender-of-interviewer effects completed thus far, Kane and Macaulay (1993) find evidence of gender-of-interviewer effects for three types of questions. They find that both men and women express more support for equality of men and women to women interviewers, that men are more supportive of gender equality in the workplace when interviewed by female interviewers, and that women are more supportive of collective action by women to deal with inequalities when interviewed by a woman than when interviewed by a man. However, when they control for factors such as the respondent's age, education, marital status, and other demographic factors, they find that the relationship between the sex of the interviewer and that of the respondent is not significant.

THE STUDIES

Three large Canadian surveys will be used to explore the extent to which the sex of the interviewer affects the reported levels of support for affirmative action. A brief description of each survey precedes the analysis. The AIDS survey (AIDS in Canada: Knowledge, Behaviour, and Attitudes of Adults) was conducted in 1988 with 2,330 Canadians.[2] The Attitudes towards Civil Liberties and the Canadian Charter of Rights and Freedoms survey (Charter of Rights study) surveyed 2,084 Canadians in 1987.[3] The Royal Commission on Electoral Reform and Party Financing survey was conducted in 1990 with 2,950 Canadians.[4]

All three surveys were done from the Institute for Social Research's centralized telephone interviewing facilities in Toronto. In order to ensure representative samples, households and respondents were selected randomly.[5] The response rate (the proportion of people who agreed to participate) for each survey was between 64 and 67 per cent.[6]

Two of the three surveys specifically asked about support for affirmative action. The AIDS survey asked, 'Do you support programs which favour the hiring and promoting of women to make up for their lack of opportunities in the past?' The Charter of Rights survey asked, 'A certain proportion of the top jobs in government should go to women' (agree or disagree). The Electoral Reform survey asked: 'As you may know, there are many more men than women in the House of Commons. In your view, how serious a problem is this?' (four-point seriousness scale).

RESULTS

The AIDS Survey

Many of the questions in the AIDS survey dealt with sensitive issues such as sexual practices, number of sexual partners, and whether the respondent knew anyone with AIDS or anyone who was homosexual. Given the nature of the questions, it is possible that the sex of the interviewer affected respondents' answers. For example, did willingness to indicate acquaintance with a homosexual or someone who had AIDS vary according to the sex of the interviewer?

For male respondents, there is a consistent pattern of responses to the AIDS items (the first four items of Table 1). When interviewed by men as opposed to women, men are less likely to report they 'know someone who is a homosexual' (41 per cent compared to 44 per cent), and 'personally know someone who has AIDS' (8 per cent compared to 11 per cent). When interviewed by women, they are also less likely to agree that an 'infected person should be required by law to name their sexual partners' (80 per cent

TABLE 1 AIDS SURVEY: RESPONSE TO QUESTIONS BY SEX OF
INTERVIEWER AND RESPONDENT

	Sex of Interviewer/Respondent			
	Male/	Female/	Male/	Female/
Interviewer: Respondent:	Male	Male	Female	Female
Question and Response	(percentage distribution)			
1. 'Personally know' someone with AIDS.	8	11	11	12
2. 'Knows someone who is a homosexual.'	41	44	40	46
3. 'A doctor carries out a blood test and finds a person has been infected with the AIDS virus. Do you think the infected person should be required by law to name his or her sexual partners?' Respondents answering 'yes'.	80[a]	84	87	87[b]
4. 'Had more than one partner in the last five years' and fear of AIDS 'stopped them from having sex' [at least once].	44	47	48	46
5. 'Efforts to prevent the sale of pornography' should be increased. Respondents saying 'yes'.	75	73	81	83
6. 'Should censors have the right to ban or require cuts to films?' Respondents answering 'yes'.	47[a]	44[a]	65[b]	61[b]
7. 'Do you approve of programs which favour the hiring and promotion of women to make up for their lack of opportunities in the past?' Respondents answering, 'yes approve'.	59[a]	68[b]	70[b]	73[b]
Minimum number of respondents (except question 3, which has approximately one-third the number of respondents).	325	790	320	860

[a]Groups marked [a] are significantly different from groups indicated [b] at the .05 level (multiple classification analysis).

compared to 84 per cent) and more likely to state they have had more than one partner over the last year (44 per cent compared to 47 per cent). Although none of these differences are statistically significant, the pattern suggests that some men give different answers to male interviewers than to female interviewers.

Questions 5, 6, and 7 in the table were part of a series of items used to determine political attitudes and ideology. These questions were included in the survey to determine the extent to which attitudes about AIDS correlated with attitudes on a number of other more common socio-political issues. The first two items show a 'gender effect'. Men, whether interviewed by men or women, are less likely than women to agree that 'efforts to prevent the sale of pornography should be increased'. (The figures are 75 and 73 per cent respectively for men interviewed by male and female interviewers; the corresponding figures for women are 81 and 83 per cent respectively.) Men are also less supportive of allowing 'censors the right to ban or cut films' than are women (between 44 and 47 per cent of men compared to 61 to 65 per cent of women, a significant difference at the .05 level).

The pattern for question 7 is quite different and reminiscent of the response pattern for the four AIDS items discussed above. Men interviewed by men are less likely to support 'programs for hiring and promoting women to make up for their lack of opportunities in the past' than are men interviewed by women (59 and 68 per cent respectively). The proportion of men supporting affirmative action programs when they were interviewed by women is close to the proportion of women supporting these programs whether interviewed by men (70 per cent) or women (73 per cent). The male/male group is significantly different from the other three groups ($p < .05$). This difference is what has been traditionally described as a 'gender-of-interviewer effect'.

There is no evidence in the AIDS survey data set to suggest the sex of the interviewer affects women's responses.

The Charter of Rights Study

The items in the Charter of Rights table can be divided into three groups. For the first two questions—'It should be against the law to speak in such a way as to promote hatred', and 'a proportion of the top government jobs should go to French Canadians'—there is no systematic variation in response according to either the sex of the respondent or the sex of the interviewer (see Table 2). This is the most common response pattern in the data set.

A gender effect, however, is present in the questions 3 and 4. Question 3, about banning or allowing 'films that show sexually explicit acts', is similar to the question in the AIDS survey about censorship of films. The results are also similar. Again men give the more 'permissive' response. When men are interviewed by men, they are more likely (but not at a level of statistical

TABLE 2 CHARTER OF RIGHTS STUDY: RESPONSES BY SEX OF
INTERVIEWER AND RESPONDENT

Question and Response	Interviewer: Respondent:	Male Male	Female Male	Male Female	Female Female
		(percentage distribution)			
1. 'It should be against the law to write or speak in such a way as to promote hatred.' *Agree*		72	70	70	74
2. 'A certain proportion of the top jobs in government should go to French Canadians.' *Agree*		35	32	26	32
3. 'Films showing sexually explicit acts should be allowed.' *Agree*		63[a]	58[a]	36[b]	35[b]
4. 'The Charter of Rights is a good thing for Canada.' *Agree*		23[b]	25[b]	34	39[a]
5. 'Large companies should have quotas for the number of women they hire.' *Agree*		65	73	70	72
6. 'It is very important to guarantee equality between men and women.' *Agree*		65	73	70	72
7. 'A certain proportion of the top jobs in government should go to women.' *Agree*		37[a]	58[b]	48[ac]	58[ad]
Minimum number of respondents (except questions 2 and 7, which has approximately half the number of cases).		275	640	260	640

[a]The difference between groups marked [a] and [b] is significant at the .05 level (multiple classification analysis).
[c]The difference between groups marked [c] and [d] is significant at the .05 level (multiple classification analysis).

significance) to say 'films that show sexually explicit acts' should be allowed (63 per cent) than when they are interviewed by women (58 per cent). The proportion of women saying these films should be allowed is significantly less than the proportion of men, but the response of women does not vary with the sex of the interviewer (36 and 35 per cent). These differences in response between men and women are statistically significant. Although the differences are less striking and not statistically significant, men (23 and 25 per cent) more often than women demonstrate support for the Canadian Charter of Rights by saying it 'is a good thing' (34 and 39 per cent).

Items 5, 6, and 7 show evidence of a gender-of-interviewer effect. As was the case in the AIDS survey, we find that when men are interviewed by other men they express less egalitarian positions than when they are interviewed by women. Thus, men interviewed by men (65 per cent) are less likely than men interviewed by women (73 per cent) and than women interviewed by men or women (70 and 72 per cent respectively) to agree that 'large companies should have quotas about the number of women they hire'. Also, in question 6, 65 per cent of men say 'it is very important to guarantee equality between men and women' when interviewed by a man, whereas 8 per cent more, or 73 per cent of men, express belief in guaranteeing equality between the sexes when interviewed by a woman. Male response, when the interviewer was a woman, is about the same as female response, which does not vary with the sex of the interviewer (70 and 72 per cent). The same pattern holds for question 7, 'a proportion of the top government jobs should be set aside for women.' Again men interviewed by other men are least supportive of this type of affirmative action (37 per cent) than men interviewed by women (58 per cent); women are more supportive, whether interviewed by men (48 per cent) or women (58 per cent). (The difference between the male/male group and the other three groups is significant at the .05 level.)

The different level and pattern of support for the two affirmative action items deserves comment. Support for 'quotas in large companies' is lower than support for 'setting aside a certain proportion of the top jobs in government' for each of the four interviewer-respondent combinations. Part of this difference may be a consequence of the tone of questions. 'Quotas' may sound more demanding and harsher than a 'certain proportion'. This difference in tone is somewhat analogous to the 'forbid' and 'not allow' experiments reported by Schuman and Presser (1981). The argument is that even though the terms have the same meaning, to 'forbid' has a harsher connotation than to 'not allow'. It is also possible that some respondents support affirmative action in government but not for large companies because they may feel that affirmative action by their government is more reasonable than a requirement imposed on a private sector organization.

In any case, neither of these two arguments provides a satisfactory answer as to why the gender-of-interviewer effect was present only in the government item. A possible hypothesis may be that the harsher connotation of 'quotas' for large companies, and the differences between private and public sector support for affirmative action, may for those men whose response is influenced by the sex of the interviewer, militate against their need to give the socially acceptable response.

Unlike the case in the AIDS survey, there is a hint of gender-of-interviewer effects for women respondents in the Charter of Rights study. In both the affirmative action items, women are more supportive of affirmative action when interviewed by other women than when interviewed by men. Five per cent more women support quotas when interviewed by women than when interviewed by men. The difference rises to 10 per cent (and is significant) in the second affirmative action item (question 7). Women may feel more comfortable expressing their support for affirmative action to other women than to men. Or they may not want to offend men, resulting in under-reporting or may feel a need to support other women, resulting in over- reporting.

The Electoral Reform Survey

As in the first two surveys, most of the questions in the Electoral Reform survey do not show either a gender-of-respondent or a gender-of-interviewer effect. The first question, asking if corporations should be allowed 'to advertise and promote their position during election campaigns', is not affected by the sex of the respondent; 46 and 45 per cent of men agree that corporations should be allowed to advertise their position, while 43 and 48 per cent of women do so. Although this pattern, where the sex of neither the respondent nor the interviewer affected the response was most common, nevertheless gender and gender-of-interviewer effects are present in the Electoral Reform survey.

Men interviewed by either men or women (67 per cent in both cases) are more supportive of 'reimbursing some of the money spent by parties and candidates during an election' than are women when interviewed by men (60 per cent) or other women (61 per cent). Likewise, men (28 and 27 per cent) are more likely than women (23 and 22 per cent) to indicate that elections work better in Canada than in the States (see Table 3).

With respect to affirmative action questions, there is strong evidence for gender-of-interviewer effects in the Electoral Reform survey. When interviewed by women, men are more likely to say that having 'many more men than women in the House of Commons' is a 'very serious' or 'serious problem' than when they are interviewed by men (30 per cent compared to 20 per cent, significant at the .05 level). The proportion of men who, when interviewed by women, think government would be 'much better' or 'better' if there were 'as many women as men in the House', is, at 44 per cent, 14 per cent higher than the number of men who think this is the case when they are interviewed by male interviewers. Finally, although the difference is very small and not significant, we also find that when men are interviewed by men they are more likely to say 'Everyone would be better off if women stayed at home and raised their children,' (26 per cent) than when they are interviewed by women (23 per cent).

The pattern of response for women, while lacking the statistical significance of the pattern for men, is also suggestive of gender-of-interviewer effects. In question 4, which asked how serious a problem under-representation of women is in the House of Commons, women who were interviewed by men are less likely to say this is a serious problem than women who are interviewed by other women. The effect of the sex of the interviewer is larger on question 5, asking if having more women would improve the quality of

Table 3 Electoral Reform Survey: Responses by sex of
Interviewer and Respondent

| | Interviewer: | Male/ | Female/ | Male/ | Female/ |
| | Respondent: | Male | Male | Female | Female |
Question and Response			(percentage distribution)		
1. 'Should corporations be allowed or not be allowed to advertise and promote their positions during election campaigns?' *Should be allowed*		46	45	43	48
2. 'Government should reimburse some of the money spent by parties and candidates during an election.' *Agree*		67	67	60	61
3. 'Elections work better in Canada than in the US.' *Agree*		28	27	23	22
4. 'As you may know, there are many more men than women in the House of Commons. In your view how serious a problem is this?' *Very serious or serious*		20[a]	30[b]	36[b]	40[b]
5. 'If there were as many women as men in the House, of Commons, government would be either much better or better.' *Agree*		30[a]	44[b]	33[a]	42[b]
6. 'Everyone would be better off if women stayed at home and raised children.' *Basically agree*		26	23	27	26
Minimum number of respondents (except first two questions which have approximately half the number of cases).		520	750	440	715

[a]The difference between groups marked [a] and [b] is significant at the .05 level (multiple classification analysis).

government (33 per cent of women interviewed by men think it would improve government, as compared to 42 per cent of women interviewed by women).

In all three studies, for the affirmative actions items, some men give different answers to female interviewers than to male interviewers. The differences range from 10 per cent on the question about women in the House of Commons to 21 per cent on the question of setting aside a proportion of top jobs in government for women. When men are asked about affirmative action issues, in each of the three surveys, the difference in the support according to the sex of the interviewer is statistically significant. There is also some evidence to suggest that some women may adjust their responses according to the sex of the interviewer. And, as was the case with men, these differences are largest for the affirmative action questions.

RELATIVE IMPORTANCE OF SEX OF INTERVIEWER

In this section the influence of the sex of both the respondent and the interviewer on responses to affirmative action questions is compared to that of other socio-demographic variables, such as age, education, income, marital status, and religiosity. Because our variables of interest are interrelated—for example higher levels of education are often associated with higher incomes—it is difficult to isolate the effect of a single variable in predicting support for affirmative action. It can be done, however, by using regression analysis, which isolates the effect of one variable while holding the effects of other variables constant (Jaeger 1990). By examining the results of a regression equation, we can compare the relative influence of each independent or predictor variable on the dependent variable.[7] In our regression equations, the dependent variable is support for affirmative action policies—as measured in each of the three surveys. The independent or predictor variables are the socio-demographic characteristics of the respondent and the sex of the interviewer.

The results of the regressions are summarized in Table 4. Three different regression equations were calculated for each survey. The way in which the gender-of-interviewer effects were measured varied in the regression equations. The effect of the non-gender variables—age, education, income, and so on—change very little for each of the three equations. For that reason in Table 4, the results of the second and third regressions include results only for the gender-of-interviewer variable. The first regression equation contains variables that measure the effect of the sex of the respondent and the interviewer on support for 'hiring and promoting women'. In Table 4 those variables are identified as sex of respondent (men compared to women); and sex of interviewer (respondents interviewed by men compared to respondents interviewed by women).[8]

The value of β in Table 4 indicates the extent to which the predictor variables cause an increase or decrease in support for hiring and promoting women. For example, a negative β value of –1.5 would indicate that the variable, after the effect of all of the other predictors are accounted for, decreases support for hiring and promoting women. (Positive β values indicate an increase in support.) As a general rule, only variables with β values that approach statistical significance—that is, β values that are very unlikely to be caused by chance—are considered predictors of response. Traditionally, probabilities of .05 or smaller, that is, results that would occur by chance five times in a hundred or less often, are considered significant.

μTABLE 4 REGRESSION RESULTS: ALL THREE SURVEYS

Variable	AIDS Survey (Hiring and promoting women)				Charter of Rights (A proportion of top jobs go to women)				Electoral Reform (Not enough women in the House)			
	β	Standard Error	Probability	Exp (β)	β	Standard Error	Probability	Exp (β)	β	Standard Error	Probability	Exp (β)
Results of First Regression												
Age	.1	.00	.074	1.000	.0	.01	.738	.998	.0	.00	.999	1.001
Education	-.1	.03	.849	.995	-.8	.04	.068	.922	1.5	.03	.000	1.174
Community size (large compared to small)	-.3	.05	.576	.972	-1.3	.06	.031	.877	—	—	—	
Religiosity (times attending worship)	-.4	.03	.208	.962	-.8	.06	.213	.926	—	—	—	
Marital status (comparing never married to others)	.1	.07	.917	1.007	.0	.11	.992	.999	—	—	—	
Employment status (employment compared to others)	-.8	.06	.194	.919	-.6	.10	.531	.938	-.3	.08	.706	.917
Union membership (yes = 1)	—	—			2.3	.10	.015	1.268	-.2	.08	.762	.966
Income	.0	.00	.375	.997	-.9	.04	.050	.919	-.3	.03	.232	.966
Sex of respondent (male = 1)	4.1	.11	.000	.659	.7	.17	.700	.937	-6.1	.13	.000	.545
Sex of interviewer (male = 1)	2.3	.11	.040	.793	6.3	.18	.001	.532	-4.0	.14	.004	.668
Results of Second Regression												
Contrast, men interviewed by men compared to all others	-16.0	.43	.000	4.954	19.0	.74	.009	6.849	28.0	.60	.000	17.509
Results of Third Regression												
Contrast, women interviewed by women compared to all others	11.4	.35	.001	.321	11.7	.56	.035	.310	17.3	.43	.000	.177

In the AIDS survey, for the first regression equation, the respondent's sex has the largest β value (–4.1) and it is significant (.000). The β value of –4.1 means that, if all other variables in the equation are held constant, male respondents significantly decrease the overall level of support for hiring and promoting women. Although the β value is smaller (–2.3), the sex of the interviewer is also found to be a significant factor in explaining responses to the question about hiring and promoting women. Once all other factors in the regression are considered, being interviewed by a man also results in a significant decrease in support for hiring and promoting women. None of the other predictor variables are significant.

Given the results of the first regression, it is not surprising that the results of the second regression show that the men/men group (men interviewed by men) is significantly different from the other three groups.[9] However, the extent of the decrease in support for hiring and promoting women is, as evidenced by the high β value (–16.0), considerably larger than the differences of 2 to 4 per cent found in the first regression. The women/women group is also significantly different from all other groups, but this group is associated with a significant increase in support for hiring and promoting women (β = 11.4). For women respondents, as for men, the results of the regression mean that knowing the sex of the interviewer will significantly improve our ability to predict the respondents' support for affirmative action.

In the Charter of Rights Survey, however, a number of variables other than gender have a significant effect on support for 'setting aside a proportion of the top jobs for women'. From the first equation we find that size of community, membership in a union, and income all are statistically significant predictor variables. (The larger the community where the respondent grew up, the more likely they are to support setting aside a proportion of the top jobs for women; and the higher the income, the less likely they are to be in favour.)

At first glance the lack of significance of the sex of the respondent in predicting response to setting aside a proportion of top jobs for women seems counter-intuitive. However, remember from Table 2 that the same proportion of men and women supported setting aside a proportion of top government jobs for women when the interviewer was a women, and that about two-thirds of all respondents in the sample were interviewed by a woman. Differences in support for setting aside jobs by the respondent's sex occur only when the interviewer was a man, and men interviewers account for a smaller proportion of the total sample. The regression confirms this finding, in that respondents interviewed by men are found to be significantly less favourable to setting aside a proportion of top jobs for women than respondents interviewed by women (β = –6.3).

As was the case in the AIDS survey, and as shown in the results of the second regression equation, the combination of male respondent and male interviewers is found to be a statistically significant predictor of response to the question about setting aside a proportion of top government jobs for women. The high and negative value of β means that this group after variation for all other factors in the equation have been taken into account, is significantly less likely to support setting aside a proportion of the top jobs for women (β = –19.0). The positive and significant β value for the women/women group indicates an increase in support.

The results of the regressions for the Electoral Reform survey show that education (β of 1.5), the sex of the respondent (β of –6.1), and the sex of the interviewer (β of –4.0) are statistically significant predictors of response to the question whether there are 'enough women in the House of Commons'. Higher levels of education are positively associated with agreeing that there are not enough women in the House, and being a man or being interviewed by man is associated with disagreeing (first regression equation). As was the case in the first two surveys, both the male/male group and the women/women groups have a statistically significant effect on response—after the effect of all other variables are accounted for (second and third regression equations).

DISCUSSION

Although gender-of-interviewer effects are not present or have limited effect on the questions central to each study, consistent evidence for gender-of-interviewer effects for affirmative action questions has been documented. The results presented in Tables 1 to 3 show that, for male respondents, the sex of the interviewer is an important determinant of response for such questions. In all three surveys men who were interviewed by women were more in agreement with affirmative action than men who were interviewed by men. The results of the regression confirm the findings of gender-of-interviewer effects for men and suggest that there are also gender-of-interviewer effects for women.

It is difficult to be certain why gender-of-interviewer effects exists, but one explanation is offered by Sudman and Bradburn (1982). They argue that respondents face a dilemma in an interview. By participating in the interview they are demonstrating a desire 'to be a good respondent and provide the information that is asked for'. At the same time they want to answer in a way 'that reflects well on themselves'. In earlier work (Bradburn et al. 1979), the authors demonstrated that seemingly innocuous questions such as whether the respondent owns a library card or is registered to vote are subject to over-reporting by 11 to 21 per cent. The questions on affirmative action are likely to be at least as sensitive. Some men may consider support for 'women's issues' to be the correct or socially acceptable response. When men are interviewed by other men, the private one-on-one situation may, for some men, create a 'conspiratorial' situation where they feel they can really say what they think. Conversely, perhaps some men are adjusting their response to suit what they believe other men (the interviewer) want to hear. The obverse may be true for women. When they are interviewed by other women, some women may feel more inclined to say honestly what they think, or they feel a need to support a position that they assume the interviewer holds. Alternatively, some women, when they are interviewed by men, may temper their support for affirmative action programs on the assumption that male interviewers are more likely to disagree with the concept.

The findings for gender-of-interviewer effects are similar to those for race-of-interviewer effects. In both cases, effects are found only for items that address issues relating to the interviewer's race or sex. Just as some whites and blacks seem to be influenced by the interviewer's race on race-related questions (Hatchett and Schuman 1975-76), some men and some women seem to be influenced by the sex of the interviewer.

The extent to which the combined influence of race and sex modify or magnify differences in reporting by respondents on topics with a gender and race component is an interesting question. How would answers from White men vary when the interviewer was a Black woman rather than a White man?

The implications of gender-of-interviewer effects for the analysis of survey data are quite straightforward. The implications for the collection of survey data are less clear. Survey organizations should routinely add interviewers' sex to their data sets. This information needs to be used by researchers when analysing data, especially data that may be sensitive to the interviewer's sex. For example, research on the 'gender gap' in politics and on attitudes towards abortion, affirmative action, and so forth needs to look at gender-of-interviewer effects. Otherwise, because most survey firms employ mainly women as interviewers, we may constantly be over-reporting male support for affirmative action and similar programs. Identification of gender-of-interviewer effects tells us as much about public attitudes as knowing the proportion of men and women who give affirmative or negative answers to questions about equity for women.

The other difficult question is whether or not survey organizations should attempt to match the sex of the interviewer to the sex of the respondent. Electing to do so would mean that the organization assumed that responses to questions that may be sensitive to the sex of the respondent are more valid when obtained from an interviewer of the same sex. This assumption may or may not be true. Certainly the variation in response by the sex of the interviewer may help to explain attitudes. Because most interviewers are women, perhaps a more reasonable solution would be for survey firms to increase the proportion of male interviewers so that the influence of the interviewers' sex on survey data can be a standard part of data analysis.

Recently, researchers have reminded us that the survey interview is as much an interaction between the respondent and interviewer as it is the use of a standardized measurement tool (Suchman and Jordan 1992). Clearly, one of the critical influences on the interaction between the respondent and the interviewer is gender.

NOTES

I would like to thank Christine Klucha, Mirka Ondrack, Anne Oram, and Michael Ornstein, colleagues at the Institute for Social Research at York University, for their considerable assistance with this paper. An earlier version of this paper was presented at the 1992 Conference of the American Association of Public Opinion Research (AAPOR), and a shortened version of that paper is included in *The Puzzles of Power*, edited by Michael Howlett and David Laycock.

1 Cotter, Cohen, and Coulter (1982) have demonstrated that race-of-interviewer effects are found in telephone surveys. Both interviewers and respondents make assumptions, which are usually accurate, about each other's race. Reese et al. (1981) have found ethnicity-of-interviewer effects in telephone surveys.

2 The survey was funded by Health and Welfare Canada' Centre for AIDS. The findings are presented in Ornstein (1989).

3 The survey was funded by the Social Sciences and Humanities Research Council of Canada. Paul M. Sniderman, Stanford University, was the principal investigator. Co-investigators were Peter H. Russell, University of Toronto, Philip E. Tetlock, University of Berkeley, and Joseph F. Fletcher, University of Toronto.

4 The results of the survey are presented in Blais and Gindengel (1992).

5 Random digit dialling (RDD) was used in all three surveys (see Groves et al. [1988: Section 3] for an explanation of the use of RDD in telephone surveys). Respondents were selected by the most-recent-birthday method in the AIDS and Electoral Reform surveys, and Kish selection methods were used to choose the respondents in the Charter of Rights Study (see O'Rourke and Blair 1983 for a description of respondent selection procedures in telephone surveys).

6 The response rate was calculated by dividing the estimated number of households in the sample by the number of interviews conducted (see Groves and Lyberg 1988 for a discussion of how to calculate response rates in survey research) and the importance of doing so.

7 Because the items of interest (support or non-support for affirmative action) are dichotomous, a logistic regression model has been used (see Aldrich and Nelson 1984).

8 In a regression model, the sex of the respondent and the interviewer are traditionally called the main effects. An interaction term was also included and, while the results are not reported in Table 4, they are consistent with the findings from the other regressions and the data presented in Tables 1 to 3.

9 Before the contrasts for the different groups were calculated an interaction term was built into a regression equation. The interaction terms were not significant, but the results were consistent with Tables 1 to 3 and with the results of the contrast presented in Table 4. Because about two-thirds of the persons interviewed were women, the male/male group has a relatively small proportion of the sample and, unless isolated in a contrast, the different findings for the group tend to be lost in the larger pool of data.

BIBLIOGRAPHY

Aldrich, John H., and Forrest D. Nelson (1984), *Linear Probability, Logit, and Probit Models* (Beverly Hills, CA: Sage).

Anderson, Barbara A., Brian D. Silver, and Paul R. Abramson (1988), 'The Effects of Race of the Interviewer on Measures of Electoral Participation by Blacks in SRC National Election Studies', *Public Opinion Quarterly* 52 (1): 53-83.

Blais, André, and Elisabeth Gidengil (1992), *Making Representative Democracy Work: The Views of Canadians*, Vol. 17 of the research studies of the Royal Commission on Electoral Reform and Party Financing (Ottawa and Toronto: RCERPF/ Dundurn).

Bradburn, Norman M. (1983), 'Response Effects', in *The Handbook of Survey Research*, eds, Peter H. Rossi, James D. Wright, and Andy B. Anderson, 289-328 (Orlando, FL: Academic).

Bradburn, Norman M., Seymour Sudman, and Associates (1979), *Improving Interview Method and Questionnaire Design* (San Francisco: Jossey-Bass).

Brodie, Janine, and Celia Chandler (1991), 'Women and the Electoral Process in Canada', in Kathy Megyery, ed., *Women in Canadian Politics: Toward Equity in Representation*, vol. 6 of the research studies of the Royal Commission on Electoral Reform and Party Financing (Ottawa and Toronto: RCERPF/Dundurn).

Campbell, Bruce A. (1981), 'Race of Interviewer Effects among Southern Adolescents', *Public Opinion Quarterly* 45 (2): 231-44.

Cotter, Patrick, Jeffery Cohen, and Philip B. Coulter (1982), 'Race-of-Interviewer Effects in Telephone Interviews', *Public Opinion Quarterly* 46 (2): 278-84.

Finkel, Steven E., Thomas M. Guterbock, and Marian J. Borg (1991), 'Race of Interviewer Effects in a Preelection Poll', *Public Opinion Quarterly* 55 (3): 313-30.

Fowler, Floyd J., Jr, and Thomas W. Mangione (1990), *Standardized Survey Interviewing: Minimizing Interviewer-Related Error* (Newbury Park, CA: Sage).

Groves, Robert M., and Lars E. Lyberg (1988), 'An Overview of Nonresponse Issues in Telephone Surveys', in Groves, Biemer, Lyberg, Massey, Nicholls II and Waksberg (1988), 191-211.

Groves, Robert M., Paul P. Biemer, Lars E. Lyberg, James T. Massey, William L. Nicholls II, and Joseph Waksberg (1988), *Telephone Survey Methodology* (New York: Wiley).

Hatchett, Shirley, and Howard Schuman (1975-76), 'White Respondents and Race of Interviewer Effects', *Public Opinion Quarterly* 39 (4): 523-8.

Howlett, Michael, and David Laycock (1994), *The Puzzles of Power: An Introduction to Political Science* (Toronto: Copp Clark Longman).

Hyman, Herbert H., J. Feldman, and C. Stember (1954), *Interviewing in Social Research* (Chicago: University of Chicago Press).

Jaeger, Richard M. (1990), *Statistics: A Spectator Sport*, 2nd ed. (Newbury Park, CA: Sage).

Johnson, Weldon T., and John D. DeLamater (1976), 'Response Effects in Sex Surveys', *Public Opinion Quarterly* 40 (1): 165-81.

Kane, Emily W., and Laura Macaulay (1993), 'Interviewer Gender and Gender Attitudes', *Public Opinion Quarterly* 57 (1): 1-28.

Kopinak, Kathryn (1987), 'Gender Differences in Political Ideology in Canada', *Canadian Review of Sociology and Anthropology* 24 (1): 23-38.

Ornstein, Michael (1989), *AIDS in Canada: Knowledge, Behaviour, and Attitudes of Adults* (Toronto: Institute for Social Research, York University).

O'Rourke, Diane, and Johnny Blair (1983), 'Improving Random Respondent Selection in Telephone Surveys', *Journal of Marketing Research* 20: 428-32.

Reiss, I.L. (1967), *The Social Context of Premarital Sexual Permissiveness* (New York: Rinehart and Winston).

Reese, Steven D., Wayne A. Danielson, Pamela J. Shoemaker, Tsan-Kuo Chang, and Huei-Ling Hsu (1981), 'Ethnicity of Interviewer Effects among Mexican Americans and Anglos', *Public Opinion Quarterly* 50 (1): 563-72.

Schofield, M. (1965), *The Sexual Behaviour of Young People* (London: Longmans).

Shapiro, Robert Y., and Harpreet Mahajan (1986), 'Gender Differences in Policy Differences: A Summary of Trends from the 1960s to the 1980s', *Public Opinion Quarterly* 50 (1): 42-61.

Schuman, Howard, and Jean M. Converse (1971), 'The Effect of Black and White Interviewers on Black Response', *Public Opinion Quarterly* 35 (1): 44-8.

Schuman, Howard, and Stanley Presser (1981), *Questions and Answers in Attitude Surveys: Experiments on Question Form, Wording, and Content* (New York: Academic).

Smith, Tom (1984), 'Gender and Attitudes towards Violence', *Public Opinion Quarterly* 48 (1B): 384-96.

Suchman, Lucy, and Brigitte Jordan (1992), 'Validity and the Collaborative Construction of Meaning in Face to Face Surveys', in *Questions About Questions: Inquiries into the Cognitive Bases of Surveys*, ed. Judith M. Tanur, 241-67 (New York: Russell Sage).

Sudman, Seymour, and Norman M. Bradburn (1982), *Asking Questions: A Practical Guide to Questionnaire Design* (San Francisco: Jossey-Bass).

Weeks, Michael F., and R. Paul Moore (1981), 'Ethnicity of Interviewer Effects on Ethnic Respondents', *Public Opinion Quarterly* 45 (2): 244-9.

Wirls, Daniel (1986), 'Reinterpreting the Gender Gap', *Public Opinion Quarterly* 50 (3): 316-30.

The Fine Line—Strategies for Change

Caroline Andrew

One way to reflect on a collection such as this one is to look at the strategy it presents for influencing the study of politics. Feminist analysis and, more generally, research on gender have, as a central element, the aim of transforming the traditional disciplines. In the past 30 years of scholarship on gender relations we have certainly learned that this is no easy task. However, we should not be totally disheartened—there have been advances. It is important to reflect on these processes and to think about how bodies of knowledge are transformed.

Nancy Adamson, Linda Briskin, and Margaret McPhail (1988) discuss this question in *Feminist Organizing for Change*. They argue that 'an effective feminist practice for change requires a tension between a politic of disengagement and one of mainstreaming' (p. 189). This tension or equilibrium between the two is the fine line evoked in my title. But what is meant by these two strategies, and do they apply to research or only to social practice?

The authors of *Feminist Organizing for Change* argue that feminists must stand both outside and inside the system and must combine 'abstract vision and concrete reality' (p. 186). Standing outside the system represents the politics of disengagement, with the aim of creating alternative structures and ideologies. It is a politics of vision, based on a radical criticism of the existing system. It is organized around thinking clearly about what should be and about how an egalitarian, non-sexist world should function.

But at the same time it is necessary to be inside the system and speak to immediate real-life concerns. The term 'politics of mainstreaming' captures the essence of this strategy: that is, that the existing system must be persuaded to change from within, that influential members of society must be moved to change their priorities and the ways they act. This strategy focuses not on what should be but on society as it is and the daily reality of women's lives.

These two strategies can be examined, not only in relation to political action aimed at improving the status of women, but also to the institutional organization of research and teaching that concentrate on gender and to intellectual reflection on gender relations. In universities and colleges, both disengagement and mainstreaming strategies exist, although the emphasis placed on one or the other certainly varies from institution to institution. The disengagement strategy is seen in specialized programs in women's studies, gender relations, and feminist theory. These programs tend to be interdisciplinary or multidisciplinary and, to greater or lesser degrees, they aim to transform existing knowledge, methodologies, and perspectives. They see themselves as introducing a fundamental critique of other pre-existing programs and administrative structures.

On the other hand, the mainstreaming strategy's intent is to introduce women into traditional disciplines, either in existing courses or in new courses in existing academic units. The purpose is to make women's perspectives or gender relations more prominent in the structure of educational institutions. The objective is to work from within to make sure that the new approaches influence the largest possible number of people in the institution. Students, whatever their field of study, should be able to see that the institution is prepared to make changes, and is capable of doing so, to better integrate women's reality.

To emphasize the complementarity of these two approaches, rather than the conflict between them, is consistent with the argument made by the authors of *Feminist Organizing for Change*. Separate programs in women's or gender studies give feminist students and professors an opportunity to work in an environment sympathetic to the study of gender relations and feminist theory. They therefore allow for new ways of thinking to be articulated. These new models can then be used in traditional courses or traditional programs to highlight better the gender relations or concerns of women. These traditional programs, which reach the most students, including of course the majority of women students, ensure that these students are at least more aware of the new approaches that are gender-sensitive or non-sexist. At the same time these courses allow these new approaches to be tested against reality; do they speak to the lives and daily experiences of large numbers of students? In this way, disengagement allows for the development and articulation of gender-sensitive theory, and mainstreaming allows it to influence the largest possible group. Disengagement keeps feminist theory intellectually stimulating, and mainstreaming keeps it visible. The two need each other. Or as Adamson, Briskin, and McPhail argue, disengagement prevents co-option and mainstreaming prevents marginalization. Separate programs in women's or gender studies do run the risk of being marginalized, but the addition of one lecture on feminism to an existing course runs the risk of leaving out the radical critique or transformative character of gender-based analysis.

In any particular field of study, these strategies can be seen as two different ways of influencing that field. In the study of politics, it is clear that some feminists, in trying to reflect on the relationships between gender and politics, have placed themselves clearly outside the conventional paradigms, subjects, or approaches of the field. For example, the study of politics has generally been defined as relating to the public sphere; therefore much of the theorizing about how gender divisions reproduce the division between public and private in society and the relegation of women to the private sphere is excluded by definition from the field of study. These questions are little discussed in basic texts on politics, and very few references are made to the literature on gender relations. Similarly the abundant feminist material that looks at violence against women and theorizes about the meaning of this issue for society is outside the study of politics—the feminist vision of politics has generally tended either to reject the existing practice completely or to construct a utopian non-violent, non-sexist, egalitarian society. There has therefore been a clear disengagement strategy—with feminist students of politics choosing to talk to, and write for, feminists rather than political scientists.

There has also been a mainstreaming strategy, by which feminist political scientists have researched some of the most traditional subjects of political science but have added women or introduced gender relations as an explicit focus. One such example is the studies that emphasize the large discrepancy all over the world between the percentages of women in the population and the percentages of women in a variety of political positions. These studies, which have used wide accepted methodologies, are fully in the mainstream of the conventional study of politics.

Once again, it is important to stress that the two strategies are complementary. The disengagement strategies have permitted the articulation of theories about the relationship of public and private sectors and the further relationship of gender to this public/private distinction. This theorizing about private-public spheres is fundamental to an understanding of the empirical research on the presence of women in formal political positions. To understand the findings of this research, it is necessary to go outside conventional political theory and to understand how the association of women with the private sphere has largely defined their place in the political system.

At the same time the studies of the gap between the number of women in the population and in formal political positions concentrate on one of the most visible parts of the political system and therefore highlight what is, in this area, the point of broadest social consensus; namely that women are dramatically under-represented in politics. These studies therefore illustrate the mainstreaming strategy; they focus on real-life questions on which it is possible to mobilize broad support for change. They use methods that are widely accepted in the study of politics, and this too adds to the acceptability of these studies. By dealing with subjects understood by the readers and using familiar categories, these studies aim to make the readers realize that gender should be a central factor in the study of politics.

It is illuminating to look at research in terms of its balance between a disengagement or a mainstreaming strategy. Elements of each are almost always present, but the balance differs. To take two examples from this collection, Meredith Ralston's 'Homeless Women and the New Right' moves more towards disengagement, whereas Alan Whitehorn and Keith Archer's 'The Gender Gap among Party Activists: A Case Study of Women and the New Democratic Party' falls more on the side of a mainstreaming strategy.

Ralston argues that to understand politics one needs to understand how the women she interviewed came to be homeless, addicted, and on welfare. An adequate political theory must be able to deal with this question since the women are full members of the body politic and therefore must be adequately accounted for. This certainly goes beyond the conventional definition of politics. The New Right theorists are political, but the effects of family violence on the life chances of those affected by this violence falls less obviously within the traditional definition of the political realm. Ralston argues that it should be considered part of politics and that therefore we can expect the New Right theorists to be able to explain this part of politics.

In addition, Ralston's argument challenges the methodology of the conventional study of politics. She argues that the women she interviewed must be listened to and that explanations of their situation must be based on these women's experiences. They become the central figures for this political analysis, and the starting point for this analysis is their interpretation of their own situation.

Ralston's argument therefore calls for a redefinition of politics, one that rejects the dichotomy of public and private and that insists that the internal dynamics of the family is an integral part of political explanation. The danger of this strategy, if we pursue the analysis of Adamson, Briskin, and McPhail (1988), is marginalization, for the readers may reject (or not understand) this redefinition of politics and therefore underestimate the pertinence of the criticism of the New Right. Readers used to traditional definitions of politics may simply feel that the argument is peripheral to the 'main business' of politics.

Alan Whitehorn and Keith Archer examine gender differences among party activists in the federal New Democratic Party. They look both at demographic differences between female and male delegates to party conventions and at differences in social and political attitudes by gender. The chapter therefore addresses well-known areas of political activity and does so with conventional methods of research. The underlying argument, that gender is an important factor in the influence of political parties and the way they operate, relates directly to the common view that political parties are essential to the functioning of political systems. The argument therefore brings questions of gender to bear on subjects that are in the centre of the study of politics.

The methods used are consistent with this approach. Quantitative survey data are widely accepted, and their use in this chapter will therefore be reassuring to traditional students of politics. The message is clear: a gender analysis of political parties helps to explain their functioning. The danger of this mainstreaming strategy, however, is that it may give the impression that the existing political system is operating fairly well and, that so indeed is the existing system of political analysis. The conclusion, that there has been progress in participation rates, could suggest that time will resolve the problems of women's participation and that the resolution of this problem does not necessarily require changes by other political actors.

In addition, this kind of study may raise the question of the actual political influence of activists within a political party and, indeed, the actual political influence of political parties. By working within familiar paradigms of what is political, the writers may be maintaining a rather formalistic definition of the political system.

Indeed, each paper in this collection can be situated according to the way it draws its fine line between mainstreaming and disengagement. David Northrup, for instance, has as his subject a very conventional and important area of political science, the methodology of survey research. But by doing the simple operation of looking at the sex of the interviewers and of the respondents, he suddenly brings about a whole reorganization of reality. What was understood as data, the answers to the interview questions, now becomes a by-product of the social relationships of interviewers and respondents.

Jane Arscott's chapter also starts from a position closer to a mainstreaming strategy, in that it presents an analysis of the report of the Royal Commission on Electoral Reform and Party Financing. Of course the analysis of government documents is an established part of the study of politics, but Arscott goes well beyond a textual analysis by bringing feminist perspectives on women's representation to bear on her analysis. The article both takes the arguments of the Commission very seriously and points out much broader perspectives from which to think about the representation of women.

In a sense, Lesley Jacobs's argument has a similar structure. He looks at the principles behind legislation and argues that recent feminist legal and political theory allows us to see these principles in a new light. Indeed, his argument is that we can now go back to earlier views about the value of realizing equality of opportunity. Jacobs's argument depends on looking at justice in families and therefore on integrating the feminist expansion of the political.

Micheline Dumont's article clearly balances mainstreaming and disengagement—the constitutional issue is a mainstreaming one in that it addresses the central question of formal politics, the maintenance of the political entity. However, to argue that women are relevant to constitutional issues is not at all mainstream. Even now, after the active involvement of women's groups in the constitutional debates, this is not seen as obvious. Answering the question about what are women's issues requires, as Dumont points out in relation to Quebec, a rethinking of what is political and what should be political.

Sandra Burt's paper falls more on the side of mainstreaming in that it hopes to convince students of public policy that there is a broad set of policies and government responses that relate to women. But by addressing Carole Pateman's (1986) distinction between domesticated and distinctive feminism, between the claims that can be accommodated within existing structures and those that cannot, the essay proposes a rethinking of reality. Policy is not just policy, it is a way of establishing how politics is envisaged.

The subject discussed by Gertrude Robinson and Armande Saint-Jean, the media coverage of women politicians, has been less central to political science, although it is essential to the public's impression of what politics is all about. To some extent, the mainstreaming thrust of the argument is to convince the reader that media coverage is an important part of politics and that the common-sense view that it *is* important is indeed correct. The fine line in the article is between our real-life belief that the media is politically important and the acquired belief that it is only of secondary importance.

Roberta Hamilton also looks at one of the central questions of political science, nationalism, and reflects on its links to feminism in Quebec. The disengagement edge to her argument is to situate debates about nationalism at the level of the practical political struggles around the conditions under which women make decisions about their own reproduction. Instead of giving the discussions about nationalism an abstract, formal basis, she situates them at the level of day-to-day choices for women and, hence, choices for everyone in the political system. One can argue that this is a woman's perspective—rooted in the practical effects of politics rather than in abstract formulations. The tension is therefore maintained between a focus on Quebec nationalism as a question of high politics and a concern for the ways in which women have organized to improve their daily lives.

Manon Tremblay also situates her subject in one of the well-understood areas of political science, legislative politics. But rather than present this in the terms of mere numbers, her essay explores legislators' attitudes towards feminism. In a fashion similar to that of Arscott, Tremblay shows that incorporating a feminist point of view on questions of representation makes us look at the political system again, and in a new way.

Women and the military is perhaps an even more contradictory juxtaposition than women and the constitution. The military, as François-Pierre Gingras states in his chapter, has been seen as an extremely masculine community. Furthermore, in Canada the political role of the military has not been discussed much. The mainstreaming strategy here is to look at attitudes that are clearly central to politics (peace and peacekeeping), whereas disengagement has its place in the choice of an unconventional milieu, the military, for looking at gender differences in political attitudes.

In his other essay in this volume, Gingras, like Robinson and Saint-Jean, looks at media coverage. He examines the daily newspapers and calculates the coverage given to women. By comparing different newspapers one sees clearly the social construction of reality, for the various descriptions of what is going on can be seen to be different organizations of reality. The study of politics must include the influence of the newspapers in defining reality and, in so arguing, Gingras is arguing for a widening of the definition of politics.

If we look at the collection as a whole, we see that although the strategies vary, the emphasis is more on mainstreaming than on disengagement. This makes it a particularly useful collection given the fact that, until now, most work on gender and politics has been closer to a disengagement strategy. The collection covers a number of topics central to the traditional view of politics as the study of the public sphere—constitutional politics, political parties, elected representatives, and public policy. Even the topics somewhat less central traditionally, such as the media and the women's movement, and the political attitudes of the military, can be related to a 'common-sense' definition of politics.

It is important to stress once again that in all the papers the strategies of mainstreaming and disengagement are intertwined as mutually complementary elements. Jane Arscott's discussion of whether the conception of the Royal Commission of Electoral Reform and Party Financing of political representation is too narrow directly addresses the definition of the political and the way that this definition is influenced by the analysis of gender influences. The strategy is both disengagement and mainstreaming, and each part depends on the relationship between the two. Or, to take another example, David Northrup's argument is mainstreaming in that it analyses survey results in areas fully within a conventional definition of polities; but it is also disengagement because the results raise significant questions about the social construction of the reality being looked at.

To return once more to Adamson, Briskin, and McPhail, successful social change requires a balance between the two approaches. The fine line of being disengaged and involved in mainstreaming at the same time is essential. If, as I have argued, the emphasis of this particular collection is somewhat more on mainstreaming, that will help to maintain the necessary balance throughout the study of gender and politics. Research is a fundamental aspect of social change—this collection moves us forward in our understanding of politics.

BIBLIOGRAPHY

Adamson, Nancy, Linda Brisken, and Margaret McPhail (1988), *Feminist Organizing for Change* (Toronto: Oxford University Press).

Pateman, Carole (1986), 'Introduction,' in *Feminist Challenges*, eds Carole Pateman and Elizabeth Gross (Sydney: Allen and Unwin).

CONTRIBUTORS

Caroline Andrew received her Ph.D. from the University of Toronto. She is a past president of the Canadian Research Institute for the Advancement of Women, the Canadian Political Science Association, and the Social Science Federation of Canada. Her research work on women and politics has dealt with women and urban development, women and the welfare state, and the forms of women's political activity. She is the co-author of several articles and books, including (with B.M. Milroy) *Life Spaces: Gender, Household, Employment*, published by the University of British Columbia Press. Recent articles are 'The Sex of Sewers, or the Construction of the Feminist City', in *Political Arrangements: Power and the City*; and 'Laughing Together: Women's Studies in Canada' in the *International Journal of Canadian Studies*. She is the current chair of the Department of Political Science at the University of Ottawa.

Keith Archer teaches political science at the University of Calgary. His fields of specialization are Canadian politics, political parties, elections, and voting behaviour. He received his Ph.D. from Duke University. His recent publications include 'Opinion Structure of Party Activists: The Reform Party of Canada' (with Faron Ellis), in the *Canadian Journal of Political Science* and *Political Choices and Electoral Consequences: A Study of Organized Labour and the New Democratic Party*. He is also the co-author (with Roger Gibbins, Rainer Knopff, and Leslie Pal) of *Parameters of Power: Canada's Political Institutions*.

Jane Arscott teaches political science at Dalhousie University in Halifax. Her research interests are the history of political thought, feminist political theory, and the general field of women and politics. She received her Ph.D. from Queen's University in 1993. She is co-editor of *In the Presence of Women: Representation and Canadian Governments* to be published in 1995. She is the author of 'Opening Up the Canon', *Studies in History and Politics*.

Sandra Burt teaches political science at the University of Waterloo, where she was the founding co-ordinator of Women's Studies. Much of her research is an investigation of different forms of political participation and an evaluation of the methods used by social scientists to measure participation. An early interest in the labels attached to women's participation has led to particular consideration of the political activism that has been part of the second wave of the women's movement. She has co-edited (with Lorraine Code and Lindsay Dorney) two editions of *Changing Patterns: Women in Canada*. More recently, she has worked with Lorraine Code on a collection of original essays on feminist methods, *Changing Methods: Feminists Transforming Practice*, to be published in 1995. Another recent work is 'What's Fair? Changing Feminist Perceptions of Justice in English Canada', in the *Windsor Yearbook of Access to Justice*.

Micheline Dumont did her graduate work at Université Laval and teaches at the Université de Sherbrooke. A specialist in women's studies and feminist theories, she has published extensively. As a member of Collectif Clio, she was co-author of *Histoire des femmes au Québec depuis quatre siècles*. Other recent publications include *L'instruction des filles au Québec* and 'Les charismes perdus: l'avenir des congrégations religieuses féminines, en l'an 2000' in *Recherches féministes*.

François-Pierre Gingras is past chair of the Political Science Department at the University of Ottawa, where he teaches research methods, comparative nationalism, and Canadian politics. He received his doctorate in sociology from Université René Descartes in Paris and is a former French editor of the *Canadian Journal of Political Science*. His eclectic research interests also cover media and politics, political sociology, and the sociology of religion. His recent publications include 'Une compagne de route: L'Église catholique, de la naissance à l'éclatement du nationalisme canadien-français', in *Études d'histoire religieuse*; 'The Peacekeepers' Attitudes Toward Peace', in *The WUNAC International Peace and Security Collection*; 'Divergences ou convergences? Les laïcs anglophones et francophones dans le catholicisme canadien', in *Sciences religieuses*; 'La vision constitutionnelle de René Lévesque', in *René Lévesque: l'homme, la nation, la démocratie*; 'La sociologie de la connaissance' and 'La théorie et le sens de la recherche' in *Recherche sociale: de la problématique à la collecte des données*; and 'Nationalism in Québec: An Incomplete Secular Revolution' (with N. Nevitte), in *Politics: Canada* (7th ed.).

Roberta Hamilton received her Ph.D. from Concordia University and now teaches sociology at Queen's University. She has special research interests in feminist theory, historical sociology, and Quebec and Canadian society. Her recent publications include 'Feminism and Motherhood' in *Resources for Feminist Research*; *Feudalism and Colonization: The Historiography of New France*; *The Politics of Diversity*, edited with Michele Barrett; and 'Feminist Theories' in *Left History*.

Lesley A. Jacobs teaches in the Department of Political Science and in the Law and Society Programme at York University. He received his Ph.D. from Oxford University. His research interests are comparative social theory and political theory, with an emphasis on rights and distributive justice. His recent publications include 'The Enabling Mode of Rights' in *Political Studies*; *Rights and Deprivation*; and *The Democratic Vision of Politics* (forthcoming). He also co-edited *Out of Apathy*.

David Northrup is a full-time researcher and manager of the Institute for Social Research at York University. He has published several articles on survey research methods. Of interest among his recent contributions are 'Psychological and Cultural Foundations of Prejudice: The Case of Anti-Semitism in Quebec' (with P.A. Sniderman, J.F. Fletcher, P.H. Russell, and P.E. Tetlock), forthcoming in the *Canadian Review of Sociology and Anthropology*; 'Public Support for the Exclusion of Unconstitutionally Obtained Evidence' (with A. Bryant, M. Gold, H.M. Stevenson), in the *Supreme Court Law Review*; and 'Public Attitudes towards the Exclusion of Evidence: Section 24(2) of the Canadian Charter of Rights and Freedoms' (with A. Bryant, M. Gold, H.M. Stevenson), in the *Canadian Bar Review*.

Meredith Ralston received her Ph.D. in political science from Dalhousie University and is now assistant professor of women's studies at Mount Saint Vincent University, in Halifax. Her area of specialization is the relationships between women, politics, and social policy. She has a special research interest in homeless women and the New Right. She is the author of 'Genderism and Contractarian Theory' in *Philosophy in Canada* and *Failures of Perception by the New Right*.

Gertrude Robinson is past director of the Graduate Program in Communications at McGill University. In addition to a special interest in women and the Canadian media, she has done research on the flows and content of international communications media in Canada and Western Europe. She received her Ph.D. from the University of Illinois (Urbana) and has been editor of the *Canadian Journal of Communication*, president of the Canadian Communication Association, and treasurer of the International Association for Mass Communication Research. She edited (with D. Sixt) *Women and Power: Canadian and German Experiences*, published in the McGill Working Papers in Communications series and is the author of 'Women and the Media in Canada: A Progress Report', in *Seeing Ourselves: Media, Power and Policy in Canada*. She wrote (with A. Saint-Jean) 'Women Politicians and Their Media Coverage: A Generational Analysis' in *Women in Politics: Toward Equity in Representation*, volume 6 of the Research Studies of the Royal Commission on Electoral Reform and Party Financing.

Armande Saint-Jean made a name for herself as a journalist and now teaches in the Department of Communications at the Université du Québec à Montréal. She is co-author (with G. Robinson) of 'Women Politicians and Their Media Coverage: A Generational Analysis' in *Women in Politics: Toward Equity in Representation*, volume 6 of the Research Studies of the Royal Commission on Electoral Reform and Party Financing.

Manon Tremblay teaches courses on women and politics as well as research methods in the Political Science department at the University of Ottawa; she has a special research interest for Canadian political parties and electoral systems. She received her Ph.D. from Université Laval. Her recent publications include 'Les femmes sont-elles candidates dans des circonscriptions perdues d'avance?' (with R. Pelletier) and 'Quand les femmes se distinguent: féminisme et représentation politique au Québec', in the *Canadian Journal of Political Science*; and 'La question de l'avortement au Parlement canadien: de l'importance du genre dans l'orientation des débats' (with G. Boivin) in *Revue Femmes et droit*.

Alan Whitehorn is a visiting professor occupying the J.S. Woodsworth chair at the Institute for the Humanities at Simon Fraser University. He normally teaches in the Department of Political and Economic Science at Royal Military College in Kingston. He received his Ph.D. from Carleton University and has special research interests in Canadian political parties, comparative politics, and political theory. He is the author of *Canadian Socialism: Essays on the CCF-NDP* and several chapters in *Party Politics in Canada*, including 'The CCF-NDP and the End of the Broadbent Era' and (with K. Archer) 'Opinion Structure of New Democrat, Liberal and Conservative Activists'. He is also the author of 'Audrey McLaughlin and the NDP's Quest For Survival', in *The Canadian General Election of 1993*.

INDEX

Note: **Boldface** number indicates a Figure.
Italic number indicates a Table.